Thomas Jefferson Morgan, William A. May

The Praise Hymnary

A Collection of Sacred Song

Thomas Jefferson Morgan, William A. May

The Praise Hymnary
A Collection of Sacred Song

ISBN/EAN: 9783744780797

Printed in Europe, USA, Canada, Australia, Japan

Cover: Foto ©Thomas Meinert / pixelio.de

More available books at **www.hansebooks.com**

THE

PRAISE HYMNARY

A Collection of Sacred Song

COMPILED AND ARRANGED BY

THOMAS J. MORGAN, D.D., LL.D.

WILLIAM A. MAY, AND PHOEBE M. HAYNES

SILVER, BURDETT AND COMPANY
NEW YORK .... BOSTON ..... CHICAGO

University Press:
JOHN WILSON AND SON, CAMBRIDGE, U.S.A.

PREFACE.

THE Praise Hymnary is a book of worship. It aims to furnish a medium for the expression of some of the profoundest and most ennobling sentiments of the human heart. Its chief note is that of praise, addressed to the Triune God, Father, Son, and Holy Spirit, ascribing to Him power, dominion, majesty, glory, recognizing Him as the giver of every good and perfect gift, gratefully acknowledging His boundless mercies, and pleading for a continuation of His loving Providence.

It is believed that both the words and the music winnowed from many sources will be found to be happily suited for their purpose. An effort has been made to take from the body of the old and the tried Hymns those that have proved most truly expressive of the adoration, hopes, and longings of the human heart. It has been the endeavor to select from the list of the new those that will make substantial addition to the old. Among the old tunes will be found many favorites without which no Hymnbook would be complete. Among the new, it is believed that the tunes composed especially for this book by Wm. A. May will be found a valuable feature. Throughout the book the constant aim has been to blend the classic and the popular by selecting the best of each, and that without sacrificing too much to either.

In determining the number of selections and the size of the book the compilers have sought to produce a work that shall not only be particularly well adapted for use in schools, colleges, Young Men's Christian Associations, and gatherings of young people, but shall also be adapted to meet the peculiar needs of those churches which desire an inexpensive, comprehensive, and choice collection of sacred songs.

This book has its own individuality, it is unlike any other; it is new; it is thoroughly usable; it is educative; its contents are varied, comprehensive, and excellent. Its use will contribute not only to the fitting expression of religious emotion but also to the enrichment of the spiritual life.

THOMAS J. MORGAN.

NEW YORK, *June* 1, 1898.

CONTENTS.

	Pages
General Praise	7–91
Lord's Day (The)	92–95
Morning and Evening	96–103
Birth of Christ	104–109
Sufferings of Christ	110–113
Resurrection of Christ	114, 115
Enthronement of Christ	116, 117
Holy Spirit	118, 119
Trust in Christ	120–123
Invitation	124–127
Repentance	128–133
Consecration	134–139
Faith and Trust	140–145
Heaven	146–149
Scriptures	150, 151
Church (The)	152, 153
Dedication	154, 155
Baptism	156, 157
Lord's Supper	158, 159
Occasional	160, 161
Missions	162–165
The New Year	166, 167
Parting Hymns	168, 169
National and Patriotic	170–183
Closing Praise	184
Index of First Lines	185
Index of Subjects	188
Alphabetical Index of Tunes	189
Index of Authors of Hymns	191

Scriptures for the Opening of Worship.

The Lord bless thee and keep thee; the Lord make His face shine upon thee and be gracious unto thee; the Lord lift up His countenance upon thee and give thee peace. (Num. vi. 24–26.)

Surely the Lord is in this place. This is none other than the house of God; and this is the gate of heaven. (Gen. xxviii. 16, 17.)

Let the words of my mouth, and the meditation of my heart, be acceptable in Thy sight, O Lord, my strength, and my redeemer. (Ps. xix. 14.)

The Lord is nigh to all that call upon Him; to all that call upon Him in truth. (Ps. cxlv. 18.)

Know ye that the Lord He is God; it is He that hath made us, and not we ourselves; we are His people, and the sheep of His pasture. Enter into His gates with thanksgiving, and into His courts with praise. For the Lord is good; His mercy is everlasting; and His truth endureth unto all generations. (Ps. c. 3–5.)

This is the day which the Lord hath made; we will rejoice and be glad in it. (Ps. cxviii. 24.)

How amiable are Thy tabernacles, O Lord of hosts. My soul longeth, yea, even fainteth for the courts of the Lord. My heart and my flesh crieth out for the living God. (Ps. lxxxiv. 1, 2.)

It is a good thing to give thanks unto the Lord, and to sing praises unto Thy name, O Most High; to show forth Thy loving-kindness in the morning, and Thy faithfulness every night. (Ps. xcii. 1, 2.)

From the rising of the sun unto the going down of the same, the Lord's name is to be praised. I love the Lord because He hath heard my voice and my supplications. Because He hath inclined His ear unto me, therefore will I call upon Him as long as I live. O give thanks unto the Lord, for He is good; for His mercy endureth forever. (Ps. cxiii. 3; cxvi. 1, 2; cxxxvi. 1.)

Come unto Me all ye that labor and are heavy laden, and I will give you rest. Take My yoke upon you, and learn of Me, for I am meek and lowly in heart, and ye shall find rest unto your souls. For My yoke is easy, and My burden is light. (Matt. xi. 28–30.)

A Scriptural Confession.

Leader: Behold the Lamb of God which taketh away the sin of the world. (John i. 29.)

Response: All we like sheep have gone astray; we have turned every one to his own way, and the Lord hath laid on Him the iniquity of us all. (Isa. liii. 6.)

Leader: Let the wicked forsake his way and the unrighteous man his thoughts, and let him return unto the Lord, and He will have mercy upon him; and to our God, for He will abundantly pardon. (Isa. lv. 7.)

Unison: O God, I acknowledge my transgressions, and my sin is ever before me. Wash me thoroughly from mine iniquity, and cleanse me from my sin. Cast me not away from Thy presence, and take not Thy Holy Spirit from me. Create in me a clean heart, O God, and renew a right spirit within me. (Ps. li. 2, 3, 10, 11.)

Leader: God was in Christ reconciling the world unto Himself, not imputing their trespasses unto them, and hath committed unto us the word of reconciliation. (2 Cor. v. 19.)

Response: There is, therefore, now no condemnation to them which are in Christ Jesus, who walk not after the flesh, but after the spirit. (Rom. viii. 1.)

Unison: Our Father which art in heaven,
Hallowed be Thy Name.
Thy kingdom come.
Thy will be done in earth as it is in heaven.
Give us this day our daily bread.
And forgive us our debts as we forgive our debtors.
And lead us not into temptation,
But deliver us from evil:
For Thine is the kingdom and the power and the glory, forever.
Amen. (Matt. vi. 9–13.)   From "People's Worship and Psalter."

THE PRAISE HYMNARY.

I PRAISE THE LORD. 7s, 4s. WELSH

1 Praise the Lord; His glories show, Alleluia, Saints within His courts below, Alleluia, Angels round His throne above, Alleluia, Praise Him all who share His love, Alleluia.

2 Earth, to Heaven exalt the strain.
　　　　　Alleluia,
Send it, Heaven, to earth again;
　　　　　Alleluia,
Age to age, and shore to shore,
　　　　　Alleluia,
Praise Him, praise Him evermore,
　　　　　Alleluia.

3 Praise the Lord; His goodness trace,
　　　　　Alleluia,
All the wonders of His grace,
　　　　　Alleluia,
All that He hath borne and done,
　　　　　Alleluia,
All He sends us through His Son.
　　　　　Alleluia.

4 Strings and voices, hands and hearts,
　　　　　Alleluia,
In the concert bear your parts;
　　　　　Alleluia,
All that breathe, your Lord adore,
　　　　　Alleluia,
Praise Him, praise Him evermore,
　　　　　Alleluia.

　　　　　HENRY F. LYTE, 1834.

THE PRAISE HYMNARY.

2 LUTHER. P. M.   MARTIN LUTHER, 1529.

1 A mighty fortress is our God, A bulwark never failing: Our Helper He, amid the flood Of mortal ills prevailing. For still our ancient foe Doth seek to work us woe; His craft and power are great, And armed with cruel hate, On earth is not his equal.

2 Did we in our own strength confide,
  Our striving would be losing;
Were not the right man on our side,
  The man of God's own choosing.
Dost ask who that may be?
Christ Jesus, it is He;
  Lord Sabaoth is His name,
  From age to age the same,
And He must win the battle.

3 And though this world, with devils filled,
  Should threaten to undo us;
We will not fear, for God hath willed
  His truth to triumph through us.
The Prince of Darkness grim, —

We tremble not for him;
His rage we can endure,
For lo! his doom is sure, —
One little word shall fell him!

4 That word above all earthly powers —
  No thanks to them — abideth;
The Spirit and the gifts are ours
  Through Him who with us sideth.
Let goods and kindred go,
This mortal life also:
The body they may kill:
God's truth abideth still,
His kingdom is forever.
    MARTIN LUTHER, 1521. Tr. F. H. HEDGE, 1853.

3 P. M.

1 REJOICE to-day with one accord,
  Sing out with exultation;
Rejoice, and praise our mighty Lord,
  Whose arm hath brought salvation;
His works of love proclaim
The greatness of His name;
For He is God alone,
Who hath His mercy shown;
  Let all His saints adore Him.

2 When in distress to Him we cried,
  He heard our sad complaining;
O trust in Him, whate'er betide,
  His love is all sustaining;
Triumphant songs of praise
To Him our hearts shall raise;
Now every voice shall say,
"O praise our God alway;"
  Let all His saints adore Him.
                  SIR HENRY W. BAKER.

GENERAL PRAISE.

4 FABEN. 8s, 7s. D. JOHN H. WILLCOX.

1 "Lord, Thy glory fills the Heaven, Earth is with its fulness stored; Unto Thee be glory given, Holy, Holy, Holy Lord!" Heaven is still with glory ringing, Earth takes up the angels' cry, "Holy, Holy, Holy!" singing, "Lord of Hosts, Thou Lord most High!"

2 Ever thus in God's high praises,
Brethren, let our tongues unite,
While our thoughts His greatness raises,
And our love His gifts excite.
With His seraph train before Him,
With His holy church below,
Thus unite we to adore Him,
Bid we thus our anthem flow:

3 "Lord, Thy glory fills the Heaven,
Earth is with its fulness stored;
Unto Thee be glory given,
Holy, Holy, Holy Lord!"
Thus, Thy glorious name confessing,
We adopt the angels' cry,
"Holy, Holy, Holy," blessing
Thee, the Lord of Hosts most High!

RICHARD MANT, *abt.* 1837.

5 8s, 7s. D.

1 CROSS, reproach, and tribulation!
Ye to me are welcome guests,
When I have this consolation,
That my soul in Jesus rests.
The reproach of Christ is glorious!
Those who here His burden bear
In the end shall prove victorious,
And eternal gladness share.

2 Bonds and stripes, and evil story,
Are our honorable crowns;
Pain is peace, and shame is glory,
Gloomy dungeons are as thrones.
Bear, then, the reproach of Jesus,
Ye who live a life of faith!
Lift triumphant songs and praises
Ev'n in martyrdom and death.

J. W. PETERSON, 1697.
Tr. from L. A. GOTTER.

THE PRAISE HYMNARY.

6 ECCLESIA. 8s, 7s. D.

2 See! the streams of living waters,
   Springing from eternal love,
  Well supply thy sons and daughters,
   And all fear of want remove:
  Who can faint, while such a river
   Ever flows their thirst t' assuage? —
  Grace which, like the Lord, the giver,
   Never fails from age to age.

3 Round each habitation hovering,
   See the cloud and fire appear,
  For a glory and a covering,
   Showing that the Lord is near!
  Thus deriving from their banner,
   Light by night, and shade by day,
  Safe they feed upon the manna
   Which He gives them when they pray.
   JOHN NEWTON, 1779.

7 VESPER. 8s, 7s, 4s. D. BORTNIANSKY.

2 Glory be to Him who loved us,
   Washed us from each spot and stain;
  Glory be to Him who bought us,
   Made us kings with Him to reign;
    Hallelujah, hallelujah,
   To the Lamb that once was slain.

3 "Glory, blessing, praise eternal!"
   Thus the choir of angels sings;
  "Honor, riches, power, dominion!"
   Thus its praise creation brings;
    Hallelujah, hallelujah,
   Glory to the King of kings!
   HORATIUS BONAR, 1868.

GENERAL PRAISE.

8 BLUMENTHAL. 7s. D. JACOB BLUMENTHAL, 1847.

1 Pleasant are Thy courts above,
In the land of light and love;
Pleasant are Thy courts below
In this land of sin and woe.
Oh, my spirit longs and faints
For the converse of Thy saints,
For the brightness of Thy face,
For Thy fulness, God of grace.

2 Happy birds that sing and fly
Round Thy altars, O Most High;
Happier souls that find a rest
In a heavenly Father's breast;
Like the wandering dove that found
No repose on earth around,
They can to their ark repair,
And enjoy it ever there.

3 Happy souls, their praises flow,
Even in this vale of woe;
Waters in the desert rise,
Manna feeds them from the skies;
On they go from strength to strength,
Till they reach Thy throne at length,
At Thy feet adoring fall,
Who hast led them safe through all.

4 Lord, be mine this prize to win,
Guide me through a world of sin,
Keep me by Thy saving grace,
Give me at Thy side a place.
Sun and shield alike Thou art,
Guide and guard my erring heart;
Grace and glory flow from Thee;
Shower, oh, shower them, Lord, on me.
                        HENRY F. LYTE, 1834.

9 7s. D.

1 SAVIOUR, when, in dust, to Thee,
Low we bend th' adoring knee;
When, repentant, to the skies,
Scarce we lift our streaming eyes;
O by all Thy pains and woe
Suffered once for man below,
Bending from Thy throne on high,
Hear Thy people while they cry.

2 By Thy birth and early years,
By Thy human griefs and fears,
By Thy fasting and distress
In the lonely wilderness;
By Thy victory in the hour
Of the subtle tempter's power; —
Jesus, look with pitying eye,
Hear Thy people while they cry.

3 By Thine hour of dark despair,
By Thine agony of prayer,
By Thy purple robe of scorn,
By Thy wounds, Thy crown of thorn,
By Thy cross, Thy pangs and cries;
By Thy perfect sacrifice; —
Jesus, look with pitying eye,
Hear Thy people while they cry.
                        SIR ROBERT GRANT, 1815. Alt.

THE PRAISE HYMNARY.

10 ADORATION. 12s, 11s. WM. A. MAY.

1 The winds that career o'er the bosom of ocean,
The shadows that curtain the face of the sky;
The stars in their beauty, the worlds in their motion
Proclaim their Creator,—our Father on high.

Copyright, 1898, by SILVER, BURDETT AND COMPANY.

2 The mountains are Thine in their mystical splendor;
The dawn of the morning springs fresh from Thy hand;
The night follows on, ever eager to render
Devotion and praise, at Thy holy command.

3 The lance of the storm, at Thine order is broken;
The lightnings are chained to their home in the clouds;
The phantoms of air, with the ills they betoken,
Return, at Thy word, to the mist of their shrouds.

4 The evening's soft beam, and the midnight's deep beauty,
Awaken the soul from its slumber of death;
All doubts disappear; I remember but duty;
Conviction sweeps on like the hurricane's breath.

5 O let me adore Thee, thou God of creation!
I turn to Thy love like a star to the sea.
O let me proclaim my eternal salvation,
My ceaseless devotion, allegiance to Thee!

E. P. ARCHBOLD, 1868.

11 12s, 11s.

1 A ROCK in the wilderness welcomed our sires,
From bondage far over the dark-rolling sea;
On that holy altar they kindled their fires,
Jehovah, which glow in our bosoms for Thee.

2 Thy blessings descended in sunshine and shower,
Or rose from the soil that was sown by Thy hand;
The mountain and valley rejoiced in Thy power,
And heaven encircled and smiled on the land.

3 The pilgrims of old an example have given
Of mild resignation, devotion, and love,
Which beams like a star in the blue vault of heaven,
A beacon-light hung in their mansion above.

4 In church and cathedral we kneel in our prayer,—
Their temple and chapel were valley and hill;
But God is the same in the aisle or the air,
And He is the Rock that we lean upon still.

GEORGE P. MORRIS.

GENERAL PRAISE.

12 SICILIAN HYMN. 8s, 7s, 4s. Italian.

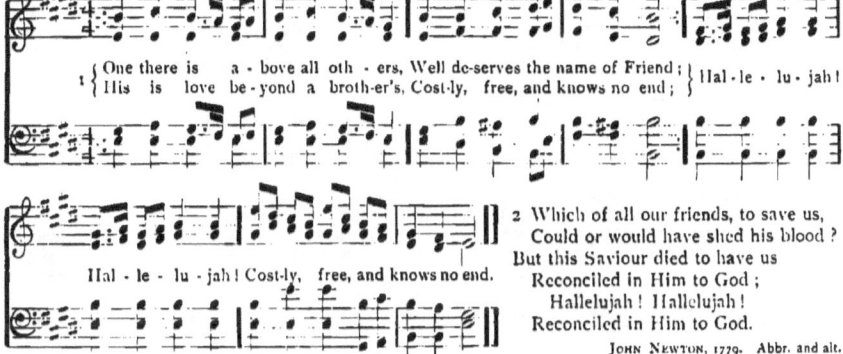

One there is a-bove all oth-ers, Well de-serves the name of Friend;
His is love be-yond a broth-er's, Cost-ly, free, and knows no end;
Hal-le-lu-jah! Hal-le-lu-jah! Cost-ly, free, and knows no end.

2 Which of all our friends, to save us,
 Could or would have shed his blood?
But this Saviour died to have us
 Reconciled in Him to God;
Hallelujah! Hallelujah!
 Reconciled in Him to God.
      JOHN NEWTON, 1779. Abbr. and alt.

13 8s, 7s, 4s.

1 SAVIOUR, send a blessing to us,
 Send a blessing from above;
All Thy truth and mercy show us,
 Be Thou here in power and love;
Grant Thy presence, grant Thy presence,
 Be it ours Thy grace to prove.

2 Nothing have we, Lord, without Thee,
 But Thy promise is our stay;
And Thy people must not doubt Thee;
 Saviour, now Thy power display,
And let gladness, and let gladness
 Fill Thy people's hearts to-day.
      THOMAS KELLY, 1840.

14 8s, 7s, 4s.

1 GOD is love; that anthem olden
 Sing the glorious orbs of light,
In their language glad and golden,
 Telling to us day and night
Their great story, blessed story,
 God is love, and God is might!

2 And the teeming earth rejoices
 In that message from above,
With ten thousand thousand voices
 Telling back from hill and grove
Her glad story, glorious story,
 God is might, and God is love.

3 Through these anthems of creation,
 Struggling up with gentle strife,
Christian songs of Christ's salvation,
 To the world with blessings rife,
Tell their story, precious story,
 God is love, and God is life!

4 Up to Him let each affection
 Daily rise, and round Him move;
Our whole lives one resurrection
 To the life of life above:
Our glad story, wondrous story,
 God is life, and God is love!
      JOHN S. B. MONSELL, 1862.

15 8s, 7s, 4s.

1 GLORY, glory everlasting
 Be to Him who bore the cross;
Who redeemed our souls by tasting
 Death, the death deserved by us;
Sound His glory, sound His glory
 While our heart with transport glows.

2 Jesus' love is love unbounded,
 Without measure, without end;
Human thought is here confounded;
 'T is too vast to comprehend;
Praise the Saviour, praise the Saviour;
 Magnify the sinner's Friend.

3 While we hear the wondrous story
 Of the Saviour's cross and shame,
Sing we, "Everlasting glory
 Be to God and to the Lamb!"
Saints and angels, saints and angels,
 Give ye glory to His name.
      THOMAS KELLY. Abt. 1809.

THE PRAISE HYMNARY.

16 C. M.

1 Arise, ye people, and adore,
  Exulting strike the chord;
  Let all the earth, from shore to shore,
  Confess the almighty Lord!

2 Glad shouts aloud, wide echoing round,
  The ascending Lord proclaim;
  The angelic choir respond the sound,
  And shake creation's frame.

3 They sing of death and hell o'erthrown
  In that triumphant hour;
  And God exalts His conquering Son
  To His right hand of power.
  Harriet Auber, 1829. Abbr.

17 C. M.

1 How rich Thy favors, God of grace!
  How various and divine!
  Full as the ocean they are poured,
  And bright as heaven they shine.

2 He to eternal glory calls,
  And leads the wondrous way
  To His own palace, where He reigns
  In uncreated day.

3 The songs of everlasting years
  That mercy shall attend,
  Which leads, through sufferings of an hour,
  To joys that never end.
  Philip Doddridge.

18 ORTONVILLE. C. M. Thomas Hastings, 1837.

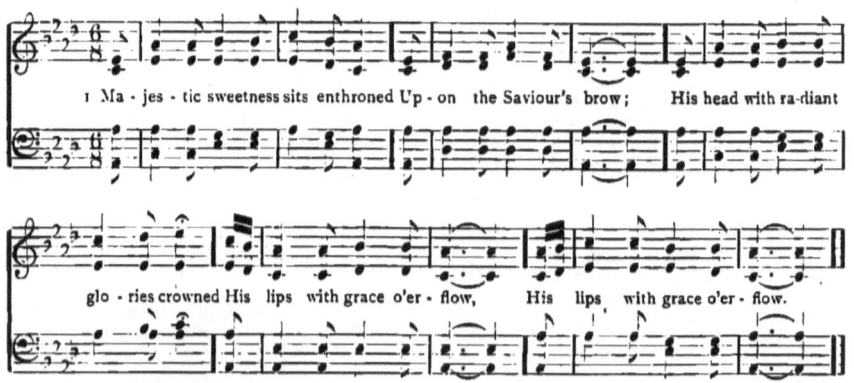

1 Majestic sweetness sits enthroned Upon the Saviour's brow; His head with radiant glories crowned His lips with grace o'er-flow, His lips with grace o'er-flow.

2 No mortal can with Him compare
  Among the sons of men;
  Fairer is He than all the fair
  That fill the heavenly train.

3 He saw me plunged in deep distress,
  He flew to my relief;
  For me He bore the shameful cross,
  And carried all my grief.

4 To Him I owe my life and breath,
  And all the joys I have;
  He makes me triumph over death,
  He saves me from the grave.

5 Since from His bounty I receive
  Such proofs of love divine,
  Had I a thousand hearts to give,
  Lord, they should all be Thine.
  Samuel Stennett, 1782. Abbr.

19 C. M.

1 O God! my heart is fully bent
  To magnify Thy name;
  My tongue, with cheerful songs of praise,
  Shall celebrate Thy fame.

2 To all the listening tribes, O Lord,
  Thy wonders I will tell;
  And to those nations sing Thy praise
  That round about us dwell;

3 Because Thy mercy's boundless height
  The highest heaven transcends;
  And far beyond the aspiring clouds
  Thy faithful truth extends.

4 Be Thou, O God, exalted high
  Above the starry frame;
  And let the world, with one consent,
  Confess Thy glorious name!
  Tate and Brady.

GENERAL PRAISE.

20 7s.

1 SWELL the anthem, raise the song,
Praises to our God belong;
Saints and angels, join to sing
Praises to the heavenly King.

2 Blessings from His liberal hand
Flow around this happy land;
Kept by Him, no foes annoy;
Peace and freedom we enjoy.

3 Here, beneath a virtuous sway
May we cheerfully obey;
Never feel oppression's rod;
Ever own and worship God.

4 Hark! the voice of nature sings
Praises to the King of kings;
Let us join the choral song,
And the grateful notes prolong.
NATHAN STRONG, 1799.

21 7s.

1 GOD eternal, Lord of all,
Lowly at Thy feet we fall:
All the earth doth worship Thee,
We amidst the throng would be.

2 All the holy angels cry,
Hail, thrice holy, God most High:
Lord of all the heavenly powers,
Be the same loud anthem ours.

3 God eternal, mighty King,
Unto Thee our praise we bring:
Seated on Thy judgment-throne,
Number us among Thine own.
JAMES E. MILLARD, 1848. Abbr. and alt.

22 DOXOLOGY. 7s.

SING we to our God above
Praise eternal as His love;
Praise Him, all ye heavenly host —
Father, Son, and Holy Ghost.
CHARLES WESLEY. 1740.

23 NUREMBURG. 7s.   JOHANN R. AHLE, 1664.

1 Praise on Thee, in Zion's gates, Daily, O Jehovah, waits; Unto Thee, O God, belong Grateful words and holy song.

2 Thou the hope and refuge art
Of remotest lands apart;
Distant isles and tribes unknown,
'Mid the ocean waste and lone.

3 Thou dost visit earth, and rain
Blessings on the thirsty plain,
From the copious founts on high,
From the rivers of the sky.

4 Thus the clouds Thy power confess,
And Thy paths drop fruitfulness,
And the voice of song and mirth
Rises from the tribes of earth!
JOSIAH CONDER.

24 7s.

1 THANK and praise Jehovah's name
For His mercies, firm and sure,
From eternity the same,
To eternity endure.

2 Praise Him, ye who know His love,
Praise Him from the depths beneath;
Praise Him in the heights above;
Praise your Maker, all that breathe.

3 For His truth and mercy stand,
Past, and present, and to be,
Like the years of His right hand,
Like His own eternity.
JAMES MONTGOMERY, 1822. Abbr.

THE PRAISE HYMNARY.

25 WE'RE MARCHING TO ZION.   Robert Lowry.

1 Come, we who love the Lord, And let our joys be known, Join in a song with sweet ac-cord, Join in a song with sweet ac-cord, And thus sur-round the throne, And thus surround the throne. We're march-ing to Zi-on, Beau-ti-ful, beau-ti-ful Zi-on, We're marching up-ward to Zi-on, The beau-ti-ful cit-y of God.

2 Let those refuse to sing,
  Who never knew our God;
But children of the heavenly King,
But children of the heavenly King,
  May speak their joys abroad,
  May speak their joys abroad.

3 The hill of Zion yields
  A thousand sacred sweets,
Before we reach the heavenly fields,
Before we reach the heavenly fields,
  Or walk the golden streets,
  Or walk the golden streets.

4 Then let our songs abound,
  And every tear be dry:
We're marching through Immanuel's ground,
We're marching through Immanuel's ground,
  To fairer worlds on high,
  To fairer worlds on high.

                            Isaac Watts. 1709.

Used by permission of Robert Lowry, owner of copyright.

GENERAL PRAISE.

26 JESUS SHALL REIGN. L. M. D. KARL WILHELM, arr.

1 Je-sus shall reign wher-e'er the sun Does his suc-ces-sive journeys run; His kingdom spread from shore to shore, Till moons shall wax and wane no more. From north to south the princes meet, To pay their hom-age at His feet; While western em - pires own their Lord, And sav-age tribes at-tend His word.

2 To Him shall endless prayer be made And endless praises crown His head; His name like sweet perfume shall rise With ev-ery morn-ing sac-ri-fice. Peo-ple and realms of ev-ery tongue Dwell on His love with sweetest song, And in-fant voi - ces shall pro-claim Their ear-ly bless-ings on His name.

ISAAC WATTS, 1719.

27 L. M. D.

1 THROUGH the new heaven what voices ring
In praise triumphant to our King?
Like many waters, hark, they pour
Their tide along the golden shore!
"All blessing, honor, power divine,
All might and majesty be Thine!
Holy and true are all Thy words,
Thou King of kings and Lord of lords!"

2 These from the martyr's bed of flame,
These from the gloomy dungeon came,
These, on the dreadful battlefield,
Stood firm till death and would not yield.
'All voices in that faithful throng,
Swell clear and true the glorious song;
"Holy and just are all Thy words,
Thou King of kings and Lord of lords."

3 These bore Thy banner o'er the sea,
Exiled and poor for love of Thee,
And found in danger and distress,
Thy presence in the wilderness.
No storm could shake, no ill could harm
So strong was Thy protecting arm,
"Holy and true are all Thy words,
Thou King of kings and Lord of lords!"

ELSIE THALHEIMER.

28 L. M.

1 Exalted Prince of life, we own
The royal honors of Thy throne;
'T is fixed by God's almighty hand,
And seraphs bow at Thy command.

2 Exalted Saviour, we confess
The mighty triumphs of Thy grace;
Where beams of gentle radiance shine,
And temper majesty divine.

3 Wide Thy resistless sceptre sway,
Till all Thine enemies obey;
Wide let Thy cross its virtues prove,
And conquer millions by its love!
Philip Doddridge.

29 L. M.

1 The Lord is King! lift up thy voice,
O earth! and all ye heavens, rejoice!
From world to world the joy shall ring —
"The Lord omnipotent is King!"

2 The Lord is King! who, then, shall dare
Resist His will, distrust His care?
Holy and true are all His ways:
Let every creature speak His praise.

3 The Lord is King! let all bow down,
Nor dare provoke His awful frown;
Ere justice blaze, His scepter kiss,
And sate thy soul with heav'nly bliss.
Josiah Conder, 1824. Abbr. and alt.

30 FEDERAL STREET. L. M.
Henry K. Oliver, 1832.

1 Thee we adore, eternal Lord! We praise Thy name with one accord;
Thy saints, who here Thy goodness see, Through all the world do worship Thee.

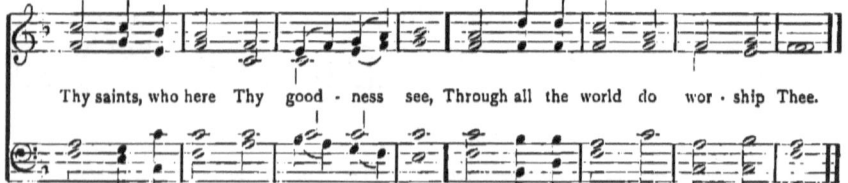

2 To Thee aloud all angels cry,
And ceaseless raise their songs on high,
Both cherubim and seraphim,
The heavens and all the powers therein.

3 The apostles join the glorious throng;
The prophets swell the immortal song;
The martyrs' noble army raise
Eternal anthems to Thy praise.

4 Thee, holy, holy, holy King
Thee, O Lord God of hosts, they sing:
Thus earth below, and heaven above,
Resound Thy glory and Thy love.
Thomas Cotterill, 1819.

31 L. M.

1 Now be my heart inspired to sing
The glories of my Saviour King;
He comes with blessings from above,
And wins the nations to His love.

2 Thy throne, O Lord, forever stands;
Grace is the sceptre in Thy hands;
Thy laws and works are just and right,
But truth and mercy Thy delight.

3 Let endless honors crown Thy head;
Let every age Thy praises spread;
Let all the nations know Thy word,
And every tongue confess Thee Lord.
Isaac Watts, 1707. Abbr.

GENERAL PRAISE.

32 S. M.

1 Awake, and sing the song
　Of Moses and the Lamb;
Wake every heart and every tongue,
　To praise the Saviour's name.

2 Sing of His dying love;
　Sing of His rising power;
Sing how He intercedes above
　For those whose sins He bore.

3 Sing till we feel our heart
　Ascending with our tongue;
Sing till the love of sin depart,
　And grace inspires our song.

4 Sing on your heavenly way,
　Ye ransomed sinners, sing;
Sing on, rejoicing every day
　In Christ the eternal King.
　　　　　Wm. Hammond, 1745.

33 S. M.

1 Now let our voices join
　To raise a sacred song;
Ye pilgrims! in Jehovah's ways,
　With music pass along.

2 See — flowers of paradise,
　In rich profusion, spring;
The sun of glory gilds the path,
　And dear companions sing.

3 See — Salem's golden spires,
　In beauteous prospect, rise;
And brighter crowns than mortals wear,
　Which sparkle through the skies.

4 All honor to His name,
　Who marks the shining way, —
To Him who leads the pilgrims on
　To realms of endless day.
　　　　　Philip Doddridge.

34 GOLDEN HILL. S. M.　　　　　Annanias Davisson, 1817.

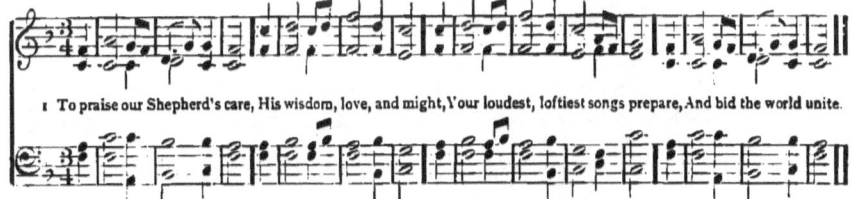

1 To praise our Shepherd's care, His wisdom, love, and might, Your loudest, loftiest songs prepare, And bid the world unite.

2 Supremely good and great,
　He tends His blood-bought fold;
He stoops, though throned in highest state,
　The feeblest to uphold.

3 He hears their softest plaint;
　He sees them when they roam;
And if His meanest lamb should faint,
　His bosom bears it home.

4 Kind Shepherd of the sheep!
　A weary flock are we;
And snares and foes are nigh; but keep
　The lambs who look to Thee.

5 And if through death's dark vale
　Our feet should early tread.
Oh, may we reach thy fold, and hail
　The love which us hath led!
　　　　　Wm. H. Havergal, 1840.

35 S. M.

1 Let every heart and tongue
　Proclaim the Saviour's praise;
He is the source of all my joy,
　His mercy crowns my days.

2 He knows my feeble frame,
　Remembers I am dust;
And though He should my life destroy,
　In Him I'll put my trust.

3 Each day He is my strength,
　My hope, my life, my all;
And, while upon His arm I lean,
　I surely cannot fall.

4 Then, to my blessed Lord
　Let grateful songs arise,
While angels bear the notes above,
　And sound them through the skies.
　　　　　W. T. Moore.

THE PRAISE HYMNARY.

36 HOSANNA! C. M.
MITCHISON'S HARMONY, Glasgow.

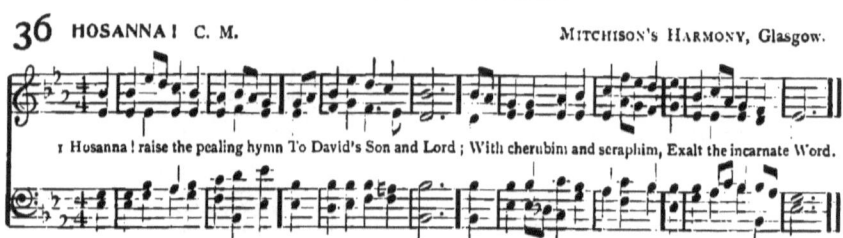

1 Hosanna! raise the pealing hymn To David's Son and Lord; With cherubim and seraphim, Exalt the incarnate Word.

37 C. M.

2 Hosanna! Sovereign, Prophet, Priest!
How vast Thy gifts, how free!
Thy blood, our life: Thy word, our feast;
Thy name, our only plea.

3 Hosanna! once Thy gracious ear
Approved a lisping throng;
Be gracious still, and deign to hear
Our poor but grateful song.

4 O Saviour! if redeemed by Thee,
Thy temple we behold,
Hosannas through eternity
We'll sing to harps of gold.
WM. H. HAVERGAL, 1833.

1 NOT only for some task sublime
Thy help do I implore;
Not only at some solemn time
Thy holy spirit pour!

2 But for each daily task of mine
I need Thy quickening power;
I need Thy presence everywhere,
I need Thee every hour.

3 Each action finds in Thee its spring,
Each joy Thy love makes bright,
Each footstep is Thine ordering,
Each grief shines in Thy light.
THOMAS H. GILL.

38 ELATION. S. M.
Arr. fr. ROSSINI.

1 Mine eyes and my de-sire Are ev-er to the Lord; I love to plead His promises, And rest upon His word.

39 S. M.

2 Lord, turn to Thee my soul;
Bring Thy salvation near:
When will Thy hand release my feet
From sin's destructive snare?

3 When shall the sovereign grace
Of my forgiving God
Restore me from those dangerous ways
My wandering feet have trod?

4 Oh, keep my soul from death,
Nor put my hope to shame!
For I have placed my holy trust
In my Redeemer's name.

5 With humble faith I wait
To see Thy face again;
Of Israel it shall ne'er be said,
He sought the Lord in vain.
ISAAC WATTS, 1719.

1 REJOICE in God alway;
When earth looks heavenly bright,
When joy makes glad the livelong day,
And peace shuts in the night.

2 Rejoice when care and woe
The fainting soul oppress;
When tears at wakeful midnight flow,
And morn brings heaviness.

3 Rejoice in hope and fear;
Rejoice in life and death;
Rejoice when threatening storms are near,
And comfort languisheth.

4 When should not they rejoice,
Whom Christ His brethren calls,
Who hear and know His guiding voice,
When on their heart it falls?
JOHN MOULTRIE.

GENERAL PRAISE.

40 STAR OF BETHLEHEM. L. M. D.   Scotch Air.

1. Now, in a song of grateful praise, To my dear Lord my voice I'll raise;
With all His saints I'll join to tell That Jesus hath done all things well.
Wisdom, and power, and love divine, In all His works, unrivalled, shine,
D.S. And force the wondering world to tell That He alone do'th all things well.

2 Howe'er mysterious are His ways,
Or dark and sorrowful my days;
And though my spirit oft rebel,
I know He still doth all things well.
And when I stand before His throne,
And all His ways are fully known,
This note in sweetest strains shall swell,
That Jesus hath done all things well.
— SAMUEL MEDLEY.

41 L. M. D.

1 To God, the great, the ever-blest,
Let songs of honor be addressed!
His mercy firm forever stands;
Give Him the thanks His love demands!
Who knows the wonder of His ways?
Who can make known His boundless praise?
Blest are the souls that fear Him still,
And learn submission to His will.
— ISAAC WATTS.

42 L. M. D.

1 My soul complete in Jesus stands!
It fears no more the law's demands;
The smile of God is sweet within,
Where all before was guilt and sin.
My soul at rest in Jesus lives:
Accepts the peace His pardon gives;
Receives the grace His death secured,
And pleads the anguish He endured.

2 My soul its every foe defies,
And cries—'T is God that justifies!
Who charges God's elect with sin?
Shall Christ, who died their peace to win?
A song of praise my soul shall sing,
To our eternal, glorious King!
Shall worship humbly at His feet,
In whom alone it stands complete.
— Mrs. GRACE W. HINSDALE.

43 L. M. D.

1 Worthy the Lamb of boundless sway,—
In earth and heaven the Lord of all!
Let all the powers of earth obey,
And low before His footstool fall.

Higher—still higher swell the strain;
Creation's voice the note prolong!
Jesus, the Lamb, shall ever reign:
Let hallelujahs crown the song.
— WALTER SHIRLEY.

THE PRAISE HYMNARY.

44 BARTIMEUS. 8s, 7s.   STEPHEN JENKS.

1 None but Christ: His merit hides me, He was faultless — I am fair;
None but Christ, His wisdom guides me, He was outcast — I'm His care.

2 None but Christ: His Spirit seals me,
  Gives me freedom with control:
  None but Christ, His bruising heals me,
  And His sorrow soothes my soul.

3 None but Christ: His life sustains me,
  Strength and song to me He is;
  None but Christ, His love constrains me,
  He is mine and I am His.
      Mrs. ANNE R. COUSIN.

45 8s, 7s.

1 HARK! the sound of holy voices,
  Chanting at the crystal sea,
  Hallelujah, hallelujah,
  Hallelujah, Lord, to Thee!

2 Multitudes, which none can number,
  Like the stars in glory stand,
  Clothed in white apparel, holding
  Palms of victory in their hands.

3 They have come from tribulation,
  And have washed their robes in blood,
  Washed them in the blood of Jesus;
  Tried they were and firm they stood.
      CHRISTOPHER WORDSWORTH, 1862.

46 JESUS, MY LORD. 6s, 4s.   WM. A. MAY.

1 Would I might love Thee more, Jesus, my Lord!
  Thy tender grace adore, (Omit .....) Jesus, my Lord!
  Teach me Thy love to me,
  O-pen mine eyes to see Thy glorious majesty, Jesus, my Lord!

Copyright, 1898, by SILVER, BURDETT & COMPANY.

2 Only in Thee I live,
  Jesus, my Lord!
  Thou only power can give,
  Jesus, my Lord!
  Thy precious truth instil,
  Teach me to know Thy will,
  All Thy commands fulfil,
  Jesus, my Lord!

3 Oh, let me love Thee more,
  Jesus, my Lord!
  Thy tender grace adore,
  Jesus, my Lord!
  Lovely indeed Thou art;
  Thyself to me impart,
  Come, dwell in my poor heart,
  Jesus, my Lord!
      ANNA HOLYOKE HOWARD.

47 6s, 4s.

1 SAVIOUR! Thy gentle voice
  Gladly we hear;
  Author of all our joys,
  Ever be near;
  Our souls would cling to Thee,
  Let us Thy fulness see,
  Let us Thy fulness see,
  Our life to cheer.

2 Fountain of life divine!
  Thee we adore;
  We would be wholly Thine
  Forevermore;
  Freely forgive our sin,
  Grant heavenly peace within,
  Grant heavenly peace within,
  Thy light restore.

3 Though to our faith unseen,
  While darkness reigns,
  On Thee alone we lean
  While life remains;
  By Thy free grace restored,
  Our souls shall bless Thee, Lord,
  Our souls shall bless Thee, Lord
  In joyful strains!
      THOMAS HASTINGS.

GENERAL PRAISE.

48 SING THE ALMIGHTY POWER OF GOD. C. M.   English.

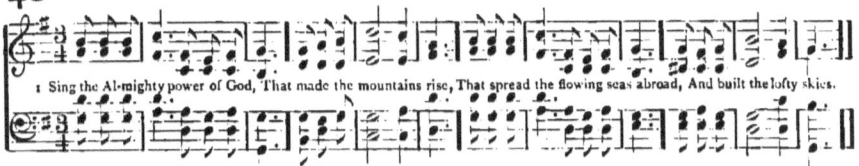

1 Sing the Almighty power of God, That made the mountains rise, That spread the flowing seas abroad, And built the lofty skies.

2 I sing the wisdom that ordained
   The sun to rule the day;
   The moon shines full at His command,
   And all the stars obey.

3 Lord! how Thy wonders are displayed
   Where'er I turn mine eye!

4 If I survey the ground I tread,
   Or gaze upon the sky!
   There 's not a plant or flower below
   But makes Thy glories known;
   And clouds arise and tempests blow,
   By order from Thy throne.
                                    ISAAC WATTS, 1715

49 C. M.

1 To Thee, my Shepherd, and my Lord,
   A grateful song I 'll raise;
   Oh let the humblest of Thy flock
   Attempt to speak Thy praise.

2 My life, my joy, my hope, I owe
   To Thine amazing love;
   Ten thousand thousand comforts here,
   And nobler bliss above.

3 To Thee my trembling spirit flies,
   With sin and grief oppressed;
   Thy gentle voice dispels my fears,
   And lulls my cares to rest.

4 Lead on, dear Shepherd! — led by Thee,
   No evil shall I fear;
   Soon shall I reach Thy fold above,
   And praise Thee better there.
                                    OTTIWELL HEGINBOTHOM, 1812.

50 LICHNER. S. M.   Arr.

1 "For - ev - er with the Lord!" — So, Jesus! let it be; Life from the dead is in that word; 'T is im-mor-tal-i-ty.

2 Here, in the body pent,
   Absent from Thee I roam;
   Yet nightly pitch my moving tent,
   A day's march nearer home.

3 "Forever with the Lord!"
   Saviour, if 't is Thy will
   The promise of that faithful word
   E'en here to me fulfil.

4 So when my latest breath
   Shall rend the vail in twain,
   By death I shall escape from death,
   And life eternal gain.

5 Knowing as I am known,
   How shall I love that word,
   And oft repeat before the throne —
   "Forever with the Lord!"
                                    JAMES MONTGOMERY, 1835.

51 S. M.

1 My soul, it is thy God
   Who calls thee by His grace;
   Now loose thee from each cumbering load,
   And bend thee to the race.

2 Make thy salvation sure;
   All sloth and slumber shun;
   Nor dare a moment's rest secure,
   Till thou the goal hast won.

3 Thy crown of life hold fast;
   Thy heart with courage stay;
   Nor let one trembling glance be cast
   Along the backward way.

4 Thy path ascends the skies,
   With conquering footsteps bright;
   And thou shalt win and wear the prize
   In everlasting light.
                                    LEONARD SWAIN, 1858.

THE PRAISE HYMNARY.

52 WARD. L. M. LOWELL MASON, 1830.

1 God is the ref-uge of His saints, When storms of sharp dis-tress in-vade;
Ere we can of-fer our com-plaints, Be-hold Him pres-ent with His aid.

53 L. M.

2 Loud may the troubled ocean roar—
  In sacred peace our souls abide;
  While every nation, every shore,
  Trembles, and dreads the swelling tide.

3 There is a stream, whose gentle flow
  Supplies the city of our God;
  Life, love, and joy, still gliding through,
  And watering our divine abode.

4 That sacred stream, Thy holy word,
  Our grief allays, our fear controls;
  Sweet peace Thy promises afford,
  And give new strength to fainting souls.

5 Zion enjoys her Monarch's love,
  Secure against a threatening hour;
  Nor can her firm foundations move,
  Built on His truth, and armed with power.
        ISAAC WATTS, 1719. Abbr.

1 AWAKE, my tongue, Thy tribute bring
  To Him who gave Thee power to sing;
  Praise Him who is all praise above,
  The source of wisdom and of love.

2 How vast His knowledge! how profound!
  A deep where all our thoughts are drowned;
  The stars He numbers, and their names
  He gives to all those heavenly flames.

3 Through each bright world above, behold
  Ten thousand thousand charms unfold;
  Earth, air, and mighty seas combine
  To speak His wisdom all divine.

4 But in redemption, Oh, what grace!
  Its wonders, Oh, what thought can trace!
  Here, wisdom shines forever bright;
  Praise Him, my soul, with sweet delight.
        JOHN NEEDHAM, 1768.

54 CAPETOWN. 7s, 5s. FRIEDRICH FILITZ, 1847.
  rall.

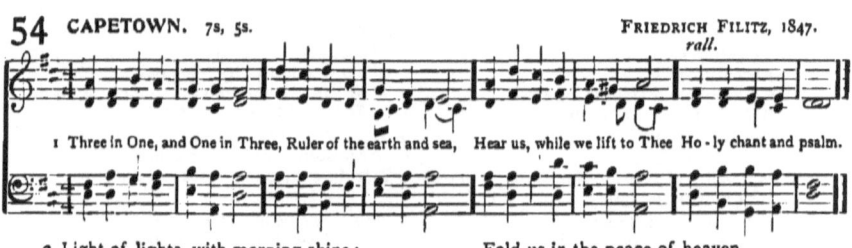

1 Three in One, and One in Three, Ruler of the earth and sea, Hear us, while we lift to Thee Ho-ly chant and psalm.

2 Light of lights, with morning shine:
  Lift on us Thy light divine;
  And let charity benign
  Breathe on us her balm.

3 Light of lights, when falls the even,
  Let it close on sin forgiven

  Fold us in the peace of heaven,
  Shed a holy calm.

4 Three in One, and One in Three,
  Dimly here we worship Thee;
  With the saints hereafter we
  Hope to bear a palm.
        GILBERT RORISON, 1859. Alt.

GENERAL PRAISE.

55 8s, 7s. D.

1 PRAISE to Thee, Thou great Creator!
  Praise to Thee from every tongue;
Join, my soul, with every creature,
  Join the universal song.
Father, source of all compassion,
  Pure, unbounded grace is Thine;
Hail the God of our salvation!
  Praise Him for His love divine.

2 For ten thousand blessings given,
    For the hope of future joy,
  Sound His praise through earth and heaven,
    Sound Jehovah's praise on high.
  Joyfully on earth adore Him,
    Till in heaven our song we raise;
  There, enraptured, fall before Him,
    Lost in wonder, love, and praise.
              JOHN FAWCETT, 1767.

56 HARWELL. 8s, 7s. D.   LOWELL MASON, 1840.

1 Hark! ten thousand harps and voices Sound the note of praise above;
  Jesus reigns, and heaven rejoices; Jesus reigns, the God of love;
  See, He sits on yonder throne;
  Jesus rules the world alone.
  Hallelujah, Hallelujah, Hallelujah! A-MEN.

2 King of glory! reign forever—
    Thine an everlasting crown;
  Nothing, from Thy love, shall sever
    Those whom Thou hast made Thine own;—
  Happy objects of Thy grace,
  Destined to behold Thy face.

3 Saviour! hasten Thine appearing;
    Bring, oh, bring the glorious day,
  When, the awful summons hearing,
    Heaven and earth shall pass away;—
  Then, with golden harps, we'll sing,—
    "Glory, glory to our King!"
              THOMAS KELLY, 1804. Abbr.

57 8s, 7s. D.

1 LORD, with glowing heart I'd praise Thee
    For the bliss Thy love bestows,
  For the pardoning grace that saves me,
    And the peace that from it flows.
  Help, O God, my weak endeavor,
    This dull soul to rapture raise;
  Thou must light the flame, or never
    Can my love be warmed to praise.

2 Praise, my soul, the God that sought thee,
    Wretched wanderer, far astray;
  Found thee lost, and kindly brought thee
    From the paths of death away.
  Praise, with love's devoutest feeling,
    Him who saw thy guilt-born fear,
  And, the light of hope revealing,
    Bade the blood-stained cross appear.

3 Lord, this bosom's ardent feeling
    Vainly would my lips express;
  Low before Thy footstool kneeling,
    Deign Thy suppliant's prayer to bless.
  Let Thy grace, my soul's chief treasure,
    Love's pure flame within me raise;
  And since words can never measure,
    Let my life show forth Thy praise.
              FRANCIS S. KEY, 1857.

THE PRAISE HYMNARY.

58 CORONATION. C. M.   OLIVER HOLDEN, 1793.

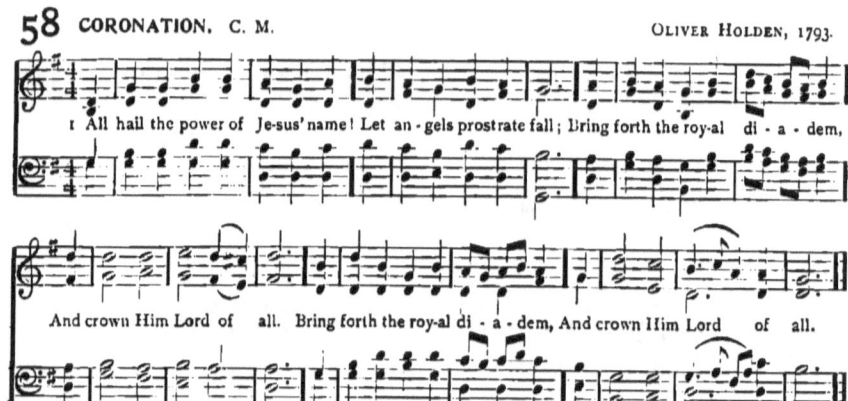

1 All hail the power of Jesus' name! Let angels prostrate fall; Bring forth the royal diadem, And crown Him Lord of all. Bring forth the royal diadem, And crown Him Lord of all.

2 Ye chosen seed of Israel's race,
Ye ransomed from the fall;
Hail Him, who saves you by His grace,
And crown Him Lord of all.

3 Sinners, whose love can ne'er forget
The wormwood and the gall;
Go, spread your trophies at His feet,
And crown Him Lord of all.

4 Let every kindred, every tribe,
On this terrestrial ball,
To Him all majesty ascribe,
And crown Him Lord of all.

5 Oh! that with yonder sacred throng,
We at His feet may fall;
We'll join the everlasting song,
And crown Him Lord of all.

EDWARD PERRONET, 1780.

59 PRAISE. P. M.    German Melody.

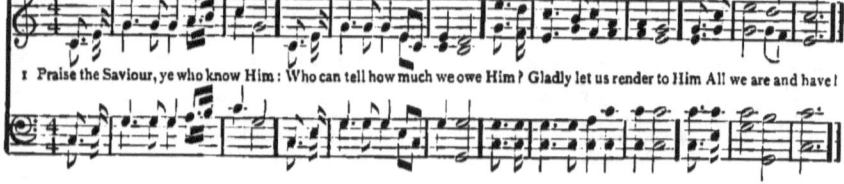

1 Praise the Saviour, ye who know Him: Who can tell how much we owe Him? Gladly let us render to Him All we are and have!

2 With His blood the Lord has bought them;
When they knew Him not, He sought them,
And from all their wanderings brought them;
His the praise alone.

3 Jesus is the name that charms us;
He for conflicts fits and arms us;
Nothing moves, and nothing harms us,
When we trust in Him.

4 Trust in Him, ye saints, forever;
He is faithful, changing never;
Neither force nor guile can sever
Those He loves from Him.

THOMAS KELLY, 1806.

60 P. M.

1 Sing of Jesus, sing forever,
Of the love that changes never.
Who or what from Him can sever
Those He makes His own?

2 Through the desert Jesus leads them,
With the bread of heaven He feeds them,
And through all the way He speeds them
To their home above.

3 There they see the Lord who bought them,
Him who came from Heaven, and sought them,
Him who by His Spirit taught them,
Him they serve and love.

THOMAS KELLY, 1815.

GENERAL PRAISE.

61 HOLLAND. C. M. D.   National Air of Holland.

1. The head that once was crowned with thorns Is crowned with glory now; A roy-al di-a-dem a-dorns The might-y Vic-tor's brow. The highest place that heaven affords Is His, is His by right, The King of kings and Lord of lords, And heaven's e-ter-nal light, And heaven's e-ter-nal light.
2. The joy of all who dwell above, The joy of all be-low, To whom He man-i-fests His love, And grants His name to know. The cross He bore is life and health, Tho' shame and death to Him, His peo-ple's hope, His peo-ple's wealth, Their ev-er-last-ing theme, Their ev-er-last-ing theme.

THOMAS KELLY, 1820.

62 C. M. D.

1 I HEARD a voice, the sweetest voice
That mortal ever heard;
Oh! how it made my heart rejoice,
And every feeling stirred!
'T was Jesus spoke to me so mild;
He called me to His side,
And said, although with heart defiled,
I might in Him confide,
I might in Him confide.

2 I saw His face, the fairest face
That mortal ever saw;
I longed the Saviour to embrace,
From Him new life to draw.
"Come unto me," He kindly said,
"And I will give Thee rest;
The ransom-price I fully paid —
Repent! believe! be blest!
Repent! believe! be blest!"

3 I felt His love, the strongest love
That mortal ever felt;
Oh! how it drew my soul above,
And made my hard heart melt!
My burden at His feet I laid,
And knew the joy of heaven,
As in my willing ear He said
The blessèd word, "*Forgiven!*"
The blessèd word, "*Forgiven!*"

P. STRYKER.

63 C. M. D.

1 THE mercies of my God and King
My tongue shall still pursue:
Oh, happy they, who, while they sing
Those mercies, share them too!
As bright and lasting as the sun,
As lofty as the sky,
From age to age, Thy word shall run,
And chance and change defy,
And chance and change defy.

2 The covenant of the King of kings
Shall stand forever sure;
Beneath the shadow of Thy wings
Thy saints repose secure.
In earth below, in heaven above,
Who, who is Lord like Thee?
Oh, spread the gospel of Thy love,
Till all Thy glories see!
Till all Thy glories see!

HENRY F. LYTE, 1834.

THE PRAISE HYMNARY.

64 COME, LET US ADORE HIM. 11s. English.

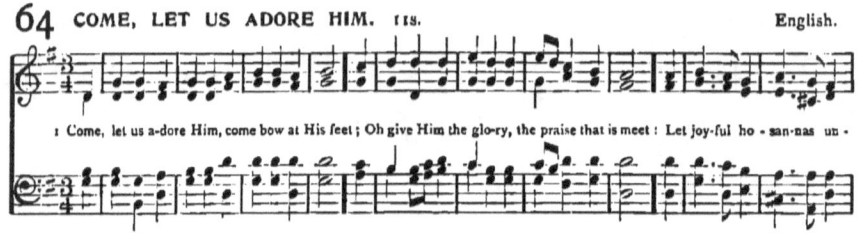

1 Come, let us a-dore Him, come bow at His feet; Oh give Him the glo-ry, the praise that is meet: Let joy-ful ho - san-nas un -

ceas-ing a - rise, And join the full cho - rus that glad-dens the skies, And join the full cho-rus that glad-dens the skies.

2 Oh! join ye the anthems of triumph that rise
From throne of the blest, from the hosts of the skies;
They sing alleluia in rapturous strains,
Hosanna! the Lord God omnipotent reigns!
Hosanna! the Lord God omnipotent reigns!

3 Rejoice! ye that love Him; His power cannot fail!
His omnipotent goodness shall surely prevail;
The triumph of evil will shortly be passed,
The Lord of all glory shall conquer at last,
The Lord of all glory shall conquer at last.

ANON.

65 11s.

1 COME, Jesus, Redeemer! abide Thou with me,
Come gladden my spirit, that waiteth for Thee;
Thy smile every shadow shall chase from my heart,
And soothe every sorrow, though keen be the smart,
And soothe every sorrow, though keen be the smart.

2 Without Thee but weakness, with Thee I am strong;
By day Thou shalt lead me, by night be my song;
Though dangers surround me, I still every fear,
Since Thou, the Most Mighty, my helper, art near,
Since Thou, the Most Mighty, my helper, art near.

3 Breathe, breathe on my spirit, oft ruffled, Thy peace,
From restless vain wishes bid Thou my heart cease;
In Thee all its longings henceforward shall end,
Till glad to Thy presence my soul shall ascend,
Till glad to Thy presence my soul shall ascend.

RAY PALMER, 1865.

66 11s.

1 FOR what shall I praise Thee, my God and my King,
For blessings, the tribute of gratitude bring?
Or praise Thee for pleasure, for health, or for ease,
For sunshine of youth, for the garden of peace?
For sunshine of youth, for the garden of peace?

2 For this I should praise; but if only for this,
I'd leave half untold the donation of bliss!
I thank Thee for sickness, for sorrow, and care,
For thorns I have gathered, the anguish I bear,
For thorns I have gathered, the anguish I bear; —

3 For nights of anxiety, for watching, and tears,
A present of pain, a prospective of fears;
I praise Thee, I bless Thee, my Lord and my God,
For blessing and trial Thy hand hath bestowed,
For blessing and trial Thy hand hath bestowed!

Mrs. CAROLINE (FRY) WILSON.

GENERAL PRAISE.

67 THE GRATEFUL SONG. L. M.　　　　　　　　　　　Old Melody.

1 From every place below the skies, The grateful song, the fervent prayer,

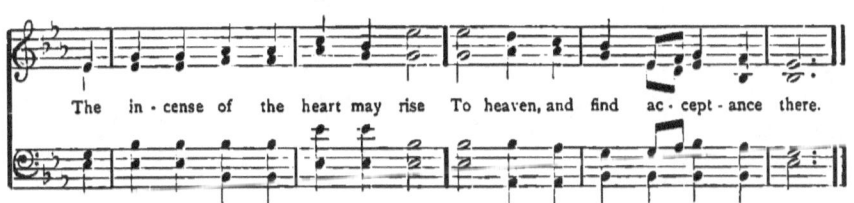

The incense of the heart may rise To heaven, and find acceptance there.

2 O Thou, to whom, in ancient time,
　The holy prophet's harp was strung,
　To Thee at last in every clime,
　Shall temples rise and praise be sung.

3 Praise God, from whom all blessings flow;
　Praise Him, all creatures here below;
　Praise Him above, ye heavenly host;
　Praise Father, Son, and Holy Ghost.

68 L. M.

1 OH, sweetly breathe the lyres above,
　When angels touch the quivering string,
　And wake, to chant Immanuel's love,
　Such strains as angel-lips can sing!

2 And sweet, on earth, the choral swell,
　From mortal tongues, of gladsome lays;
　When pardoned souls their raptures tell,
　And grateful, hymn Immanuel's praise.

3 Jesus, Thy name our souls adore;
　We own the bond that makes us Thine;
　And carnal joys that charmed before,
　For Thy dear sake we now resign.

4 Our hearts, by dying love subdued,
　Accept Thine offered grace to-day;
　Beneath the cross, with blood bedewed,
　We bow, and give ourselves away.

5 In Thee we trust,—on Thee rely;
　Though we are feeble, Thou art strong;
　Oh, keep us till our spirits fly
　To join the bright, immortal throng!

　　　　　　　　　　　RAY PALMER, 1842.

69 L. M.

1 COME, Christians, brethren, ere we part,
　Join every voice and every heart;
　One solemn hymn to God we raise,
　One final song of grateful praise.

2 Christians, we here may meet no more,
　But there is yet a happier shore;
　And there, released from toil and pain,
　Soon, brethren, we may meet again.

　　　　　　　　　　HENRY KIRKE WHITE, 1806

THE PRAISE HYMNARY.

70 7s. 6l.

1 OH! give thanks to Him who made
Morning light and evening shade;
Source and giver of all good,
Nightly sleep and daily food;
Quickener of our wearied powers;
Guard of our unconscious hours.

2 Oh! give thanks to nature's King,
Who made every breathing thing:
His, our warm and sentient frame,
His, the mind's immortal flame.
Oh, how close the ties that bind
Spirits to the Eternal Mind!

3 Oh! give thanks with heart and lip,
For we are His workmanship;
And all creatures are His care:
Not a bird that cleaves the air
Falls unnoticed; but who can
Speak the Father's love to man?

4 Oh! give thanks to Him that came
In a mortal, suffering frame —
Temple of the Deity —
Came, for rebel man to die;
In the path Himself hath trod,
Leading back His saints to God.

JOSIAH CONDER.

71 SABBATH. 7s. 6l. LOWELL MASON, 1824.

1 Cen-ter of our hopes Thou art, End of our enlarged de-sires: Stamp Thine image on our heart; Fill us now with heavenly fires:
Joined to Thee by love di-vine, Seal our souls for-ev-er Thine, Joined to Thee by love divine, Seal our souls for-ev-er Thine.

2 All our works in Thee be wrought,
  Levelled at one common aim:
Every word and every thought
  Purge in the refining flame;
Lead us, through the paths of peace,
On to perfect holiness.

3 Let us all together rise, —
  To Thy glorious life restored;
Here regain our Paradise, —
  Here prepare to meet our Lord:
Here enjoy the earnest given:
Travel hand in hand to heaven.

CHARLES WESLEY, 1749.

72 DOXOLOGY. 7s. 6l.

1 PRAISE the Name of God most high;
Praise Him, all below the sky;
Praise Him, all ye heavenly host —
Father, Son, and Holy Ghost:
As through countless ages past,
Evermore His praise shall last.

ANON, 1827.

73 7s. 6l.

1 LORD of mercy and of might,
  God and Father of us all,
Lord of day, and Lord of Night,
  Listen to our solemn call:
Listen, whilst to Thee we raise
Songs of prayer and songs of praise.

2 Shed within our hearts, oh, shed
  Thine own Spirit's living flame —
Love for all whom Thou hast made,
  Love for all who love Thy name:
Young and old together bless,
Clothe our souls with righteousness.

3 Father, give to us Thy peace:
  May our life on earth be blest;
When our trials here shall cease,
  May we enter into rest, —
Rest within our home above,
Thee to praise, and Thee to love.

REGINALD HEBER, 1827.

GENERAL PRAISE.

74 WILMOT. 8s, 7s. C. M. Von Weber.

1 Praise the Lord! ye heavens, adore Him, Praise Him, angels, in the height;
Sun and moon, rejoice before Him; Praise Him, all ye stars of light!

2 Praise the Lord, for He hath spoken;
Worlds His mighty voice obeyed;
Laws which never shall be broken,
For their guidance He hath made.

3 Praise the Lord — for He is glorious;
Never shall His promise fail;
God hath made His saints victorious,
Sin and death shall not prevail.

4 Praise the God of our salvation,
Hosts on high His power proclaim;
Heaven and earth, and all creation,
Laud and magnify His name.
JOHN KEMPTHORN, 1796.

75 8s, 7s.

1 THINE forever, Thine forever!
May Thy face upon us shine;
Help, oh, help our weak endeavor,
Lord, forever to be Thine.

2 Thine forever, Thine forever!
Armed with faith, and strong in Thee,
Ever fighting, fainting never,
May we march to victory!

3 Daily in the grace increasing
Of thy Spirit, more and more,
Watching, praying without ceasing,
May we reach the heavenly shore!
CHRISTOPHER WORDSWORTH, 1860.

76 8s, 7s.

1 FRIEND of sinners! Lord of Glory!
Lowly, Mighty! Brother, King!
Musing o'er Thy wondrous story,
Fain would I Thy praises sing.

2 Friend to help us, comfort, save us,
In whom power and pity blend,
Praise we must the grace which gave us
Jesus Christ, the sinner's Friend.

3 Friend who never fails nor grieves us,
Faithful, tender, constant, kind!
Friend who at all times receives us,
Friend who came the lost to find!

4 Sorrow soothing, joys enhancing,
Loving until life shall end,
Then conferring bliss entrancing,
Still in heaven the sinner's Friend.

5 Oh, to love and serve Thee better!
From all evil set us free;
Break, Lord, every sinful fetter,
Be each thought conformed to Thee.

6 Looking for Thy bright appearing,
May our spirits upward tend;
Till no longer doubting, fearing,
We behold the sinner's Friend!
NEWMAN HALL, 1859.

THE PRAISE HYMNARY.

77 HENDON. 7s.   C. H. A. MALAN, 1828.

1 Now be-gin the heaven-ly theme, Sing a-loud in Je-sus' name; Ye who Je-sus' kind-ness prove, Tri-umph in re-deem-ing love, Tri-umph in re-deem-ing love.

2 Ye who see the Father's grace
Beaming in the Saviour's face,
As to Canaan on ye move,
Praise and bless redeeming love.

3 Mourning souls, dry up your tears;
Banish all your guilty fears;
See your guilt and curse remove,
Cancelled by redeeming love.

4 Welcome, all by sin opprest,
Welcome to His sacred rest;
Nothing brought Him from above,
Nothing but redeeming love.

5 Hither, then, your music bring,
Strike aloud each joyful string;
Mortals, join the host above,
Join to praise redeeming love.
                JOHN LANGFORD, 1761. Abbr.

78 7s.

1 HOLY, holy, holy Lord,
Be Thy glorious name adored !
Lord, Thy mercies never fail;
Hail, celestial Goodness, hail !

2 Though unworthy, Lord, Thine ear,
Deign our humble songs to hear;
Purer praise we hope to bring,
When around Thy throne we sing.

3 While on earth ordained to stay,
Guide our footsteps in Thy way,
Till we come to dwell with Thee,
Till we all Thy glory see.

4 Then with angel-harps again
We will wake a nobler strain;
There, in joyful songs of praise,
Our triumphant voices raise.
                BENJAMIN WILLIAMS, 1778. Abbr.

79 7s.

1 PRAISE our glorious King and Lord,
Angels waiting on His word,
Saints that walk with Him in white,
Pilgrims walking in His light:

2 Glory to the Eternal One,
Glory to His only Son,
Glory to the Spirit be
Now, and through eternity.
                ALEXANDER R. THOMPSON, 1869.

80 7s.

1 THEE to laud in songs divine,
Angels and archangels join,
We with them our voices raise,
Echo Thine eternal praise:

2 Holy, holy, holy Lord,
Live, by heaven and earth adored,
Full of Thee, they ever cry,
Glory be to God on high.
                CHARLES WESLEY, 1780.

GENERAL PRAISE.

81 ST. ALKMUND. L. M.   Arr. fr. Ancient Melody.

1 My God, my King, Thy various praise Shall fill the remnant of my days; Thy grace employ my humble tongue, Till death and glory raise the song.

2 The wings of every hour shall bear
Some thankful tribute to Thine ear,
And every setting sun shall see
New works of duty done for Thee.

3 But who can speak Thy wondrous deeds?
Thy greatness all our thoughts exceeds:
Vast and unsearchable Thy ways;
Vast and immortal be Thy praise.
                     ISAAC WATTS, 1709. Abbr.

83 L. M.

1 Now let our souls, on wings sublime,
Rise from the vanities of time;
Draw back the parting veil, and see
The glories of eternity.

2 Born by a new, celestial birth,
Why should we grovel here on earth?
Why grasp at vain and fleeting toys,
So near to heaven's eternal joys?

3 Shall aught beguile us on the road,
While we are walking back to God?
As strangers into life we come,
And dying is but going home.
                     THOMAS GIBBONS, 1762.

82 L. M.

1 THERE seems a voice in every gale,
A tongue in every opening flower,
Which tells, O Lord! the wondrous tale
Of Thy indulgence, love, and power.

2 The birds that rise on soaring wing
Unite to hymn their Maker's praise;
And all the mingling sounds of spring
To Thee a general pæan raise.

3 And shall my voice, great God! alone
Be mute 'midst nature's loud acclaim?
No; let my heart with answering tone
Breathe forth in praise Thy holy name.

4 And nature's debt is small to mine:
Thou bad'st her being bounded be;
But — matchless proof of love divine —
Thou gav'st eternal life to me.
                     Mrs. A. OPIE.

84 DOXOLOGY. L. M.

1 To Father, Son, and Holy Ghost,
The God whom earth and heaven adore,
Be glory as it was of old,
Is now, and shall be evermore!
                     TATE AND BRADY, 1696. Alt.

THE PRAISE HYMNARY.

85 6s, 4s.

1 BREAK forth, ye heavens, in song!
Shout, bright angelic throng,
   Jehovah's praise!
Saints, clad in robes of white,
On Zion's glittering height,
Laud ye the God of might,
   Ancient of Days!

2 Let star respond to star
Through firmaments afar,
   Glory to God!
Earth, fling the joyful sound
Through ether's blue profound
To vocal spheres around,
   Glory to God!

3 Father, in light concealed,
Christ, Light of light revealed,
   Spirit Divine,
In glory streaming down
From Father and from Son,
Blest Three, forever one,
   All praise be Thine!

Z. EDDY.

86 ITALIAN HYMN. 6s, 4s.   FELICE GIARDINI, 1765.

1 Glo-ry to God on high, Let prais-es fill the sky! Praise ye His name. An-gels His name a-dore, Who all our sor-rows bore, And saints cry ev-er-more, "Worth-y the Lamb!"

2 All they around the throne
Cheerfully join in one,
   Praising His name.
We who have felt His blood
Sealing our peace with God,
Spread His dear fame abroad:
   "Worthy the Lamb!"

3 Join all the human race,
Our Lord and God to bless;
   Praise ye His name!
In Him we will rejoice,
Making a cheerful noise,
And say with heart and voice,
   "Worthy the Lamb!"

4 Though we must change our place,
Our souls shall never cease
   Praising His name;
To Him we'll tribute bring,
Laud Him our gracious King,
And through all ages sing,
   "Worthy the Lamb!"

JAMES ALLEN, 1761.

87 6s, 4s.

1 COME, all ye saints of God,
Through all the earth abroad,
   Spread Jesus' fame:
Tell what His love hath done;
Trust in His name alone;
Shout to His lofty throne,
   "Worthy the Lamb!"

2 Hence, gloomy doubts and fears!
Dry up your mournful tears;
   Join our glad theme:
Beauty for ashes bring;
Strike each melodious string;
Join heart and voice to sing,
   "Worthy the Lamb!"

3 Hark! how the choirs above,
Filled with the Saviour's love,
   Dwell on His name!
There, too, may we be found,
With light and glory crowned,
While all the heavens resound,
   "Worthy the Lamb!"

JAMES BODEN, 1801.

GENERAL PRAISE.

88 6s, 4s.

1 LET us awake our joys;
 Strike up with cheerful voice;
  Each creature sing:
 Angels! begin the song;
 Mortals! the strain prolong,
 In accents sweet and strong,
  "Jesus is King!"

2 Proclaim abroad His name;
 Tell of His matchless fame;
  What wonders done!
 Above, beneath, around,
 Let all the earth resound,
 Till heaven's high arch rebound,
  "Victory is won!"

3 He vanquished sin and hell,
 And our last foe will quell:
  Mourners, rejoice!
 His dying love adore;
 Praise Him, now raised in power!
 Praise Him forevermore,
  With joyful voice.

4 All hail the glorious day,
 When, through the heavenly way,
  Lo, He shall come!
 While they who pierced Him wail,
 His promise shall not fail;
 Saints, see your King prevail:
  Great Saviour, come!
  WILLIAM KINGSBURY, 1806.

89 6s, 4s.

1 COME, Thou Almighty King,
 Help us Thy name to sing,
  Help us to praise;
 Father all glorious,
 O'er all victorious,
 Come, and reign over us,
  Ancient of days.

2 Come, thou Incarnate Word,
 Gird on Thy mighty sword,
  Our prayer attend;
 Come, and Thy people bless,
 And give Thy word success:
 Spirit of holiness,
  On us descend.

3 Come, Holy Comforter,
 Thy sacred witness bear,
  In this glad hour;
 Thou, who almighty art,
 Now rule in every heart,
 And ne'er from us depart,
  Spirit of power.

4 To the great One in Three
 The highest praises be,
  Hence evermore.
 His sovereign majesty
 May we in glory see,
 And, to eternity,
  Love and adore!
  CHARLES WESLEY, 1757. Abbr.

90 6s, 4s.

1 LET the still air rejoice —
 Be every youthful voice
  Blended in one;
 While we renew our strain
 To Him, with joy again,
 Who sends the evening rain,
  And morning sun.

2 His hand in beauty gives
 Each flower and plant that lives,
  Each sunny rill;
 Springs! which our footsteps meet —
 Fountains! our lips to greet —
 Waters! whose taste is sweet,
  On rock and hill.

3 Each summer bird that sings,
 Drinks from dear Nature's springs,
  Her early dew;
 And the refreshing shower
 Falls on each herb and flower,
 Giving it life and power,
  Fragrant and new.
  JOHN PIERPONT. Abbr.

91 6s, 4s.

1 THOU, whose almighty Word
 Chaos and darkness heard,
  And took their flight;
 Hear us, we humbly pray,
 And where the Gospel's day
 Sheds not its glorious ray,
  "Let there be light."

2 Thou, who didst come to bring
 On Thy redeeming wing
  Healing and sight,
 Health to the sick in mind,
 Sight to the inly blind,
 Oh, now to all mankind
  "Let there be light."

3 Spirit of truth and love,
 Life-giving, holy Dove,
  Speed forth Thy flight;
 Move o'er the water's face,
 Bearing the lamp of grace,
 And in earth's darkest place
  "Let there be light."
  JOHN MARRIOTT, 1813.

THE PRAISE HYMNARY.

92 LYONS. 10s, 11s. F. J. HAYDN, 1770.

1 O worship the King, all glorious above, And gratefully sing His wonderful love; Our Shield and Defender, the Ancient of days, Pavilioned in splendor and girded with praise.

2 Thy bountiful care, what tongue can recite?
It breathes in the air, it shines in the light;
It streams from the hills, it descends to the plain,
And sweetly distils in the dew and the rain.

3 Frail children of dust, and feeble as frail,
In Thee do we trust, nor find Thee to fail;
Thy mercies, how tender! how firm to the end,
Our Maker, Defender, Redeemer, and Friend!

4 Our Father and God, how faithful Thy love!
While angels delight to hymn Thee above,
The humbler creation, though feeble their lays,
With true adoration shall lisp to Thy praise.

SIR ROBERT GRANT, 1839.

93 10s, 11s.

1 YE servants of God, your Master proclaim,
And publish abroad His wonderful name:
The name, all victorious, of Jesus extol;
His kingdom is glorious, and rules over all.

2 God ruleth on high, almighty to save;
And still He is nigh, His presence we have:
The great congregation His triumph shall sing,
Ascribing salvation to Jesus our King.

3 "Salvation to God, who sits on the throne,"
Let all cry aloud, and honor the Son;
Our Saviour's high praises the angels proclaim,—
Fall down on their faces, and worship the Lamb.

CHARLES WESLEY, 1744.

GENERAL PRAISE.

94 C. M.

1 BEHOLD the glories of the Lamb,
  Amid His Father's throne;
  Prepare new honors for His name,
  And songs before unknown.

2 Let elders worship at His feet,
  The church adore around,
  With vials full of odors sweet,
  And harps of sweeter sound.

3 Now to the Lamb that once was slain,
  Be endless blessings paid!
  Salvation, glory, joy, remain
  Forever on Thy head!

4 Thou hast redeemed our souls with blood,
  Hast set the prisoners free,
  Hast made us kings and priests to God,
  And we shall reign with Thee.
      ISAAC WATTS, 1692.

95 C. M.

1 THE Saviour! Oh, what endless charms
  Dwell in that blissful sound!
  Its influence every fear disarms
  And spreads delight around.

2 Here pardon, life, and joy divine
  In rich profusion flow
  For guilty rebels, lost in sin,
  And doomed to endless woe.

3 The mighty Former of the skies
  Descends to our abode,
  While angels view with wondering eyes,
  And hail the incarnate God.

4 How rich the depths of love divine!
  Of bliss, a boundless store!
  Dear Saviour, let me call Thee mine;
  I cannot wish for more.
      ANNE STEELE, 1760.

96 DOWNS. C. M.   LOWELL MASON, 1832.

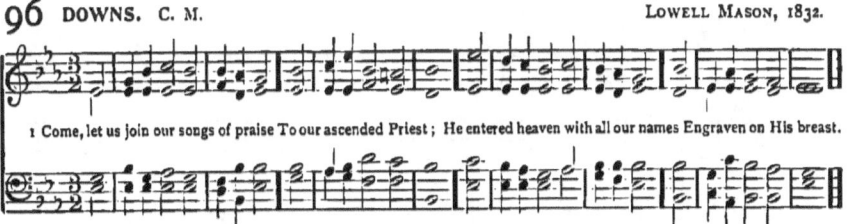

1 Come, let us join our songs of praise To our ascended Priest; He entered heaven with all our names Engraven on His breast.

2 Below, He washed our guilt away,
  By His atoning blood;
  Now He appears before the throne,
  And pleads our cause with God.

3 Clothed with our nature still, He knows
  The weakness of our frame,
  And how to shield us from the foes
  Which He himself o'ercame.

4 Nor time, nor distance, e'er shall quench
  The fervor of His love;
  For us He died in kindness here,
  For us He lives above.

5 Oh! may we ne'er forget His grace,
  Nor blush to bear His name;
  Still may our hearts hold fast His faith —
  Our lips His praise proclaim.
      ALEXANDER PIRIE, 1782.

97 C. M.

1 WHAT grace, O Lord, and beauty shone
  Around Thy steps below;
  What patient love was seen in all
  Thy life and death of woe!

2 For, ever on Thy burdened heart
  A weight of sorrow hung;
  Yet no ungentle, murmuring word
  Escaped Thy silent tongue.

3 Thy foes might hate, despise, revile,
  Thy friends unfaithful prove;
  Unwearied in forgiveness still,
  Thy heart could only love.

4 O give us hearts to love like Thee!
  Like Thee, O Lord, to grieve
  Far more for others' sins than all
  The wrongs that we receive.
      EDWARD DENNY, 1839.

THE PRAISE HYMNARY.

98 L. M.

1 Bless, O my soul, the Living God!
Call home thy thoughts that rove abroad;
Let all the powers within me join
In work and worship so divine.

2 Bless, O my soul, the God of grace!
His favors claim thy highest praise;
Why should the wonders He hath wrought
Be lost in silence and forgot?

3 'Tis He, my soul, that sent His son
To die for crimes which thou hast done;
He owns the ransom, and forgives
The hourly follies of our lives.

4 Let the whole earth His power confess;
Let the whole earth adore His grace:
The Gentile with the Jew shall join
In work and worship so divine.

ISAAC WATTS, 1719. Abbr.

99 L. M.

1 Servants of God! in joyful lays,
Sing ye the Lord Jehovah's praise;
His glorious name let all adore,
From age to age, for evermore.

2 Who is like God? so great, so high,
He bows Himself to view the sky;
And yet, with condescending grace,
Looks down upon the human race.

3 He hears the uncomplaining moan
Of those who sit and weep alone;
He lifts the mourner from the dust;
In Him the poor may safely trust.

4 Oh then, aloud, in joyful lays,
Sing to the Lord Jehovah's praise.
His saving name let all adore,
From age to age, forevermore.

JAMES MONTGOMERY.

100 GRATITUDE. L. M.   P. A. D. BOST, 1837. Arr.

1 God of my life! through all my days
My grateful powers shall sound Thy praise;
The song shall wake with opening light,
And warble to the silent night.

2 When anxious cares would break my rest,
And griefs would tear my throbbing breast,
Thy tuneful praises, raised on high,
Shall check the murmur and the sigh.

3 When death o'er nature shall prevail,
And all its powers of language fail,
Joy through my swimming eyes shall break,
And mean the thanks I cannot speak.

4 Soon shall I learn the exalted strains,
Which echo o'er the heavenly plains,
And emulate, with joy unknown,
The glowing seraphs round Thy throne.

PHILIP DODDRIDGE, 1740.

101 L. M.

1 Oh, render thanks to God above,
The fountain of eternal love;
Whose mercy firm, through ages past,
Hath stood, and shall forever last.

2 Who can His mighty deeds express,
Not only vast — but numberless?
What mortal eloquence can raise
His tribute of immortal praise?

3 Extend to me that favor, Lord,
Thou to Thy chosen dost afford;
When Thou return'st to set them free,
Let Thy salvation visit me.

TATE AND BRADY.

GENERAL PRAISE.

102 C. M.

1 LET children hear the mighty deeds,
　Which God performed of old;
　Which in our younger years we saw,
　And which our fathers told.

2 He bids us make His glories known,
　His works of power and grace;
　And we'll convey His wonders down
　Through every rising race.

3 Our lips shall tell them to our sons,
　And they again to theirs,
　That generations yet unborn
　May teach them to their heirs.

4 Thus shall they learn, in God alone
　Their hope securely stands;
　That they may ne'er forget His works,
　But practise His commands.
　　　　　　　　ISAAC WATTS, 1719.

103 C. M.

1 LET songs of praises fill the sky:
　Christ, our ascended Lord,
　Sends down His Spirit from on high,
　According to His word.

2 The Spirit, by His heavenly breath,
　New life creates within;
　He quickens sinners from the death
　Of trespasses and sin.

3 The things of Christ the Spirit takes,
　And shows them unto men;
　The fallen soul His temple makes,
　God's image stamps again.

4 Come, Holy Spirit, from above,
　With Thy celestial fire;
　Come, and with flames of zeal and love,
　Our hearts and tongues inspire.
　　　　　　THOMAS COTTERILL, 1819. Abbr.

104 WARWICK. C. M.　　　　SAMUEL STANLEY, 1800.

1 Come, let us join our cheerful songs
With angels round the throne;
Ten thousand thousand are their tongues,
But all their joys are one.

105 C. M.

1 AGAIN the Lord of light and life
　Awakes the kindling ray,
　Unseals the eyelids of the morn,
　And pours increasing day.

2 This day be grateful homage paid,
　And loud hosannas sung;
　Let gladness dwell in every heart,
　And praise on every tongue.

3 Ten thousand different lips shall join
　To hail this welcome morn,
　Which scatters blessings from its wings
　To nations yet unborn.
　　　Mrs. ANNA L. BARBAULD, 1773. Abbr. and alt.

2 "Worthy the Lamb that died," they cry,
　"To be exalted thus:"
　"Worthy the Lamb," our lips reply,
　"For He was slain for us."

3 Jesus is worthy to receive
　Honor and power divine;
　And blessings more than we can give,
　Be, Lord, forever Thine.

4 The whole creation join in one
　To bless the sacred name
　Of Him who sits upon the throne,
　And to adore the Lamb.
　　　　　　　　ISAAC WATTS, 1707.

THE PRAISE HYMNARY.

106 PELTON. S. M.   WM. A. MAY.

1 Oh, sing amid the storm, When high life's billows roll! For thou art one, art one with God, My deathless, dauntless soul!

Copyright, 1898, by SILVER, BURDETT AND COMPANY.

2 Oh, sing amid the storm,
   Spirit divine of birth!
For thou art, thou art mightier
   Than anything of earth.

3 Be nevermore dismayed,
   Nor yield to any fate.
Thou 'rt kin to God, to God Himself:
   Then claim thy high estate.

4 Oh, sing amid the storm,
   In faith's triumphant tone!
For time nor space, nor life nor death,
   Can part Him from His own.
            ELIZA M. HICKOK. Alt.

107 S. M.

1 To God the only wise,
   Who keeps us by His word,
Be glory now and evermore,
   Through Jesus Christ our Lord.

2 Hosanna to the Word,
   Who from the Father came;
Ascribe salvation to the Lord,
   And ever bless His name.

3 The grace of Christ our Lord,
   The Father's boundless love,
The Spirit's blest communion, too,
   Be with us from above.
            ISAAC WATTS, 1709.

108 LISCHER. H. M.   From the German by LOWELL MASON, 1841.

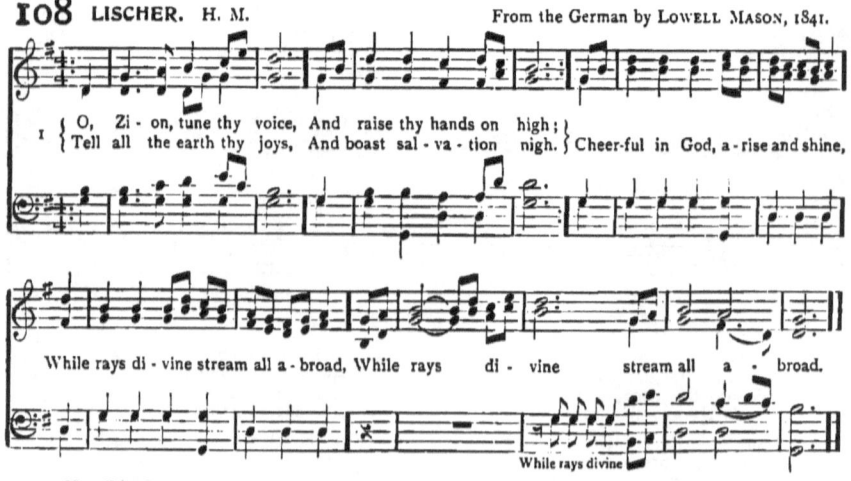

1 O, Zion, tune thy voice, And raise thy hands on high;
Tell all the earth thy joys, And boast salvation nigh.
Cheerful in God, arise and shine, While rays divine stream all abroad, While rays divine stream all abroad.

2 He gilds thy mourning face
   With beams that cannot fade;
   His all-resplendent grace
   He pours around thy head;
The nations round thy form shall view,
With lustre new divinely crowned.

3 There on His holy hill
   A brighter sun shall rise,
   And with His radiance fill
   Those fairer, purer skies;
While round His throne ten thousand stars,
In nobler spheres, His influence own.
            PHILIP DODDRIDGE. Abbr.

GENERAL PRAISE.

109 AUSTRIAN HYMN. 8s, 7s. D. F. J. HAYDN, 1797.

1. Father, Thine elect who lovest
With an everlasting love;
Saviour, who the bar removest
From the holy home above;
Spirit, daily meetness bringing
For the glory there upstored;
List to Thy glad people singing,
"Holy, holy, holy Lord!"

2. Lord, with sin-bound souls Thou bearest,
Struggling towards this strain divine;
Glad on mortal lips Thou hearest
That thrice awful name of Thine.
But Thou listenest, O how sweetly!
When from holy lips outpoured,
Rings through heaven this strain full meetly,
"Holy, holy, holy Lord!"

3. Shall we, Lord, meet voices never
Bring to that eternal hymn?
Hallow us to help the endeavor
Of Thy pure-lipped Seraphim:
Hark! their own high strain we bring Thee,
Listen to the full accord!
Sweet the song we ever sing Thee,
"Holy, holy, holy Lord!"

THOMAS H. GILL, 1860.

110 8s, 7s. D.

1. BLEST be Thou, O God of Israel!
Thou, our Father and our Lord!
Majesty is Thine forever;
Ever be Thy name adored.
Thine, O Lord, are power and greatness;
Glory, victory, are Thine own;
All is Thine in earth and heaven,
Over all Thy boundless throne.

2. Riches come of Thee, and honor;
Power and might to Thee belong;
Thine it is to make us prosper,
Only Thine to make us strong.
Lord, our God, for these, Thy bounties,
Hymns of gratitude we raise;
To Thy name, forever glorious,
Ever we address our praise.

HENRY U. ONDERDONK, 1826.

THE PRAISE HYMNARY.

111 PARK STREET. L. M.   F. M. A. VENUA, 1768.

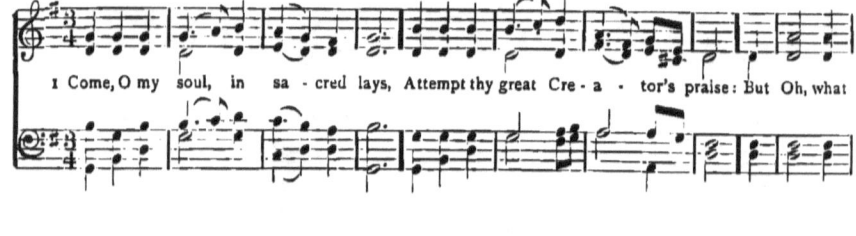

1 Come, O my soul, in sacred lays, Attempt thy great Creator's praise: But Oh, what

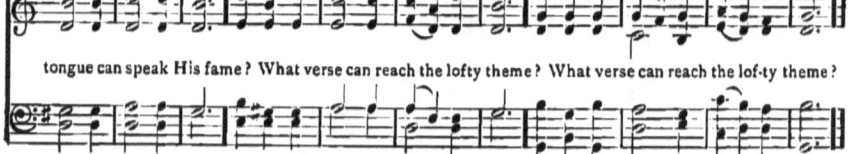

tongue can speak His fame? What verse can reach the lofty theme? What verse can reach the lofty theme?

2 Enthroned amid the radiant spheres,
He, glory like a garment wears;
To form a robe of light divine,
Ten thousand suns around Him shine.

3 In all our Maker's grand designs,
Almighty power with wisdom, shines;
His works, through all this wondrous frame,
Declare the glory of His name.

4 Raised on devotion's lofty wing,
Do thou, my soul, His glories sing;
And let His praise employ thy tongue
Till listening worlds shall join the song.
                  THOMAS BLACKLOCK, 1754.

113 L. M.

1 ZION, awake! thy strength renew;
Put on thy robes of beauteous hue;
Church of our God, arise and shine,
Bright with the beams of truth divine.

2 Soon shall thy radiance stream afar,
Wide as the heathen nations are;
Gentiles and kings thy light shall view,
All shall admire and love thee, too.
                  WILLIAM SHRUBSOLE.

114 DOXOLOGY. L. M.

1 To God the Father, God the Son,
And God the Spirit, Three in One,
Be honor, praise, and glory given,
By all on earth, and all in heaven.
                  ISAAC WATTS, 1709. Abbr.

112 L. M.

1 BE Thou exalted, O my God,
Above the heavens, where angels dwell;
Thy power on earth be known abroad,
And land to land Thy wonders tell.

2 My heart is fixed; my song shall raise
Immortal honors to His name;
Awake, my tongue, to sound His praise,
His wondrous goodness to proclaim!

3 High o'er the earth His mercy reigns,
And reaches to the utmost sky;
His truth to endless years remains,
When lower worlds dissolve and die.
                  ISAAC WATTS.

115 L. M.

1 THERE'S nothing bright, above, below,
From flowers that bloom to stars that glow,
But in its light my soul can see
Some features of the Deity.

2 There's nothing dark, below, above,
But in its gloom I trace Thy love,
And meekly wait the moment when
Thy touch shall make all bright again.

3 The light, the dark, where'er I look,
Shall be one pure and shining book,
Where I may read, in words of flame,
The glories of Thy wondrous name.
                  THOMAS MOORE, 1816.

GENERAL PRAISE.

116 C. M.

1 To our Redeemer's glorious name
   Awake the sacred song;
   O may His love immortal flame!
   Tune every heart and tongue.

2 His love, what mortal thought can reach!
   What mortal tongue display!
   Imagination's utmost stretch
   In wonder dies away.

3 He left His radiant throne on high,
   Left the bright realms of bliss,
   And came to earth to bleed and die.
   Was ever love like this?

4 Blest Lord, while we adoring pay
   Our humble thanks to Thee,
   May every heart with rapture say,
   "The Saviour died for me!"

ANNE STEELE, 1760.

117 C. M.

1 SING, all ye ransomed of the Lord,
   Your great Deliverer sing;
   Ye pilgrims, now for Zion bound,
   Be joyful in your King.

2 His hand divine shall lead you on,
   Through all the blissful road,
   Till to the sacred mount you rise,
   And see your gracious God.

3 Bright garlands of immortal joy
   Shall bloom on every head;
   While sorrow, sighing, and distress,
   Like shadows, all are fled.

4 March on in your Redeemer's strength,
   Pursue His footsteps still;
   And let the prospect cheer your eye
   While laboring up the hill.

PHILIP DODDRIDGE, 1740.

118 BOARDMAN. C. M. From L. DEVEREAUX, arr. by KINGSLEY, 1853.

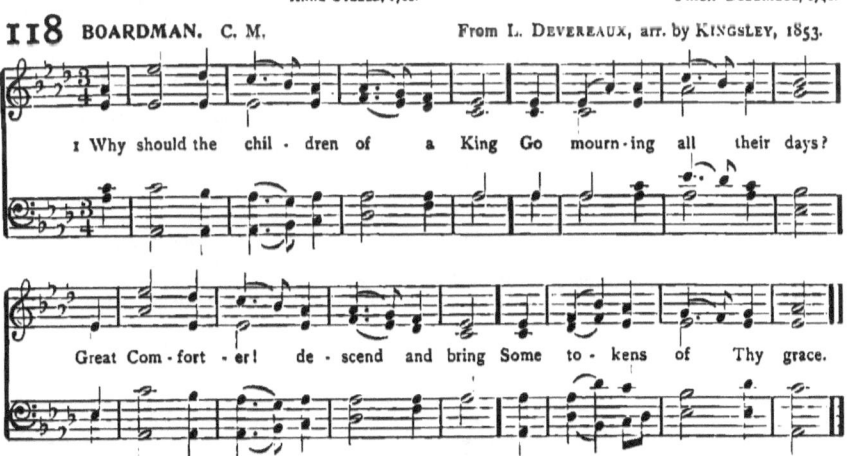

1 Why should the children of a King Go mourning all their days?
Great Comforter! descend and bring Some tokens of Thy grace.

2 Dost Thou not dwell in all the saints,
   And seal the heirs of heaven?
   When wilt Thou banish my complaints,
   And show my sins forgiven?

3 Assure my conscience of her part
   In the Redeemer's blood;
   And bear Thy witness with my heart
   That I am born of God.

4 Thou art the earnest of His love,
   The pledge of joys to come;
   And Thy soft wings, celestial Dove,
   Will safe convey me home.

ISAAC WATTS, 1709.

119 C. M.

1 LIFT up to God the voice of praise,
   Whose breath our souls inspired;
   Loud, and more loud the anthem raise,
   With grateful ardor fired.

2 Lift up to God the voice of praise,
   Whose goodness, passing thought,
   Loads every minute as it flies,
   With benefits unsought.

3 Lift up to God the voice of praise,
   From whom salvation flows,
   Who sent His Son, our souls to save
   From everlasting woes.

RALPH WARDLAW, 1803. Abbr.

THE PRAISE HYMNARY.

120 PORTUGUESE HYMN. 11s.   M. A. PORTAGALLO, 1790. Arr.

1 How firm a foundation, ye saints of the Lord, Is laid for your faith in His excellent word! What more can He say, than to you He hath said,—To you, who, for refuge, to Je-sus have fled, To you, who, for refuge, to Je-sus have fled?

2 "Fear not, I am with thee, oh, be not dismayed,
For I am thy God, I will still give thee aid;
I'll strengthen thee, help thee, and cause thee to stand,
Upheld by my gracious, omnipotent hand.

3 "When through the deep waters I call thee to go,
The rivers of sorrow shall not overflow;
For I will be with thee thy trouble to bless,
And sanctify to thee thy deepest distress.

4 "When through fiery trials thy pathway shall lie,
My grace, all-sufficient, shall be thy supply;
The flame shall not hurt thee; I only design
Thy dross to consume, and thy gold to refine.

5 "Even down to old age all my people shall prove
My sovereign, eternal, unchangeable love;
And then, when gray hairs shall their temples adorn,
Like lambs they shall still in my bosom be borne.

6 "The soul that on Jesus hath leaned for repose,
I will not—I will not desert to his foes;
That soul—though all hell should endeavor to shake,
I'll never—no, never—no, never forsake!"

GEORGE KEITH, 1787.

121 KIMMEL. 11s.   W. T. MOORE.

1 O Jesus! the giver of all we enjoy! Our lives to Thine honor we wish to employ; With praises unceasing we'll sing of Thy name,
D. C. Thy goodness increasing, Thy love we'll proclaim.

2 The wonderful name of our Jesus we'll sing,
And publish the fame of our Captain and King;
With sweet exultation His goodness we prove;
His name is Salvation—His nature is love.

3 And when to the regions of glory we rise,
And join the bright legions that shout through the skies,
We'll tell the glad story of Jesus' kind grace,
And give Him the glory, the honor, and praise.

ANON.

GENERAL PRAISE.

122 HOMEWARD. 7s. 6l. FRANZ ABT, arr.

1 Rock of Ages, cleft for me, Let me hide myself in Thee; Let the water and the blood, From Thy wounded side that flowed Be of sin the double cure— Cleanse me from its guilt and power.

CHORUS.
Rock of Ages, cleft for me, Let me hide myself in Thee, Let me hide myself in Thee.

2 Not the labors of my hands
Can fulfil Thy law's demands;
Could my zeal no respite know,
Could my tears forever flow,
All for sin could not atone;
Thou must save, and Thou alone.

3 Nothing in my hand I bring;
Simply to Thy cross I cling;
Naked, come to Thee for dress;

Helpless, look to Thee for grace;
Foul, I to the fountain fly;
Wash me, Saviour, or I die.

4 While I draw this fleeting breath,
When mine eyelids close in death,
When I soar to worlds unknown,
See Thee on Thy judgment throne,
Rock of Ages, cleft for me,
Let me hide myself in Thee.

AUGUSTUS M. TOPLADY, 1776. Sl. alt.

TOPLADY. 7s. 6l. THOMAS HASTINGS, 1830.

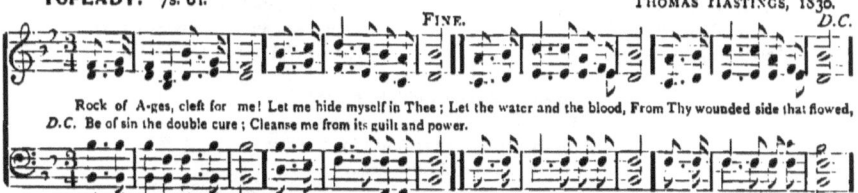

Rock of Ages, cleft for me! Let me hide myself in Thee; Let the water and the blood, From Thy wounded side that flowed,
D.C. Be of sin the double cure; Cleanse me from its guilt and power.

THE PRAISE HYMNARY.

123 BRADFORD. C. M.   G. F. HANDEL, 1741.

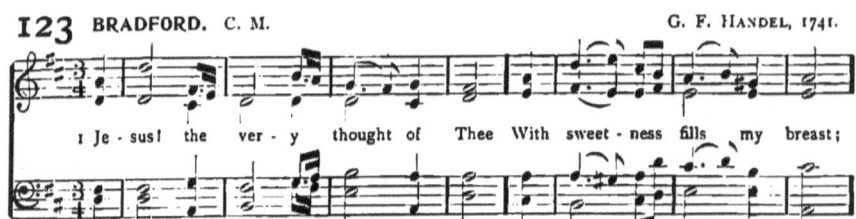

1 Jesus! the very thought of Thee With sweetness fills my breast;

But sweeter far Thy face to see, And in Thy presence rest.

2 Nor voice can sing, nor heart can frame,
   Nor can the memory find
A sweeter sound than Thy blest name,
   O Saviour of mankind!

3 O Hope of every contrite heart,
   O Joy of all the meek!
To those who fall, how kind Thou art!
   How good to those who seek!

4 But what to those who find? Ah, this
   Nor tongue nor pen can show:
The love of Jesus, what it is,
   None but His loved ones know.

5 Jesus, our only joy be Thou!
   As Thou our prize wilt be;
Jesus, be Thou our glory now,
   And through eternity!
      BERNARD OF CLAIRVAUX, 1153; tr. by E. CASWALL, 1849.

124   C. M.

1 JESUS, I love Thy charming name,
   'Tis music to mine ear;
Fain would I sound it out so loud
   That earth and heaven should hear.

2 Yes, Thou art precious to my soul,
   My transport, and my trust;
Jewels to Thee are gaudy toys,
   And gold is sordid dust.

3 All my capacious powers can wish,
   In Thee doth richly meet;
Nor to mine eyes is light so dear,
   Nor friendship half so sweet.

4 Thy grace still dwells upon my heart,
   And sheds its fragrance there;
The noblest balm of all its wounds,
   The cordial of its care.

5 I'll speak the honors of Thy name
   With my last laboring breath;
Then, speechless, clasp Thee in mine arms,
   The antidote of death.
              PHILIP DODDRIDGE, 1755.

GENERAL PRAISE.

125 SNELLING. L. M. D.   WM. A. MAY.

1 My hope is built on nothing less Than Jesus' blood and righteousness. I dare not trust the sweetest frame, But wholly lean on Jesus' name. On Christ, the Solid Rock, I stand, All other ground is sinking sand! On Christ, the Solid Rock, I stand, All other ground is sinking sand.

Copyright, 1892, by SILVER, BURDETT & COMPANY.

2 When darkness veils His lovely face,
I rest on His unchanging grace;
In every high and stormy gale,
My anchor holds within the veil:
On Christ, the Solid Rock, I stand,
All other ground is sinking sand.
On Christ, the Solid Rock, I stand,
All other ground is sinking sand.

3 His oath, His covenant and blood,
Support me in the whelming flood:
When all around my soul gives way,
He then is all my hope and stay:
On Christ, the Solid Rock, I stand,
All other ground is sinking sand.
On Christ, the Solid Rock, I stand,
All other ground is sinking sand.

EDWARD MOTE, 1836.

126 L. M. D.

1 Now I have found the ground wherein
Sure my soul's anchor may remain;
The wounds of Jesus, for my sin,
Before the world's foundation slain;
On Christ, the Solid Rock, I stand,
All other ground is sinking sand.
On Christ, the Solid Rock, I stand,
All other ground is sinking sand.

2 O love, thou bottomless abyss!
My sins are swallowed up in thee;
Covered is my unrighteousness,
From condemnation now I'm free;
On Christ, the Solid Rock, I stand,
All other ground is sinking sand.
On Christ, the Solid Rock, I stand,
All other ground is sinking sand.

3 With faith I plunge me in this sea,
Here is my hope, my joy, my rest;
Hither, when hell assails, I flee.
I look into my Saviour's breast.
On Christ, the Solid Rock, I stand,
All other ground is sinking sand.
On Christ, the Solid Rock, I stand,
All other ground is sinking sand.

4 Though waves and storms go o'er my head,
Though strength, and health, and friends be gone;
Though joys be withered all, and dead;
Though every comfort be withdrawn—
On Christ, the Solid Rock, I stand,
All other ground is sinking sand.
On Christ, the Solid Rock, I stand,
All other ground is sinking sand.

JOHANN A. ROTHE.
Tr. JOHN WESLEY, 1740.

THE PRAISE HYMNARY.

127 EWING. 7s, 6s. D.   ALEXANDER EWING, 1853.

1 Je-ru-sa-lem, the gold-en, With milk and hon-ey blest! Be-neath thy con-tem-pla-tion Sink heart and voice op-pressed: I know not, oh, I know not What so-cial joys are there, What ra-dian-cy of glo-ry, What light be-yond com-pare!

2 They stand, those halls of Zion,
   All jubilant with song,
And bright with many an angel,
   And all the martyr throng;
The Prince is ever in them,
   The daylight is serene;
The pastures of the blessèd
   Are decked in glorious sheen.

3 There is the throne of David;
   And there, from care released,
The song of them that triumph,
   The shout of them that feast:
And they who, with their Leader,
   Have conquered in the fight
Forever and forever
   Are clad in robes of white.
      BERNARD OF CLUNY, 1130. J. M. NEALE, tr. 1851. Abbr.

129 DOXOLOGY. 7s, 6s. D.

1 To Thee be praise forever,
   Thou glorious King of kings;
Thy wondrous love and favor
   Each ransomed spirit sings:
We'll celebrate Thy glory,
   With all the saints above,
And shout the joyful story
   Of Thy redeeming love.
      THOMAS HAWEIS, 1792, alt.

128 7s, 6s. D.

1 THE heavens declare His glory,
   Their Maker's skill the skies;
Each day repeats the story,
   And night to night replies.
Their silent proclamation
   Throughout the earth is heard
The record of creation,
   The page of nature's word.

2 So pure, so soul-restoring,
   Is truth's diviner ray;
A brighter radiance pouring
   Than all the pomp of day:
The wanderer surely guiding,
   It makes the simple wise;
And, evermore abiding,
   Unfailing joy supplies.

3 Thy Word is richer treasure
   Than lurks within the mine;
And daintiest fare less pleasure
   Yields than this food divine.
How wise each kind monition!
   Led by Thy counsels, Lord,
How safe the saints' condition,
   How great is their reward!
      JOSIAH CONDER.

GENERAL PRAISE.

130 ONSET. C. M.
WM. A. MAY.

1 With joyful praise, and homage sweet, Make all your wishes known; And, pleading at the mercy-seat, God's loving-kindness own.

Copyright, 1898, by SILVER, BURDETT AND COMPANY.

2 In just accordance with His will,
Your heart's petition frame,
Desiring that the glory still
Be rendered to His name.

3 He who hath taught us how to pray,
Can all our wants relieve,
He bids us come without delay,
And of His grace receive.

4 With simple, steadfast faith, O Lord,
Thy blessing we implore,
Pleading the promise of Thy word —
Till time shall be no more!

LOUISA E. LITZSINGER.

131 C. M.

1 ETERNAL Source of life and light!
Supremely good and wise!
To Thee we bring our grateful vows,
To Thee lift up our eyes.

2 Our dark and erring minds illume
With truth's celestial rays;
Inspire our hearts with sacred love,
And tune our lips to praise.

3 Safely conduct us, by Thy grace,
Through life's perplexing road;
And place us, when that journey's o'er,
At Thy right hand, O God!

PHILIP DODDRIDGE, 1755.

132 CHRISTMAS. C. M.
G. F. HANDEL, 1728.

1 Am I a sol-dier of the cross, A fol-lower of the Lamb? And shall I fear to own His cause, Or blush to speak His name? Or blush to speak His name?

2 Must I be carried to the skies
On flowery beds of ease,
While others fought to win the prize,
And sailed through bloody seas?

3 Are there no foes for me to face?
Must I not stem the flood?

Is this vile world a friend to grace,
To help me on to God?

4 Sure I must fight, if I would reign;
Increase my courage, Lord;
I'll bear the toil, endure the pain,
Supported by Thy word.

ISAAC WATTS, 1720. Abbr.

133 L. M.

1 ETERNAL Spirit, we confess
And sing the wonders of Thy grace:
Thy power conveys our blessings down
From God the Father and the Son.

2 Enlightened by Thy heavenly ray,
Our shades and darkness turn to day;
Thine inward teachings make us know
Our danger and our refuge too.

3 Thy power and glory work within,
And break the chains of reigning sin;
All our imperious lusts subdue,
And form our wretched hearts anew.
ISAAC WATTS, 1709. Abbr.

134 L. M.

1 To us the light of truth display,
And make us know and choose Thy way;
Plant holy fear in every heart,
That we from God may ne'er depart.

2 Lead us to holiness — the road
That we must take to dwell with God;
Lead us to Christ, the living way,
Nor let us from His precepts stray.

3 Lead us to God, our final rest,
To be with Him forever blest;
Lead us to heaven, its bliss to share —
Fulness of joy forever there!
S. BROWNE, 1720.

135 DUKE STREET. L. M.

JOHN HATTON, 1790. Abt.

1 Now to the Lord a noble song! Awake, my soul, awake, my tongue,

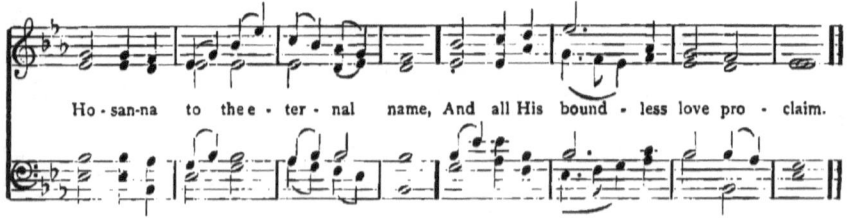

Hosanna to the eternal name, And all His boundless love proclaim.

2 See where it shines in Jesus' face, —
The brightest image of His grace;
God, in the person of His Son,
Has all His mightiest works outdone.

3 Grace! 't is a sweet, a charming theme;
My thoughts rejoice at Jesus' name;
Ye angels, dwell upon the sound;
Ye heavens, reflect it to the ground.

4 O may I reach the happy place,
Where He unveils His lovely face,
His beauties there may I behold,
And sing His name to harps of gold.
ISAAC WATTS, 1707. Abbr.

136 L. M.

1 As when in silence, vernal showers
Descend, and cheer the fainting flowers,
So, in the secrecy of love,
Falls the sweet influence from above.

2 That heavenly influence let me find
In holy silence of the mind,
While every grace maintains its bloom,
Diffusing wide its rich perfume.

3 Nor let these blessings be confined
To me, but poured on all mankind,
Till earth's wild wastes in verdure rise,
And a young Eden bless our eyes.
THOMAS GIBBONS, 1784.

GENERAL PRAISE.

137 BALERMA. C. M. Adapted from the Spanish by R. SIMPSON.

1 Oh for a heart to praise my God, A heart from sin set free; A heart that always feels Thy blood, So free-ly spilt for me.

2 A heart resigned, submissive, meek,
  My dear Redeemer's throne;
Where only Christ is heard to speak,
  Where Jesus reigns alone.

3 A heart in every thought renewed,
  And full of love divine;
Perfect, and right, and pure, and good,
  A copy, Lord, of Thine.

4 Thy nature, dearest Lord, impart;
  Come quickly from above;
Write Thy new name upon my heart,
  Thy new, best name of love.
               CHARLES WESLEY, 1742.

138 DOXOLOGY. C. M.

To Father, Son, and Holy Ghost,
  The God whom we adore,
Be glory, as it was, is now,
  And shall be evermore.
               TATE AND BRADY, 1696.

139 C. M.

1 I WORSHIP Thee, sweet Will of God,
  And all Thy ways adore;
And every day I live, I seem
  To love Thee more and more.

2 I love to kiss each print where Thou
  Hast set Thine unseen feet:
I cannot fear Thee, blessed Will,
  Thine empire is so sweet.

3 I have no cares, O blessed Will,
  For all my cares are Thine;
I live in triumph, Lord, for Thou
  Hast made Thy triumphs mine.

4 Ill that He blesses is our good,
  And unblest good is ill;
And all is right that seems most wrong,
  If it be His sweet will.
               FREDERICK W. FABER, 1849.

140 PRAISE YE THE LORD. Old German.

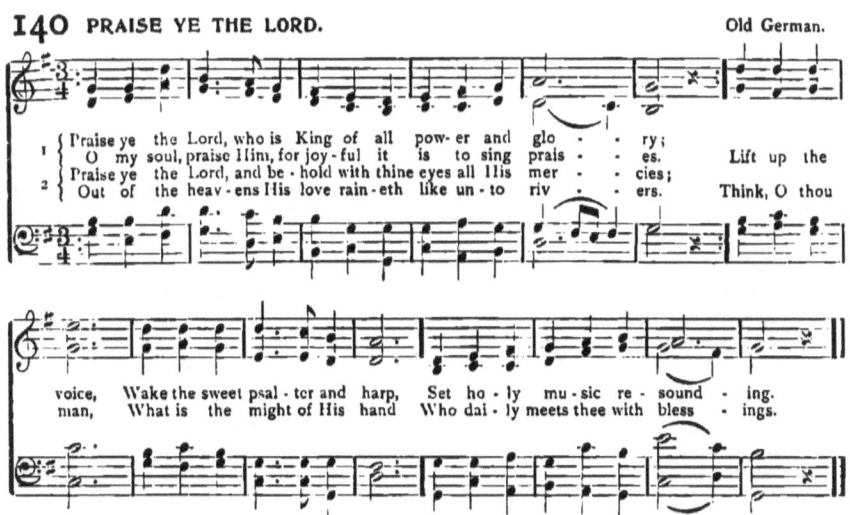

1 { Praise ye the Lord, who is King of all pow-er and glo - ry;
    O my soul, praise Him, for joy-ful it is to sing prais - es. Lift up the
2 { Praise ye the Lord, and be-hold with thine eyes all His mer - cies;
    Out of the heav-ens His love rain-eth like un-to riv - ers. Think, O thou

voice, Wake the sweet psal-ter and harp, Set ho-ly mu-sic re-sound - ing.
man, What is the might of His hand Who dai-ly meets thee with bless - ings.

THE PRAISE HYMNARY.

141 PEACE. C. M.   J. G. F.

1 Great peace have they who love Thy law, Whose mind is stayed on Thee,
My peace I give, My peace I leave, Sweet peace ye have in me.

CHORUS.
Oh, Thou wilt keep him in per-fect peace, Yes, Thou wilt keep him in per-fect peace, Whose mind is stayed on Thee, Whose mind is stayed on Thee.

This Hymn is *free* to be used for the glory of God.

2 'T was peace on earth the angels sang,
    To weary ones there's rest,
  Sweet peace was made through Jesus' blood,
    Which cannot be expressed.

3 No peace have they in wicked ways,
    They're like the troubled sea,
  Peace, peace they say, when they have none;
    From sin they do not flee.

4 "Fear not, little flock," our Saviour said,
    It is your Father's will,
  A glorious kingdom to bestow;
    His word He will fulfil.

5 If fiery trials fill our way,
    Like Jesus tempted sore,
  Oh! "It is I, be not afraid;"
    Said Jesus o'er and o'er.

JOHN.

GENERAL PRAISE.

142 BEECHER. 8s, 7s. D.   JOHN ZUNDEL, 1870.

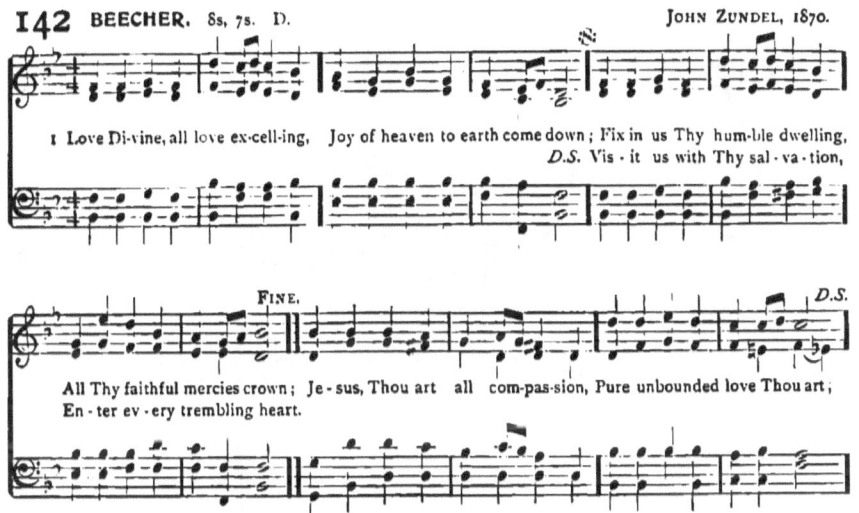

1 Love Divine, all love excelling, Joy of heaven to earth come down; Fix in us Thy humble dwelling, All Thy faithful mercies crown; Jesus, Thou art all compassion, Pure unbounded love Thou art; Visit us with Thy salvation, Enter every trembling heart.

2 Breathe, O breathe, Thy loving Spirit
   Into every troubled breast;
Let us all in Thee inherit,
   Let us find Thy promised rest;
Take away our love of sinning,
   Alpha and Omega be,
End of faith, as its beginning,
   Set our hearts at liberty.

3 Come, almighty to deliver,
   Let us all Thy life receive;
Speedily return, and never,
   Never more Thy temples leave.
Thee we would be always blessing,
   Serve Thee as Thy hosts above,
Pray, and praise Thee without ceasing,
   Glory in Thy perfect love.

4 Finish then Thy new creation,
   Pure and spotless let us be;
Let us see Thy great salvation
   Perfectly restored in Thee:
Changed from glory unto glory,
   Till in heaven we take our place
Till we cast our crowns before Thee,
   Lost in wonder, love, and praise.
             CHARLES WESLEY, 1747.

143 8s, 7s. D.

1 HALLELUJAH! sing to Jesus!
   His the scepter, His the throne;
Hallelujah! His the triumph,
   His the victory alone;
Hark! the songs of peaceful Zion
   Thunder like a mighty flood;
Jesus out of every nation
   Hath redeemed us by His blood.

2 Hallelujah! not as orphans
   Are we left in sorrow now;
Hallelujah! He is near us,
   Faith believes, nor questions how:
Though the cloud from sight received Him
   When the forty days were o'er;
Shall our hearts forget His promise,
   "I am with you evermore?"

3 Hallelujah! Bread of angels,
   Thou on earth our food, our stay!
Hallelujah! hear the sinful
   Flee to Thee from day to day;
Intercessor, Friend of sinners,
   Earth's Redeemer, plead for me,
Where the songs of all the sinless
   Sweep across the crystal sea.
             WILLIAM C. DIX, 1868.

THE PRAISE HYMNARY.

144. THE LOVE OF GOD TO ME.
Wm. A. May.

1 As flows the riv-er, calm and deep, In si-lence to the sea, So floweth ev-er, flow-eth ev-er, And ceaseth nev-er, ceaseth nev-er The love of God to me! The love of God to me!

Copyright, 1898, by SILVER, BURDETT AND COMPANY.

2 He kindly keepeth those He loves
   Secure from every fear,
From eye that weepeth, eye that weepeth,
While yet one sleepeth, yet one sleepeth
   He gently dries the tear;
   He gently dries the tear!

3 What peace He bringeth to my heart —
   A deep unfathomed sea!
How sweetly singeth, sweetly singeth,

The soul that clingeth, soul that clingeth
   My loving Lord, to Thee,
   My loving Lord, to Thee!

4 As calmly sinketh daylight clear,
   Within the golden west
All tempests o'er, tempests o'er,
On heavenly shore, on heavenly shore,
   I'll find my longed-for rest,
   I'll find my longed-for rest.

Arr. W. A. M.

145. COME, YE DISCONSOLATE. 11s, 10s.
Samuel Webbe, 1800.

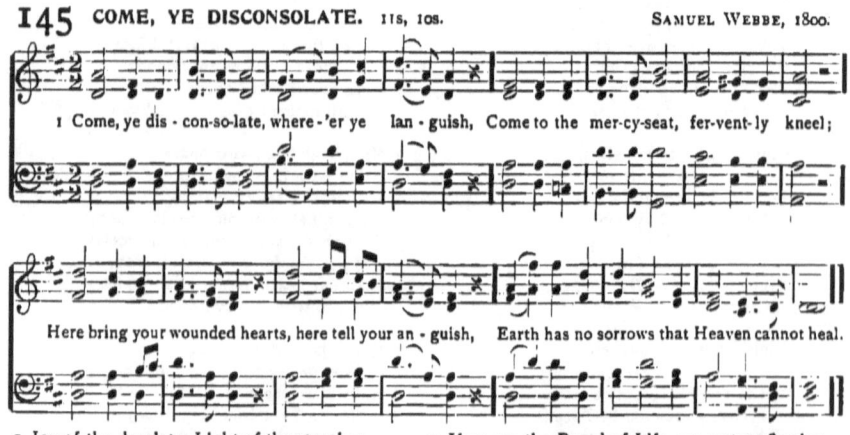

1 Come, ye dis-con-so-late, where-'er ye lan-guish, Come to the mer-cy-seat, fer-vent-ly kneel; Here bring your wounded hearts, here tell your an-guish, Earth has no sorrows that Heaven cannot heal.

2 Joy of the desolate, Light of the straying,
   Hope of the penitent, fadeless and pure;
Here speaks the Comforter, tenderly saying,
   Earth has no sorrows that Heaven cannot cure.

3 Here see the Bread of Life, see waters flowing
   Forth from the throne of God, pure from above;
Come to the feast prepared, come, ever knowing
   Earth has no sorrows but Heaven can remove.

Thomas Moore, 1816, vs. 1, 2. Alt.
Thomas Hastings, v. 3.

GENERAL PRAISE.

146 WE PRAISE THEE AGAIN. 10s, 11s. J. J. HUSBAND, 1798.

1 We praise Thee, O God! for the Son of Thy love, For Jesus who died, and is now gone above. Hallelujah! Thine the glory, Hallelujah! Amen. Hallelujah! Thine the glory, We praise Thee again.

2 We praise Thee, O God! for Thy Spirit of light,
Who has shown us our Saviour, and scattered our night.

3 All glory and praise to the Lamb that was slain,
Who has borne all our sins, and has cleansed ev'ry stain.

4 All glory and praise to the God of all grace,
Who has bought us, and sought us, and guided our ways.

5 Revive us again: fill each heart with Thy love;
May each soul be rekindled with fire from above.

WM. P. MACKAY, 1866. Alt.

147 10s, 11s.

1 REJOICE and be glad: the Redeemer has come!
Go look on His cradle, His cross and His tomb.

> CHORUS.—Sound His praises, tell the story
> Of Him who was slain,
> Sound His praises, tell with gladness,
> He liveth again.

2 Rejoice and be glad: for the blood has been shed;
Redemption is finished, the price has been paid.

3 Rejoice and be glad: for the Lamb that was slain,
O'er death is triumphant, and liveth again.

4 Rejoice and be glad: for our King is on high;
He pleadeth for us on His throne in the sky.

5 Rejoice and be glad: for He cometh again—
He cometh in glory, the Lamb that was slain.

HORATIUS BONAR, 1874.

THE PRAISE HYMNARY.

148 LOVING-KINDNESS. L. M.   Western Melody, 1830.

1 Awake, my soul, to joyful lays,
And sing thy great Redeemer's praise;
He justly claims a song from me;
His loving kindness, oh, how free!

REFRAIN.
Loving kindness, loving kindness,
His loving kindness, oh, how free!

2 He saw me ruined by the fall,
Yet loved me, notwithstanding all;
He saved me from my lost estate:
His loving kindness, oh, how great!

3 Though mighty hosts of cruel foes,
Though earth and hell my way oppose,
He safely leads my soul along:
His loving kindness, oh, how strong!

4 When trouble, like a gloomy cloud,
Has gathered thick and thundered loud,
He near my soul has always stood:
His loving kindness, oh, how good!

5 So when I pass death's gloomy vale,
And all my mortal powers must fail,
Oh, may my last expiring breath
His loving kindness sing in death!

SAMUEL MEDLEY, 1787.

149 L. M.

1 OF Him who did salvation bring,
I could forever think and sing;
Arise, ye needy, He'll relieve;
Arise, ye guilty, He'll forgive.

2 Ask but His grace, and lo, 'tis given!
Ask, and He turns your hell to heaven;
Though sin and sorrow wound my soul,
Jesus, Thy balm will make me whole.

3 'T is Thee I love, for Thee alone,
I shed my tears, and make my moan!
Where'er I am, where'er I move,
I meet the object of my love.

4 Insatiate to this spring I fly;
I drink, and yet am ever dry;
Ah! who against Thy charms is proof?
Ah! who that loves can love enough?

BERNARD OF CLAIRVAUX, tr. by A. W. BOEHM, 1712.

GENERAL PRAISE.

150 HOW I LOVE JESUS. C. M.   American Spiritual.

1 There is a name I love to hear, I love to sing its worth; It sounds like music in mine ear—The sweetest name on earth.

REFRAIN.
Oh, how I love Jesus, Oh, how I love Jesus, Oh, how I love Jesus, Because He first loved me.

2 It tells me of a Saviour's love,
  Who died to set me free;
It tells me of His precious blood,
  The sinner's perfect plea.

3 It tells me what my Father hath
  In store for every day,
And, though I tread a darksome path,
  Yields sunshine all the way.

4 It tells of One, whose loving heart
  Can feel my deepest woe,
Who in each sorrow bears a part,
  That none can bear below.

          FREDERICK WHITFIELD, 1859.

151 C. M.

1 How sweet the name of Jesus sounds
  In a believer's ear;
It soothes his sorrow, heals his wounds,
  And drives away his fear.

2 It makes the wounded spirit whole,
  And calms the troubled breast;
'Tis manna to the hungry soul,
  And to the weary, rest.

3 Dear Name, the rock on which I build,
  My shield and hiding-place;
My never-failing treasure, filled
  With boundless stores of grace.

4 Jesus, my Shepherd, Saviour, Friend,
  My Prophet, Priest, and King,
My Lord, my Life, my Way, my End,
  Accept the praise I bring.

5 I would Thy boundless love proclaim
  With every fleeting breath,
So shall the music of Thy name
  Refresh my soul in death.

          JOHN NEWTON, 1779.

THE PRAISE HYMNARY.

152 AUTUMN. 8s, 7s. D.   Spanish Melody from MARECHO.

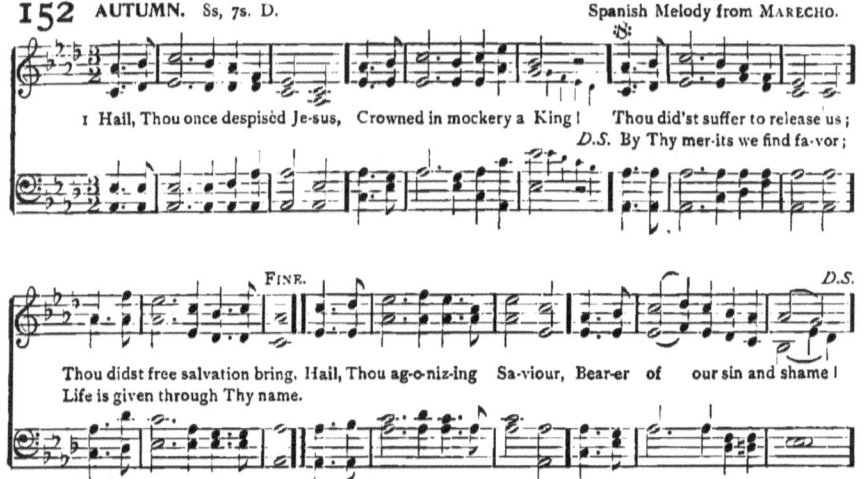

1 Hail, Thou once despisèd Jesus, Crowned in mockery a King! Thou did'st suffer to release us;
D.S. By Thy merits we find favor;
Thou didst free salvation bring. Hail, Thou agonizing Saviour, Bearer of our sin and shame!
Life is given through Thy name.

2 Jesus, hail! enthroned in glory,
  There forever to abide,
All the heavenly hosts adore Thee,
  Seated at Thy Father's side;
There for sinners Thou art pleading;
  There Thou dost our place prepare;
Ever for us interceding,
  Till in glory we appear.

3 Worship, honor, power, and blessing
  Thou art worthy to receive;
Loudest praises, without ceasing,
  Meet it is for us to give!
Help, ye bright angelic spirits,
  Bring your sweetest, noblest lays;
Help to sing our Saviour's merits,
  Help to chant Immanuel's praise.
            JOHN BAKEWELL, 1760.

153 8s, 7s. D.

1 TAKE, my soul, thy full salvation,
  Rise o'er sin, and fear, and care;
Joy to find in every station
  Something still to do or bear.
Think what Spirit dwells within thee;
  What a Father's smile is thine;
What a Saviour died to win thee!
  Child of heaven, shouldst thou repine?

2 Haste thee on from grace to glory,
  Armed by faith, and winged by prayer;
Heaven's eternal day's before thee,
  God's own hand shall guide thee there.
Soon shall close thy earthly mission,
  Swift shall pass thy pilgrim days,
Hope will change to glad fruition,
  Faith to sight, and prayer to praise.
            HENRY F. LYTE, 1825

154 8s, 7s. D.

1 HEAVENLY Shepherd, guide us, feed us,
  Through our pilgrimage below,
And beside the waters lead us,
  Where Thy flock rejoicing go.
Lord, Thy guardian presence ever,
  Meekly bending, we implore;
We have found Thee, and would never,
  Never wander from Thee more.
            JOHN BICKERSTETH, 1819.

155 8s, 7s. D.

1 LORD, dismiss us with Thy blessing,
  Bid us now depart in peace;
Still on heavenly manna feeding,
  Let our faith and love increase:
Fill each breast with consolation;
  Up to Thee our hearts we raise;
When we reach our blissful station,
  Then we'll give Thee nobler praise.
            ROBERT HAWKER. 1794.

GENERAL PRAISE.

156 JEWETT. 6s. D.   C. M. VON WEBER, 1820.

1 My Jesus, as Thou wilt: O may Thy will be mine; Into Thy hand of love I would my all resign. Through sorrow or through joy, Conduct me as Thine own, And help me still to say, "My Lord, Thy will be done."

2 My Jesus, as Thou wilt:
    Though seen through many a tear,
Let not my star of hope
    Grow dim or disappear.
Since Thou on earth hast wept
    And sorrowed oft alone,
If I must weep with Thee,
    "My Lord, Thy will be done."

3 My Jesus, as Thou wilt:
    All shall be well for me;
Each changing future scene
    I gladly trust with Thee.
Straight to my home above,
    I travel calmly on,
And sing in life or death,
    "My Lord, Thy will be done."
BENJAMIN SCHMOLKE, 1716, tr. by Miss JANE BORTHWICK, 1853.

157 6s. D.

1 THERE is a blessèd home
    Beyond this land of woe,
Where trials never come,
    Nor tears of sorrow flow;
Where faith is lost in sight,
    And patient hope is crowned,
And everlasting light
    Its glory throws around.

2 There is a land of peace,
    Good angels know it well;
Glad songs that never cease
    Within its portals swell;
Around its glorious throne
    Ten thousand saints adore
Christ, with the Father One,
    And Spirit, evermore.

3 Look up, ye saints of God,
    Nor fear to tread below
The path your Saviour trod
    Of daily toil and woe;
Wait but a little while
    In uncomplaining love,
His own most gracious smile
    Shall welcome you above.
SIR HENRY W. BAKER, 1861.

THE PRAISE HYMNARY.

158 HALLADALE. 8s, 7s. D. WM. A. MAY.

1 { Come, Thou fount of ev'ry blessing, Tune my heart to sing Thy grace; }
  { Streams of mer-cy nev-er ceas-ing *Omit* . . . . } Call for songs of loudest praise.

  { Teach me some melodious son-net, Sung by flaming tongues above, }
  { Praise the mount, I'm fixed upon it, *Omit* . . . . } Mount of God's unchanging love.

Copyright, 1898, by SILVER, BURDETT & COMPANY.

2 Here I raise my Ebenezer;
  Hither by Thy help I'm come;
  And I hope, by Thy good pleasure,
  Safely to arrive at home:
  Jesus sought me when a stranger,
  Wandering from the fold of God;
  He to save my soul from danger,
  Interposed His precious blood.

3 O, to grace how great a debtor
  Daily I'm constrained to be!
  Let that grace, Lord, like a fetter,
  Bind my wandering heart to Thee.
  Prone to wander, Lord, I feel it;
  Prone to leave the God I love;
  Here's my heart; Lord, take and seal it;
  Seal it from Thy courts above.
                                ROBERT ROBINSON, 1757.

159 NETTLETON. 8s, 7s. D. ASAHEL NETTLETON, 1825.

1 { Crown His head with endless blessing Who, in God, the Father's name, }
  { With compassion nev-er ceas-ing, Comes salvation to pro-claim. } Lo, Jehovah, we adore Thee,— Thee, our Saviour,— Thee, our God;
  D.C. From Thy throne Thy beams of glory Shine through all the world abroad.

2 Jesus! Thee our Saviour hailing,
  Thee our God in praise we own;
  Highest honors, never failing,
  Rise eternal round Thy throne.
  Now, ye saints, His power confessing,
  In your grateful strains adore;
  For His mercy, never ceasing,
  Flows, and flows forevermore.
                                WILLIAM GOODE, 1811.

160 DOXOLOGY. 8s, 7s. D.

PRAISE the God of all creation;
  Praise the Father's boundless love.
Praise the Lamb, our Expiation,
  Priest and King enthroned above;
Praise the Fountain of Salvation,
  Him by whom our spirits live:
Undivided adoration
  To the One Jehovah, give.
                                JOSIAH CONDER, 1836.

GENERAL PRAISE.

161 SWEETLY SING. Arr.

2 Angels bright, angels bright,
Robed in garments pure and white,
Chant His praise, chant His praise,
In melodious lays:
But from that bright, happy throng,
Ne'er can come this sweetest song—
Redeeming love, redeeming love,
Brought us here above.

3 Far away, far away,
We in sin's dark valley lay,
Jesus came, Jesus came,
Blessed be His name!
He redeemed us by His grace,
Then prepared in heaven a place
To receive — to receive
All who will believe.

4 Now we know — now we know
We to heaven must shortly go,
Soon the call — soon the call
Comes to one and all.
Saviour! when our time shall come,
Take us to our heavenly home,
There we'll raise notes of praise,
Through unending days.

Miss J. W. Sampson.

162 ARLINGTON. C. M. Thomas A. Arne, 1744.

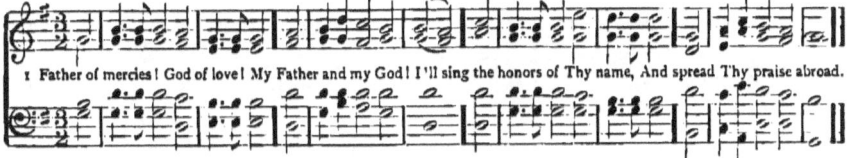

2 In every period of my life
Thy thoughts of love appear;
Thy mercies gild each transient scene,
And crown each passing year.

3 In all Thy mercies, may my soul
A Father's bounty see;
Nor let the gifts Thy grace bestows
Estrange my heart from Thee.

Ottiwell Heginbothom, 1794.

163 C. M.

1 Glory to God! Who deigns to bless
His people every day,
Unfolds His wondrous promises,
And makes it sweet to pray.

2 Glory to God! who deigns to hear
The humblest sigh we raise,
And answers every heartfelt prayer,
And hears our hymn of praise.

Anon.

THE PRAISE HYMNARY.

164 THATCHER. S. M.
From HANDEL, 1732, arr.

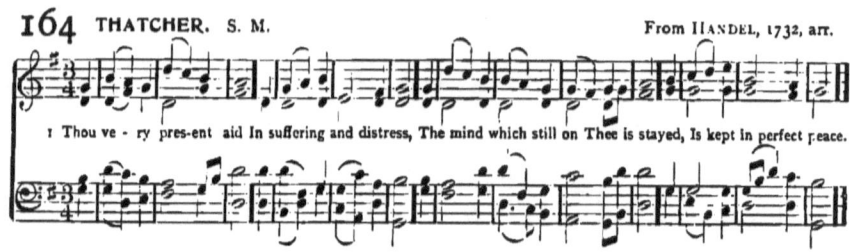

1 Thou ve-ry pres-ent aid In suffering and distress, The mind which still on Thee is stayed, Is kept in perfect peace.

165 S. M.

2 The soul by faith reclined
  On the Redeemer's breast,
'Mid raging storms, exults to find
  An everlasting rest.

3 Sorrow and fear are gone,
  Whene'er Thy face appears;
It stills the sighing orphan's moan,
  And dries the widow's tears.

4 Jesus, to whom I fly,
  Doth all my wishes fill;
What though created streams are dry?
  I have the fountain still.

5 Stripped of each earthly friend,
  I find them all in One,
And peace and joy which never end,
  And heaven, in Christ, alone.

CHARLES WESLEY, 1749.

1 WHAT cheering words are these;
  Their sweetness who can tell?
In time, and to eternal days,
  "'T is with the righteous well!"

2 Well when they see His face,
  Or sink amidst the flood;
Well in affliction's thorny maze,
  Or on the mount with God.

3 'T is well when joys arise,
  'T is well when sorrows flow,
'T is well when darkness vails the skies,
  And strong temptations grow.

4 'T is well when Jesus calls,—
  "From earth and sin arise,
To join the hosts of ransomed souls,
  Made to salvation wise!"

JOHN KENT, 1803.

166 KENTUCKY. S. M.
AARON CHAPIN, 1822.

1 Blest be the tie that binds Our hearts in Christian love, The fel-low-ship of kin-dred minds Is like to that a-bove.

2 Before our Father's throne
  We pour our ardent prayers;
Our fears, our hopes, our aims are one,
  Our comforts and our cares.

2 We share our mutual woes,
  Our mutual burdens bear;
And often for each other flows
  The sympathizing tear.

4 When we asunder part,
  It gives us inward pain;
But we shall still be joined in heart,
  And hope to meet again.

5 This glorious hope revives
  Our courage by the way;
While each in expectation lives,
  And longs to see the day.

6 From sorrow, toil, and pain,
  And sin, we shall be free,
And perfect love and friendship reign
  Through all eternity.

JOHN FAWCETT, 1772.

GENERAL PRAISE.

167 C. M. D.

1 On Jordan's rugged banks I stand,
    And cast a wishful eye
To Canaan's fair and happy land,
    Where my possessions lie.
Oh, the transporting, rapturous scene,
    That rises to my sight!
Sweet fields arrayed in living green,
    And rivers of delight!

2 O'er all those wide extended plains
    Shines one eternal day;
There God, the Son, forever reigns,
    And scatters night away.

No chilling winds, or poisonous breath,
    Can reach that healthful shore;
Sickness and sorrow, pain and death,
    Are felt and feared no more.

3 When shall I reach that happy place,
    And be forever blest?
When shall I see my Father's face,
    And in His bosom rest?
Filled with delight, my raptured soul
    Can here no longer stay;
Though Jordan's waves around me roll,
    Fearless I'd launch away.

SAMUEL STENNETT, 1787.

168 VARINA. C. M. D.   From C. H. RINCK. Arr. by GEO. F. ROOT, 1846.

1 There is a land of pure delight, Where saints immortal reign;
  In - fin - ite day excludes the night, And pleasures banish pain;
  There ev-er last-ing spring a-bides,
  And nev-er-withering flowers: Death, like a nar-row sea, di-vides This heavenly land from ours.

2 Sweet fields beyond the swelling flood
    Stand dressed in living green;
So to the Jews old Canaan stood,
    While Jordan rolled between.
But timorous mortals start and shrink
    To cross this narrow sea,
And linger, shivering on the brink,
    And fear to launch away.

3 Oh, could we make our doubts remove,
    These gloomy doubts that rise,
And see the Canaan that we love
    With unbeclouded eyes: —
Could we but climb where Moses stood,
    And view the landscape o'er,
Not Jordan's stream, nor death's cold flood,
    Should fright us from the shore.

ISAAC WATTS, 1709.

169 C. M. D.

1 I HEARD the voice of Jesus say,
    "Come unto me and rest:
Lay down, thou weary one, lay down
    Thy head upon my breast:"
I came to Jesus as I was,
    Weary, and worn, and sad;
I found in Him a resting-place,
    And He has made me glad.

2 I heard the voice of Jesus say,
    "Behold, I freely give
The living water! thirsty one
    Stoop down, and drink, and live."

I came to Jesus, and I drank
    Of that life-giving stream:
My thirst was quenched, my soul revived,
    And now I live in Him.

3 I heard the voice of Jesus say,
    "I am this dark world's light:
Look unto me; thy morn shall rise,
    And all the day be bright."
I looked to Jesus, and I found
    In Him my Star, my Sun;
And in that light of life I'll walk
    Till all my journey's done.

HORATIUS BONAR, 1857.

THE PRAISE HYMNARY.

170 LAND OF BEULAH. 8s, 7s. D.   J. W. Dadmun, arr.

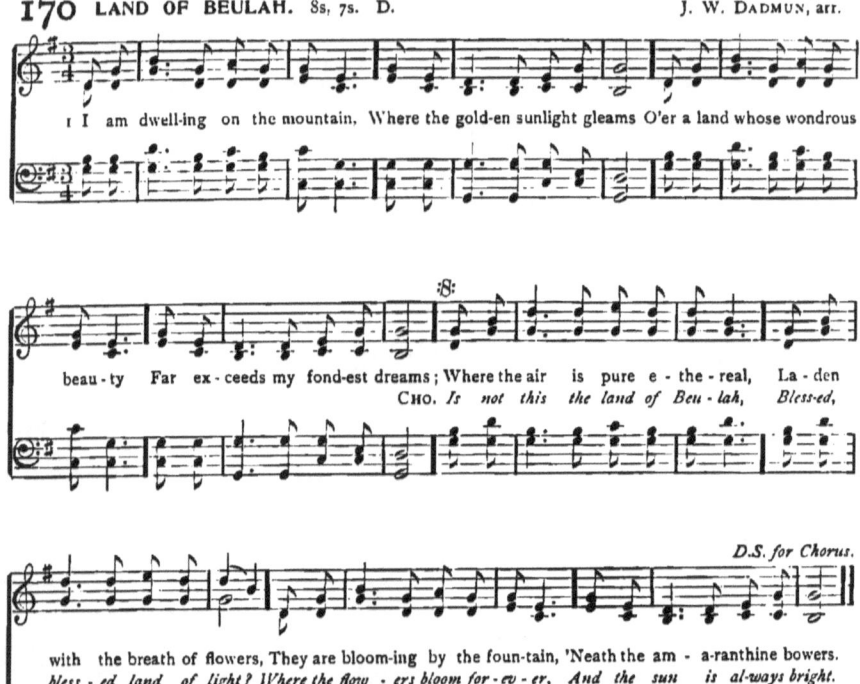

1. I am dwelling on the mountain, Where the golden sunlight gleams O'er a land whose wondrous beauty Far exceeds my fondest dreams; Where the air is pure ethereal, Laden with the breath of flowers, They are blooming by the fountain, 'Neath the amaranthine bowers.

Cho. Is not this the land of Beulah, Blessed, blessed land of light? Where the flowers bloom forever, And the sun is always bright.

2 I am drinking at the fountain,
  Where I ever would abide;
For I've tasted life's pure river,
  And my soul is satisfied;
There's no thirsting for life's pleasures,
  Nor adorning, rich and gay,
For I've found a richer treasure,
  One that fadeth not away.

3 Tell me not of heavy crosses,
  Nor the burdens hard to bear,
For I've found this great salvation
  Makes each burden light appear;
And I love to follow Jesus,
  Gladly counting all but dross,
Worldly honors all forsaking
  For the glory of the cross.

4 Oh, the cross has wondrous glory!
  Oft I've proved this to be true;
When I'm in the way so narrow
  I can see a pathway through;
And how sweetly Jesus whispers:
  Take the cross, thou needst not fear,
For I've tried this way before thee,
  And the glory lingers near.

                     Rev. Wm. Hunter. Abbr.

GENERAL PRAISE.

171 LOUVAN. L. M. — Virgil C. Taylor, 1847.

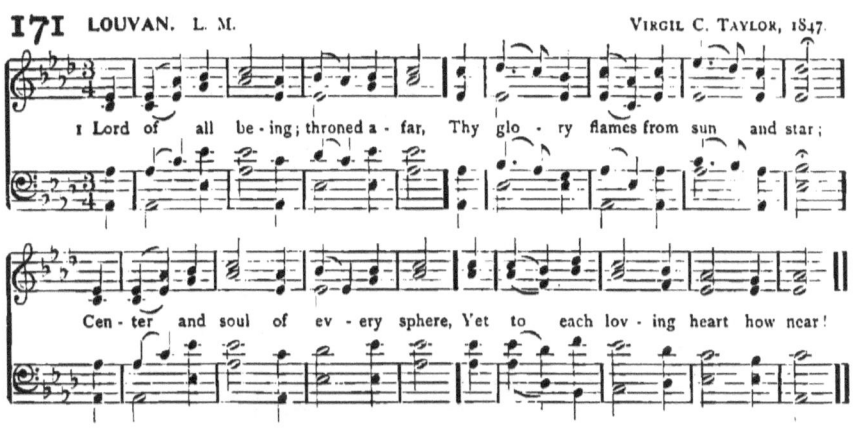

1 Lord of all being; throned afar, Thy glory flames from sun and star; Center and soul of every sphere, Yet to each loving heart how near!

2 Sun of our life, Thy quickening ray
Sheds on our path the glow of day;
Star of our hope, Thy softened light
Cheers the long watches of the night.

3 Our midnight is Thy smile withdrawn;
Our noontide is Thy gracious dawn;
Our rainbow arch Thy mercy's sign;
All, save the clouds of sin, are Thine!

4 Lord of all life, below, above,
Whose light is truth, whose warmth is love,
Before Thy ever-blazing throne
We ask no luster of our own.

5 Grant us Thy truth to make us free,
And kindling hearts that burn for Thee,
Till all Thy living altars claim
One holy light, one heavenly flame!
   OLIVER W. HOLMES, 1848.

172 L. M.

1 How sweet the praise, how high the theme,
To sing of Him who rules supreme;
Who dwells at God's right hand on high,
Yet looks on us with tender eye!

2 The angelic host, in countless throngs,
Recount His glories in their songs,
And golden harps salute His ear;
Yet our weak praise He deigns to hear.

3 The planets roll their orbits round;
Unnumbered worlds, in space profound,
Are ruled by Him, by Him controlled;
Yet He's the Shepherd of our fold.

4 Exalted high upon His throne,
The universe is all His own;
Untold the honors He doth wear;
Yet we are objects of His care.
   BENJAMIN SKENE.

173 DE FLEURY. 8s. D. — Lewis Edson, 1782.

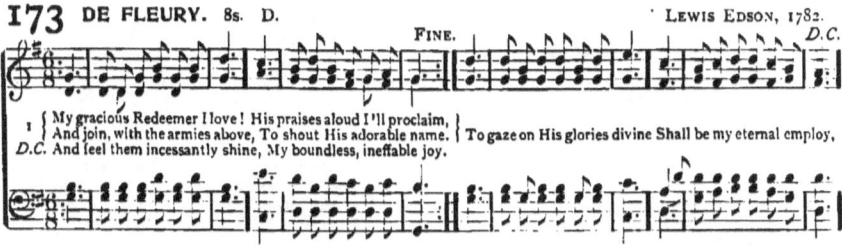

1 My gracious Redeemer I love! His praises aloud I'll proclaim,
And join, with the armies above, To shout His adorable name.
D.C. And feel them incessantly shine, My boundless, ineffable joy.
To gaze on His glories divine Shall be my eternal employ,

2 You palaces, scepters, and crowns,
   Your pride with disdain I survey;
   Your pomps are but shadows and sounds,
   And pass in a moment away.
The crown that my Saviour bestows
   Yon permanent sun shall outshine;
   My joy everlastingly flows —
   My God, my Redeemer, is mine.
      BENJAMIN FRANCIS, 1787. Abbr.

THE PRAISE HYMNARY.

174 LUX BENIGNA. 10s, 4s, 10s. JOHN B. DYKES, 1861.

1 Lead, kindly Light, amid the encircling gloom, Lead Thou me on; The night is dark, and I am far from home, Lead Thou me on; Keep Thou my feet; I do not ask to see The distant scene, one step enough for me.

2 I was not ever thus, nor prayed that Thou
    Shouldst lead me on;
I loved to choose and see my path; but now
    Lead Thou me on!
I loved the garish day, and, spite of fears,
Pride ruled my will. Remember not past years!

3 So long Thy Power hast blest me, sure it still
    Will lead me on
O'er moor and fen, o'er crag and torrent, till
    The night is gone,
And with the morn those angel faces smile
Which I have loved long since, and lost awhile!
                   JOHN H. NEWMAN, 1833.

175 HORTON. 7s. XAVIER S. VON WARTENSEE, 1786.

1 Wait, my soul, upon the Lord, To His gracious promise flee, Laying hold upon His word, "As thy days thy strength shall be."

2 If the sorrows of thy case
  Seem peculiar still to thee,
God has promised needful grace —
  "As thy days thy strength shall be."

3 Days of trial, days of grief,
  In succession thou mayst see;

This is still thy sweet relief —
  "As thy days thy strength shall be."

4 Rock of Ages, I'm secure,
  With Thy promise full and free;
Faithful, positive, and sure —
  "As thy days thy strength shall be."
                  WILLIAM F. LLOYD, 1835.

176 7s.

1 PRINCE of Peace, control my will;
Bid this struggling heart be still;
Bid my fears and doubtings cease;
Hush my spirit into peace.

2 Thou hast bought me with Thy blood,
Opened wide the gate to God;
Peace I ask — but peace must be,
Lord, in being one with Thee.

3 May Thy will, not mine, be done;
May Thy will and mine be one;
Chase these doubtings from my heart;
Now Thy perfect peace impart.

4 Saviour, at Thy feet I fall;
Thou my life, my Lord, my all!
Let Thy happy servant be
One forevermore with Thee!
                 MARY A. S. BARBER, 1838.

GENERAL PRAISE.

177 ELLESDIE. 8s, 7s. D.
JOHANN C. W. A. MOZART, arr.

1 Sweet the moments, rich in blessing,
Which before the cross I spend;
Life and health and peace possessing,
From the sinner's dying Friend.
Here I'll sit, forever viewing
Mercy's streams in streams of blood.
D.S. Precious drops, my soul bedewing,
Plead and claim my peace with God.

2 Truly blessèd is the station,
  Low before His cross to lie,
While we see divine compassion
  Beaming in His gracious eye.
Lord, in ceaseless contemplation
  Fix our hearts and eyes on Thee,
Till we taste Thy whole salvation,
  And Thine unveiled glories see.

3 For Thy sorrows we adore Thee,
  For the pains that wrought our peace;
Gracious Saviour, we implore Thee,
  In our hearts Thy love increase.
Here we feel our sins forgiven,
  While upon the Lamb we gaze;
And our thoughts are all of heaven,
  And our lips o'erflow with praise.
  JAMES ALLEN, 1757. WALTER SHIRLEY, 1774. Alt.

178 8s, 7s. D.

1 GLORY to the almighty Father,
    Fountain of eternal love,
  Who, His wandering sheep to gather,
    Sent a Saviour from above.
  To the Son all praise be given,
    Who, with love unknown before
  Left the bright abode of heaven,
    And our sin and sorrows bore.

2 Equal strains of warm devotion
    Let the Spirit's praise employ;
  Author of each pure emotion;
    Source of wisdom, peace, and joy.
  Thus, while our glad hearts, ascending,
    Glorify Jehovah's name,
  Heavenly songs with ours are blending;
    There the theme is still the same.
      WILLIAM H. BATHURST, 1831. Abbr.

179 8s, 7s. D.

1 ALWAYS with us, always with us,
    Words of cheer, and words of love,
  Thus the risen Saviour whispers,
    From His dwelling-place above.
  With us when the storm is sweeping,
    O'er our pathway dark and drear,
  Waking hope within our bosoms,
    Stilling every anxious fear.

2 With us in the lonely valley,
    When we cross the chilling stream;
  Lighting up the steps to glory
    Like the ancient prophet's dream.
  Always with us, always with us,
    Pilot on the surging main,
  Guiding to the distant haven,
    Where we shall be home again.
      EDWIN H. NEVIN, 1858. Abbr.

THE PRAISE HYMNARY.

180 ARMSTRONG. 8s, 7s. D. — Arr. by EMMELAR.

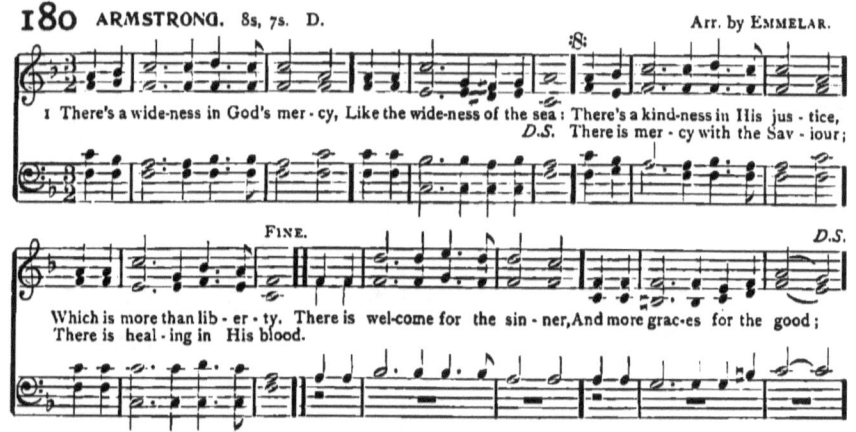

1 There's a wide-ness in God's mer-cy, Like the wide-ness of the sea: There's a kind-ness in His jus-tice, Which is more than lib-er-ty. There is wel-come for the sin-ner, And more grac-es for the good; There is heal-ing in His blood.
D.S. There is mer-cy with the Sav-iour;

2 There is no place where earth's sorrows
Are more felt than up in heaven;
There is no place where earth's failings
Have such kindly judgment given.
There is plentiful redemption
In the blood that has been shed;
There is joy for all the members
In the sorrows of the Head.

3 For the love of God is broader
Than the measure of man's mind;
And the heart of the Eternal
Is most wonderfully kind.
If our love were but more simple,
We should take Him at His word;
And our lives would be all sunshine
In the sweetness of our Lord.
FREDERICK W. FABER, 1849. Abbr.

181 8s, 7s. D.

1 YES, for me, for me He careth
With a brother's tender care;
Yes, with me, with me He shareth
Every burden, every fear.
Yes, o'er me, o'er me He watcheth,
Ceaseless watcheth, night and day;
Yes, e'en me, e'en me He snatcheth
From the perils of the way.

2 Yes, for me He standeth pleading
At the mercy-seat above;
Ever for me interceding,
Constant in untiring love.

Yes, in me abroad He sheddeth
Joys unearthly, love and light;
And to cover me He spreadeth
His paternal wing of might.

3 Yes, in me, in me He dwelleth;
I in Him, and He in me!
And my empty soul He filleth,
Here and through eternity.
Thus I wait for His returning,
Singing all the way to heaven;
Such the joyful song of morning,
Such the tranquil song of even.
HORATIUS BONAR, 1857.

182 8s, 7s. D.

1 WHAT a friend we have in Jesus,
All our griefs and sins to bear!
What a privilege to carry
Everything to God in prayer!
Oh, what peace we often forfeit,
Oh, what needless pain we bear,
All because we do not carry
Everything to God in prayer!

2 Have we trials and temptations?
Is there trouble anywhere?
We should never be discouraged,
Take it to the Lord in prayer;

Can we find a friend so faithful,
Who will all our sorrows share?
Jesus knows our every weakness;
Take it to the Lord in prayer.

4 Blessed Jesus, Thou hast promised
Thou wilt all our burdens bear,
May we ever, Lord, be bringing
All to Thee in earnest prayer.
Soon in glory, bright, unclouded,
There will be no need for prayer;
Rapture, praise, and endless worship,
Shall be our sweet portion there.
JOSEPH SCRIVEN, 1855. Abbr

GENERAL PRAISE.

183 REFUGE. 7s. D.
JOSEPH P. HOLBROOK.

Used by per.

1. Jesus! lover of my soul,
Let me to Thy bosom fly
While the billows near me roll,
While the tempest still is high;
Hide me, O my Saviour! hide,
Till the storm of life is past;
Safe into the haven guide;
Oh, receive my soul at last!

2. Other refuge have I none;
Hangs my helpless soul on Thee;
Leave, ah! leave me not alone,
Still support and comfort me.
All my trust on Thee is stayed;
All my help from Thee I bring;
Cover my defenceless head
With the shadow of Thy wing.

3. Thou, O Christ! art all I want;
More than all in Thee I find;
Raise the fallen, cheer the faint,
Heal the sick, and lead the blind.
Just and holy is Thy name,
I am all unrighteousness;
Vile and full of sin I am,
Thou art full of truth and grace.

4. Plenteous grace with Thee is found,—
Grace to pardon all my sin;
Let the healing streams abound,
Make and keep me pure within;
Thou of life the fountain art,
Freely let me take of Thee;
Spring Thou up within my heart,
Rise to all eternity.

CHARLES WESLEY, 1740.

MARTYN. 7s. D.
SIMEON B. MARSH, 1834.

1. Jesus! lover of my soul, Let me to Thy bosom fly
While the billows near me roll, While the tempest still is high;
Hide me, O my Saviour! hide, Till the storm of life is past;
D.C. Safe into the haven guide; Oh, receive my soul at last!

184 FERGUSON. S. M. *George Kingsley, 1843.*

1 Raise your triumphant songs
To an immortal tune;
Wide let the earth resound the deeds
Celestial grace has done.

2 Sing how eternal love
 Its chief Beloved chose,
And bade Him raise our wretched race
 From their abyss of woes.

3 Now, sinners, dry your tears,
 Let hopeless sorrow cease;
Bow to the scepter of His love,
 And take the offered peace.

4 Lord, we obey Thy call;
 We lay an humble claim
To the salvation Thou hast brought,
 And love and praise Thy name.
          Isaac Watts, 1719.

185 S. M.

1 God is the fountain whence
 Ten thousand blessings flow;
To Him my life, my health, and friends,
 And every good, I owe.

2 The comforts He affords
 Are neither few nor small;
He is the source of fresh delights,
 My portion and my all.

3 He fills my heart with joy,
 My lips attunes for praise;
And to His glory I'll devote
 The remnant of my days.
          Anon.

186 MAITLAND. C. M. *George N. Allen, 1849.*

1 Must Jesus bear the cross alone, And all the world go free? No: there's a cross for every one, And there's a cross for me.

2 How happy are the saints above,
 Who once went sorrowing here!
But now they taste unmingled love,
 And joy without a tear.

3 The consecrated cross I'll bear,
 Till death shall set me free;
And then go home my crown to wear,
 For there's a crown for me.

4 Oh, precious cross! oh, glorious crown!
 Oh, resurrection day!
Ye angels from the stars come down,
 And bear my soul away.
          Thomas Shepherd, 1692.
          George N. Allen, alt. 1852.

187 C. M.

1 Thou dear Redeemer, dying Lamb,
 I love to hear of Thee;
No music's like Thy charming name,
 Nor half so sweet can be.

2 My Jesus shall be still my theme,
 While in this world I stay;
I'll sing my Jesus' lovely name
 When all things else decay.

3 When I appear in yonder cloud,
 With all Thy favored throng,
Then will I sing more sweet, more loud,
 And Christ shall be my song.
          John Cennick, 1745.

GENERAL PRAISE.

188 STILL WATER. 11s, 10s. Spiritual Songs, 1833.

1 The Lord is my Shepherd, He makes me repose
Where the pastures in beauty are growing,
He leads me afar from the world and its woes,
Where in peace the still waters are flowing.

2 He strengthens my spirit, He shows me the path,
Where the arms of His love shall enfold me,
And when I walk through the dark valley of death,
His rod and His staff will uphold me!

WILLIAM KNOX.

189 11s, 10s.

1 Oh! TELL me, Thou life and delight of my soul,
Where the flock of Thy pasture are feeding;
I seek Thy protection, I need Thy control,
I would go where my Shepherd is leading.

2 Oh! tell me the place where Thy flock are at rest,
Where the noontide will find them reposing.
The tempest now rages, my soul is distressed,
And the pathway of peace I am losing.

3 Oh! why should I stray with the flocks of Thy foes,
'Mid the desert where now they are roving,
Where hunger and thirst, where affliction and woes,
And temptations their ruin are proving?

4 Oh! when shall my foes and my wandering cease?
And the follies that fill me with weeping!
Thou Shepherd of Israel, restore me that peace
Thou dost give to the flock Thou art keeping.

5 A voice from the Shepherd now bids thee return
By the way where His footprints are lying:
No longer to wander, no longer to mourn;
O lone one, now homeward be flying!

THOMAS HASTINGS, 1833 Abbr

THE PRAISE HYMNARY.

190 MARCHING AS TO WAR. 6s, 5s. D. WM. A. MAY.

1 Onward, Christian soldiers, Marching as to war, With the Cross of Jesus Going on before.
Christ, the Royal Master, Leads against the foe, Forward into battle See His banners go!

REFRAIN.
Onward, Christian soldiers, Marching as to war, With the Cross of Jesus Going on before.

Copyright, 1891, by WM. A. MAY.

2 Like a mighty army
  Moves the Church of God;
  Brothers, we are treading
  Where the saints have trod.
  We are not divided,
  All one body we,
  One in hope, and doctrine,
  One in charity.

3 Crowns and thrones may perish,
  Kingdoms rise and wane,
  But the Church of Jesus
  Constant will remain ;
  Gates of hell can never
  'Gainst that Church prevail ;
  We have Christ's own promise,
  And that cannot fail!

4 Onward then, ye people,
  Join the happy throng,
  Blend with ours your voices,
  In triumphant song !
  Glory, laud and honor,
  Unto Christ the King,
  This through countless ages
  Men and angels sing !
  SABINE BARING-GOULD, 1865. Abbr.

191 PILOT. 7s. 6l. J. E. GOULD.

1 Jesus, Saviour, pilot me Over life's tempestuous sea ; Unknown waves before me roll, Hiding rock and treacherous shoal ;
D.C. Chart and compass come from Thee : Jesus, Saviour, pilot me.

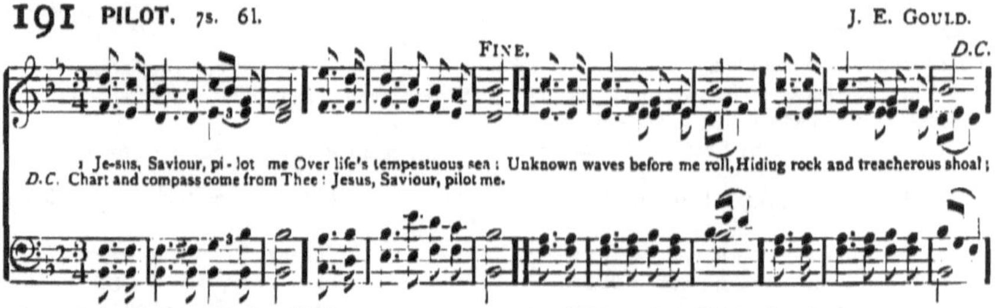

2 As a mother stills her child,
  Thou canst hush the ocean wild ;
  Boisterous waves obey Thy will
  When Thou say'st to them " Be still ! "
  Wondrous Sovereign of the sea,
  Jesus, Saviour, pilot me.

3 When at last I near the shore,
  And the fearful breakers roar
  'Twixt me and the peaceful rest,
  Then, while leaning on Thy breast,
  May I hear Thee say to me,
  " Fear not, I will pilot Thee ! "
  EDWARD HOPPER, 1871.

GENERAL PRAISE.

192 PRAISES TO OUR KING. 6s, 5s. D. SIR ARTHUR S. SULLIVAN, 1872.

1 Saviour, blessed Saviour, Listen while we sing; Hearts and voices raising Praises to our King.
All we have to offer, All we hope to be, Body, soul, and spirit, All we yield to Thee.

REFRAIN.
Saviour, blessed Saviour, Listen while we sing; Hearts and voices raising Praises to our King.
Listen while we sing; Hearts and voices raising

2 Higher, then, and higher,
  Bear the ransomed soul,
  Earthly toils forgotten,
  Saviour, to its goal;

Where, in joys unthought of,
  Saints with angels sing,
  Never weary, raising
  Praises to their King.
      GODFREY THRING, 1862. Abbr.

193 BOWRING. 8s, 7s. SIR JOHN BOWRING, arr.

1. Worship, honor, glory, blessing, Lord! we offer to Thy name; Young and old, Thy praise expressing, Join their Saviour to proclaim.

2 As the saints in heaven adore Thee,
  We would bow before Thy throne;
  As Thine angels serve before Thee,
  So on earth Thy will be done.
      EDWARD OSLER, 1836.

194 DOXOLOGY. 8s, 7s.
PRAISE the Father, earth and heaven,
  Praise the Son, the Spirit praise,
  As it was, and is, be given
  Glory through eternal days.
      AVON, 1827.

195 8s, 7s.
1 MAY the grace of Christ, the Saviour,
  And the Father's boundless love,
  With the Holy Spirit's favor,
  Rest upon us from above.

2 Thus may we abide in union
  With each other and the Lord,
  And possess, in sweet communion,
  Joys which earth cannot afford.
      JOHN NEWTON, 1779.

THE PRAISE HYMNARY.

196 AMAZING GRACE. C. M. — Old Melody.

Amazing grace! how sweet the sound That saved a wretch like me, I once was lost, but now am found, Was blind, but now I see, Was blind, but now I see,
D. S. To meet to part no more

Was blind, but now I see, I once was lost, but now am found, Was blind, but now I see.
On Canaan's hap-py shore, Then we shall meet at Je-sus' feet, Shall meet to part no more.

Coda (to be sung or omitted at pleasure).

Oh, that will be joy-ful, joy-ful, joy-ful, Oh, that will be joy-ful, To meet to part no more.

2 'T was grace that taught my heart to fear,
And grace my fears relieved;
How precious did that grace appear,
The hour I first believed!

3 Through many dangers, toils, and snares,
I have already come;
'T is grace has brought me safe thus far,
And grace will lead me home.

4 The Lord has promised good to me,
His word my hope secures;
He will my shield and portion be,
As long as life endures.

5 Yes, when this flesh and heart shall fail,
And mortal life shall cease,
I shall possess, within the vail,
A life of joy and peace.

6 The earth shall soon dissolve like snow,
The sun forbear to shine;
But God, who called me here below,
Will be forever mine.

JOHN NEWTON, 1779.

197 C. M.

1 LET saints below in concert sing
With those to glory gone;
For all the servants of our King,
In earth and heaven, are one.

2 One family — we dwell in Him —
One church above, beneath,
Though now divided by the stream —
The narrow stream of death;

3 One army of the living God,
To His command we bow;
Part of the host have crossed the flood,
And part are crossing now.

4 Even now, by faith, we join our hands
With those that went before,
And greet the ransomed blessèd bands
Upon the eternal shore.

5 Lord Jesus! be our constant guide;
And, when the word is given,
Bid death's cold flood its waves divide,
And land us safe in heaven.

CHARLES WESLEY, 1759. Abbr.

GENERAL PRAISE.

198 DENNIS. S. M.
HANS. G. NAGELI, arr., 1849.

1 How gentle God's commands! How kind His precepts are!
Come, cast your burdens on the Lord, And trust His constant care.

2 Beneath His watchful eye
His saints securely dwell;
That hand which bears creation up
Shall guard His children well.

3 Why should this anxious load
Press down your weary mind?
Haste to your heavenly Father's throne,
And sweet refreshment find.

4 His goodness stands approved,
Unchanged from day to day:
O drop your burden at His feet,
And bear a song away.
PHILIP DODDRIDGE, 1755.

199 C. M.

1 My Saviour, my Almighty Friend,
When I begin Thy praise,
Where will the growing numbers end,
The numbers of Thy grace?

2 Thou art my everlasting trust,
Thy goodness I adore;
And since I knew Thy graces first,
I speak Thy glories more.

3 My feet shall travel all the length
Of the celestial road,
And march with courage in Thy strength
To see my Father, God.
ISAAC WATTS, 1719. Abbr.

200 EVAN. C. M.
WM. H. HAVERGAL, 1847.

1 How sweet, how heavenly is the sight, When those who love the Lord In one another's peace delight, And so ful-fil His word!

2 Let love, in one delightful stream,
Through every bosom flow;
And union sweet, and dear esteem
In every action glow.

3 Love is the golden chain that binds
The happy souls above;
And he's an heir of heaven who finds
His bosom glow with love.
JOSEPH SWAIN, 1792. Abbr.

201 C. M.

1 My soul shall praise Thee, O my God,
Through all my mortal days,
And in eternity prolong
Thy vast, Thy boundless praise.

2 In every smiling, happy hour,
Be this my sweet employ;
Thy praise refines my earthly bliss,
And heightens all my joy.
OTTIWELL HEGINBOTHOM, 1791. Abbr.

THE PRAISE HYMNARY.

202   THE PEACE OF GOD. P. M.   WM. A. MAY.

How blest the heart that knows Thy peace, The peace that flow-eth as a riv- er; So calm, so clear, it ne'er shall cease, But broad and deep, flows on for-ev- - er.

Copyright, 1891, by WM. A. MAY.

2 Thou careth for me, Thou say'st, my Lord;
  And Thou art God! there's none above Thee!
  All things according to Thy word,
  Shall work for good to them that love Thee.

3 Then let me cast on Thee my care;
  Dwell in Thy smile when days are dreary,
  Trust Thee through all, howe'er it fare:
  Rest in Thine arms when faint and weary.

4 But, more than all, grant me the grace,
  To do Thy will, O gracious giver;
  Then may I hope to know Thy peace —
  The peace that floweth as a river.

ELSIE DUNDEE, Arr.

203   HAPPY DAY. L. M.   EDWARD F. RIMBAULT, arr.

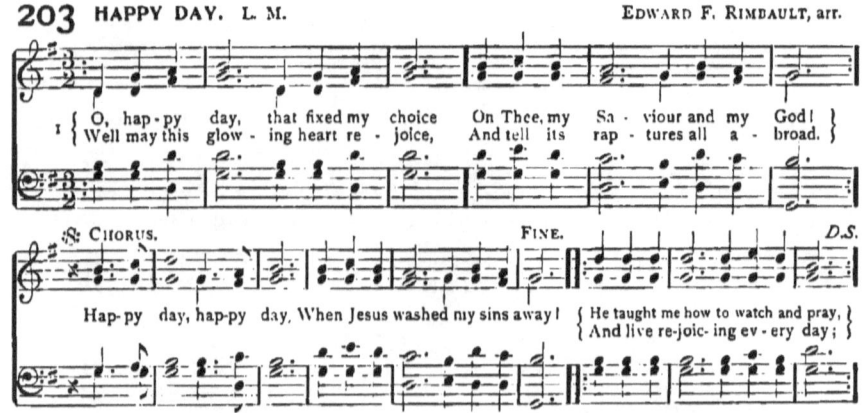

O, hap-py day, that fixed my choice On Thee, my Sa- viour and my God!
Well may this glow- ing heart re- joice, And tell its rap- tures all a- broad.

Hap-py day, hap-py day, When Jesus washed my sins away! He taught me how to watch and pray,
And live re-joic- ing ev- ery day;

2 'T is done, — the great transaction's done;
  I am my Lord's, and He is mine;
  He drew me, and I followed on,
  Rejoiced to own the call divine.

3 Now rest, my long-divided heart,
  Fixed on this blissful centre, rest;
  Here have I found a nobler part,
  Here heavenly pleasures fill my breast.

4 High heaven that hears the solemn vow,
  That vow renewed shall daily hear;
  Till in life's latest hour I bow,
  And bless in death a bond so dear.

PHILIP DODDRIDGE, 1755.

GENERAL PRAISE.

204 COMFORT. 6s, 9s. R. D. HUMPHREYS, 1826.

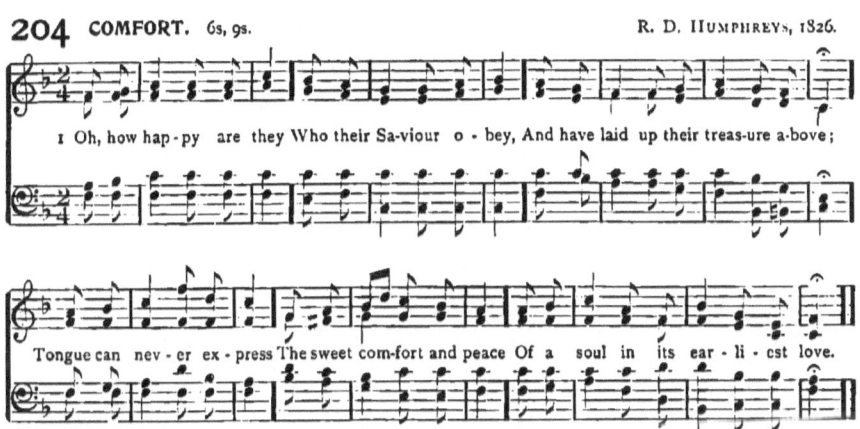

1 Oh, how happy are they Who their Saviour obey, And have laid up their treasure above; Tongue can never express The sweet comfort and peace Of a soul in its earliest love.

2 That sweet comfort is mine,
When the favor divine
I have found in the blood of the Lamb.
When I truly believe
What great joy I receive!
What a heaven in Jesus' sweet name!

3 'T is a heaven below
My Redeemer to know;
And the angels could do nothing more
Than to fall at His feet,
And the story repeat,
And the Lover of sinners adore.

4 Jesus all the day long
Is my joy and my song:
Oh, that all His salvation might see!
"He hath loved me," I cry,
"He did suffer and die
To redeem such a rebel as me."

5 Oh, the rapturous height
Of that holy delight
Which I feel in the life-giving blood!
Of my Saviour possessed,
I am perfectly blest,
As if filled with the fulness of God.

CHARLES WESLEY, 1749. Sl. alt.

205 WOODSTOCK. C. M. DEODATUS DUTTON, JR., 1829.

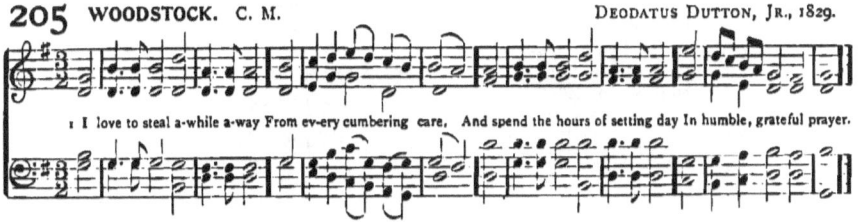

1 I love to steal awhile away From every cumbering care, And spend the hours of setting day In humble, grateful prayer.

2 I love in solitude to shed
The penitential tear,
And all His promises to plead,
Where none but God can hear.

3 I love to think on mercies past,
And future good implore,
And all my cares and sorrows cast
On Him whom I adore.

4 I love by faith to take a view
Of brighter scenes in heaven;
The prospect doth my strength renew,
While here by tempests driven.

5 Thus, when life's toilsome day is o'er,
May its departing ray
Be calm as this impressive hour,
And lead to endless day.

Mrs. PHOEBE H. BROWN, 1818.

206 EVARTS. 7s, 6s. D. ANON.

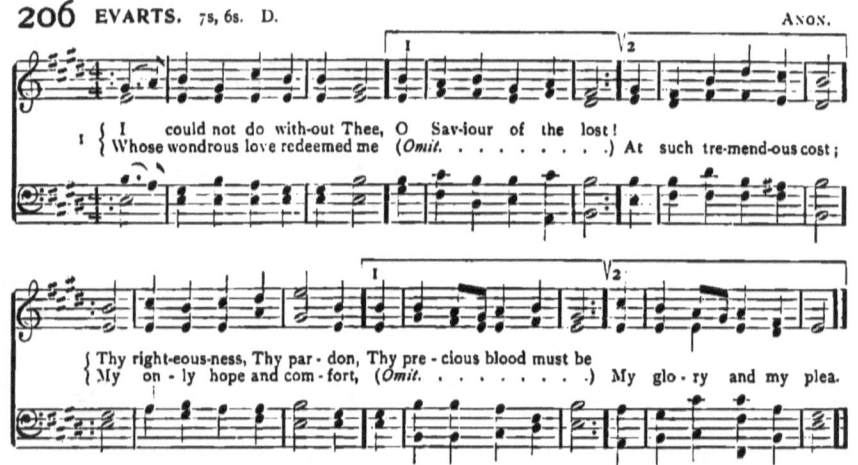

1 I could not do with-out Thee, O Saviour of the lost!
  Whose wondrous love redeemed me (*Omit* . . . .) At such tremendous cost;
  Thy righteousness, Thy pardon, Thy precious blood must be
  My only hope and comfort, (*Omit* . . . .) My glory and my plea.

2 I could not do without Thee,
    I cannot stand alone,
  I have no strength or goodness,
    No wisdom of my own;
  But Thou, beloved Saviour,
    Art all in all to me,
  And perfect strength in weakness
    Is theirs who lean on Thee.

3 I could not do without Thee,
    For, oh, the way is long,
  And I am often weary,
    And sigh replaces song.
  How could I do without Thee?
    I do not know the way;
  Thou knowest, and Thou leadest,
    And wilt not let me stray.

4 I could not do without Thee!
    For life is fleeting fast,
  And soon in solemn loneness
    The river must be past.
  But Thou wilt never leave me,
    And though the waves roll high,
  I know Thou wilt be with me,
    And whisper, "It is I."
        FRANCES R. HAVERGAL, 1873.

207 7s, 6s. D.

1 IN heavenly love abiding,
    No change my heart shall fear,
  And safe is such confiding,
    For nothing changes here:
  The storm may roar without me,
    My heart may low be laid,
  But God is round about me,
    And can I be dismayed?

2 Wherever He may guide me,
    No want shall turn me back;
  My Shepherd is beside me,
    And nothing can I lack:
  His wisdom ever waketh,
    His sight is never dim;
  He knows the way He taketh,
    And I will walk with Him.

3 Green pastures are before me,
    Which yet I have not seen;
  Bright skies will soon be o'er me,
    Where darkest clouds have been:
  My hope I cannot measure;
    My path to life is free;
  My Saviour has my treasure,
    And He will walk with me.
        ANNA L. WARING, 1850.

208 7s, 6s. D.

1 WHEN shall the voice of singing
    Flow joyfully along?
  When hill and valley, ringing
    With one triumphant song,
  Proclaim the contest ended,
    And Him who once was slain,
  Again to earth descended,
    In righteousness to reign?

2 Then from the craggy mountains
    The sacred shout shall fly;
  And shady vales and fountains
    Shall echo the reply:
  High tower and lowly dwelling
    Shall send the hymn around,
  All hallelujah swelling
    In one eternal sound!
        JAMES EDMESTON, 1822. Alt.

GENERAL PRAISE.

209 C. M.

1 HOLY and reverend is the name
  Of our eternal King;
  Thrice holy Lord! the angels cry;
  Thrice holy! let us sing.

2 The deepest reverence of the mind,
  Pay, O my soul! to God;
  Lift with thy hands a holy heart
  To His sublime abode.

3 With sacred awe pronounce His name
  Whom words nor thoughts can reach;
  A broken heart shall please Him more
  Than noblest forms of speech.

4 Thou holy God! preserve our souls
  From all pollution free:
  The pure in heart are Thy delight,
  And they Thy face shall see.
  JOHN NEEDHAM, 1768.

210 C. M.

1 GOD's glory is a wondrous thing,
  Most strange in all its ways,
  And, of all things on earth, least like
  What men agree to praise.

2 Workman of God! O lose not heart,
  But learn what God is like;
  And in the darkest battle-field
  Thou shalt know where to strike.

3 Oh, learn to scorn the praise of men!
  Oh, learn to lose with God!
  For Jesus won the world thro' shame,
  And beckons thee His road.

4 And right is right, since God is God;
  And right the day must win;
  To doubt would be disloyalty,
  To falter would be sin!
  FREDERICK W. FABER, 1848. Abbn.

211 MANOAH. C. M.
F. J. HAYDN, arr., 1851.

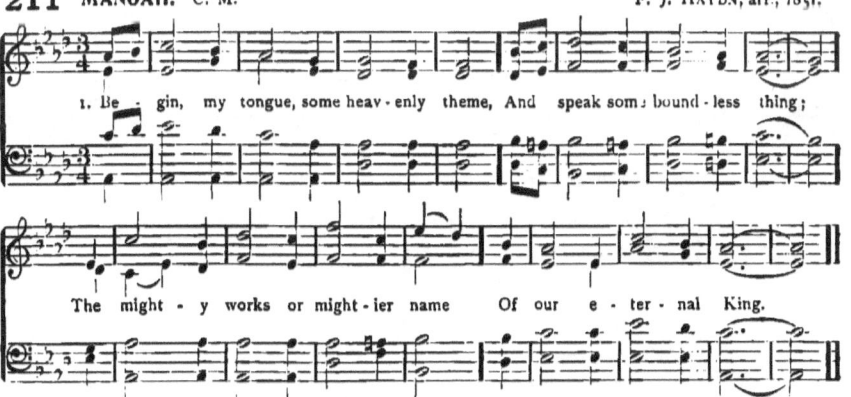

1. Begin, my tongue, some heavenly theme, And speak some boundless thing; The mighty works or mightier name Of our eternal King.

2 Tell of His wondrous faithfulness,
  And sound His power abroad;
  Sing the sweet promise of His grace,
  And the performing God.

3 His very word of grace is strong,
  As that which built the sky;
  The voice that rolls the stars along,
  Proclaims it from on high.

4 O might I hear Thy heavenly tongue
  But whisper, "Thou art mine!"
  Those gentle words should raise my song
  To notes almost divine.
  ISAAC WATTS, 1707.

212 DOXOLOGY. C. M.

LET God the Father, and the Son,
  And Spirit, be adored,
Where there are works to make Him known,
  Or saints to love the Lord!
  ANON.

213 C. M.

1 COME, ye that know and fear the Lord,
  And raise your souls above;
  Let every heart and voice accord
  To sing that God is love.

2 This precious truth His word declares,
  And all His mercies prove;
  While Christ, the atoning Lamb, appears
  To show that God is love.

3 Behold, His loving kindness waits
  For those who from Him rove,
  And calls of mercy reach their hearts,
  To teach them God is love.

4 O may we all, while here below,
  This blest of blessings prove;
  Till warmer hearts, in brighter worlds,
  Shall shout that God is love.
  GEORGE BURDER, 1784.

THE PRAISE HYMNARY.

214 PRAISE SONG. S. M. D.   Felix Mendelssohn-Bartholdy.

1 I bless the Christ of God, I rest on love divine, And with unfaltering lip and heart, I call the Saviour mine. His cross dispels each doubt; I bury in His tomb Each thought of unbelief and fear, Each lingering shade of gloom.

2 I praise the God of peace;
   I trust His truth and might;
He calls me His, I call Him mine,
   My God, my joy, my light.
In Him is only good,
   In me is only ill;
My ill but draws His goodness forth,
   And me He loveth still.

3 'T is He who saveth me,
   And freely pardon gives;
I love because He loveth me;
   I live because He lives.
My life with Him is hid,
   My death has passed away,
My clouds have melted into light,
   My midnight into day.
             Horatius Bonar, 1863. Abbr.

215 S. M. D.

1 Come, sound His praise abroad,
   And hymns of glory sing:
Jehovah is the sovereign God,
   The universal King.
He formed the deeps unknown;
   He gave the seas their bound;
The watery worlds are all His own,
   And all the solid ground.

2 Come, worship at His throne,
   Come, bow before the Lord:
We are His work, and not our own,
   He formed us by His word.
To-day attend His voice,
   Nor dare provoke His rod;
Come, like the people of His choice,
   And own our gracious God.
             Isaac Watts, 1719.

GENERAL PRAISE.

216 MORGAN. 10s. Wm. A. May.

1 Wilt Thou me guide, as o'er life's rugged way, Footsore and weak I wander, day by day? And when to me there cometh sin's un-rest, Wilt Thou me guide in - to Thy ref-uge blest?

Copyright, 1898, by SILVER, BURDETT AND COMPANY.

2 Wilt Thou me guide, when joy fills all my soul,
   And I in strength press forward toward my goal?
   Lest I should fail, and tempted, turn aside,
   Wilt Thou me guide, O, wilt Thou, wilt Thou guide?

3 Wilt Thou me guide, when grief on me has flung
   A bitter woe, and sorrow's song is sung?
   When hope hath fled and faith is almost gone,
   Wilt Thou me guide, wilt Thou me guide alone?

4 Wilt Thou me guide, when, at life's twilight hour
   The shadows fall on me with chilling power?
   When evening comes, may I in Thee confide,
   That, in the darkness, Thou may'st be my guide?

Wm. A. May.

217 WOODLAND. C. M. 51. Nathaniel D. Gould, 1832.

1 There is an hour of peaceful rest To mourning wanderers given; There is a joy for souls distrest, A balm for every wounded breast, 'Tis found above, in heaven.

2 There is a home for weary souls
   By sin and sorrow driven;
   When tossed on life's tempestuous shoals,
   Where storms arise, and ocean rolls,
   And all is drear but heaven.

3 There, fragrant flowers, immortal, bloom,
   And joys supreme are given;
   There, rays divine disperse the gloom:
   Beyond the confines of the tomb
   Appears the dawn of heaven.

William B. Tappan, 1818. Abbr.

THE PRAISE HYMNARY.

218 PLEYEL'S HYMN. 7s.
IGNACE J. PLEYEL, 1800.

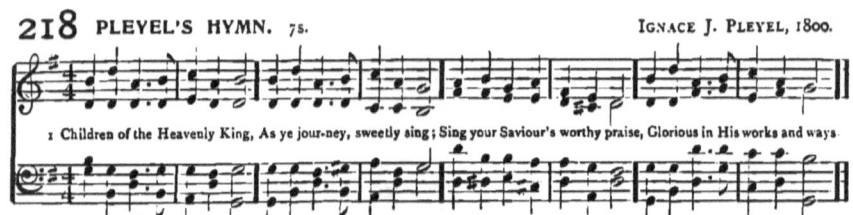

1 Children of the Heavenly King, As ye jour-ney, sweetly sing; Sing your Saviour's worthy praise, Glorious in His works and ways.

2 We are traveling home to God,
   In the way the fathers trod:
   They are happy now; and we
   Soon their happiness shall see.

3 Shout, ye little flock, and blest,
   You on Jesus' throne shall rest;
   There your seat is now prepared,
   There your kingdom and reward.

4 Lift your eyes, ye sons of Light,
   Zion's city is in sight;

There our endless home shall be,
There our Lord we soon shall see.

5 Fear not, brethren; joyful stand
   On the borders of your land:
   Jesus Christ, your Father's Son,
   Bids you undismayed go on.

6 Lord, obediently we go,
   Gladly leaving all below;
   Only 'Thou our leader be,
   And we still will follow Thee.
               JOHN CENNICK, 1742.

219 AMSTERDAM. 7s, 6s. D.
JAMES NARES, 1778.

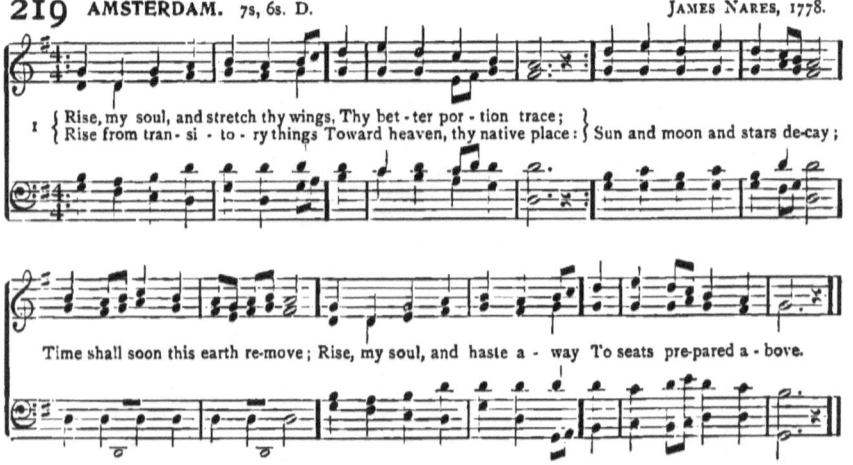

1 { Rise, my soul, and stretch thy wings, Thy bet-ter por-tion trace; }
   { Rise from tran-si-to-ry things Toward heaven, thy native place: } Sun and moon and stars de-cay;
Time shall soon this earth re-move; Rise, my soul, and haste a-way To seats pre-pared a-bove.

2 Rivers to the ocean run,
   Nor stay in all their course;
  Fire ascending seeks the sun;
   Both speed them to their source:
  So a soul that's born of God,
   Pants to view His glorious face;
  Upward tends to His abode,
   To rest in His embrace.

3 Cease, ye pilgrims, cease to mourn,
   Press onward to the prize;
  Soon our Saviour will return
   Triumphant in the skies:
  Yet a season,—and you know
   Happy entrance will be given,
  All our sorrows left below,
   And earth exchanged for heaven.
       ROBERT SEAGRAVE, 1748. Abbr.

GENERAL PRAISE.

220 8s, 7s, 4s.

1 GOD of our salvation! hear us;
    Bless, oh, bless us, ere we go;
  When we join the world, be near us,
    Lest we cold and careless grow.
      Saviour! keep us;
    Keep us safe from every foe.

2 As our steps are drawing nearer
    To our everlasting home,
  May our view of heaven grow clearer,
    Hope more bright of joys to come;
      And, when dying,
    May Thy presence cheer the gloom.
                            THOMAS KELLY, 1809.

221 8s, 7s, 4s.

1 KEEP us, Lord, oh, keep us ever:
    Vain our hope, if left by Thee;
  We are Thine; oh, leave us never,
    Till Thy glorious face we see;
      Then to praise Thee
    Through a bright eternity.

2 Precious is Thy word of promise,
    Precious to Thy people here;
  Never take Thy presence from us,
    Jesus, Saviour, still be near:
      Living, dying,
    May Thy name our spirits cheer.
                            THOMAS KELLY, 1809.

222 GREENVILLE. 8s, 7s, 4s. JEAN J. ROUSSEAU, 1750.

1 Lord, dis-miss us with Thy bless-ing, Fill our hearts with joy and peace; Let us each, Thy love possessing, Triumph in re-deem-ing grace; Oh, re-fresh us, oh, re-fresh us, Traveling through this wilderness.

2 Thanks we give, and adoration,
    For Thy gospel's joyful sound,
  May the fruits of Thy salvation
    In our hearts and lives abound;
      May Thy presence
    With us evermore be found.

3 So, whene'er the signal's given,
    Us from earth to call away;
  Borne on angels' wings to heaven,
    Glad to leave our cumbrous clay,
      May we, ready,
    Rise and reign in endless day.
              JOHN FAWCETT, 1774. Abbr.

223 8s, 7s, 4s.

1 GOD Almighty and All-seeing!
    Holy One, in whom we all
  Live, and move, and have our being,
    Hear us when on Thee we call;
      Father, hear us,
    As before Thy throne we fall.

2 Of all good art Thou the Giver:
    Weak and wandering ones are we;
  Then forever, yea, forever,
    In Thy presence would we be;
      Oh, be near us,
    That we wander not from Thee.
                            JOHN PIERPONT.

225 L. M. D.

1 He leadeth me! O blessed thought!
   O words with heavenly comfort fraught!
   Whate'er I do, where'er I be
   Still 't is God's hand that leadeth me!

REFRAIN.
   He leadeth, leadeth me!
   He leadeth, leadeth me!
   By His own love, constraineth me.
   His faithful servant I would be,
   For by His love He leadeth me!

2 Sometimes 'mid scenes of deepest gloom,
   Sometimes where Eden's bowers bloom,
   By waters still, o'er troubled sea, —
   Still 't is His hand that leadeth me!

3 Lord, I would clasp Thy hand in mine,
   Nor ever murmur nor repine;
   Content whatever lot I see,
   Since 't is my God that leadeth me.

4 And when my task on earth is done,
   When by Thy grace the victory 's won,
   Even death's cold wave I will not flee,
   Since God through Jordan leadeth me.

J. H. GILMORE, 1859. Sl. alt.

GENERAL PRAISE.

226 GRACE IS FREE. 7s. ANON.

1 Lord, I perish! save, I cried When the storm was raging high; In Thy mercy let me hide, Jesus, save me, or I die.

CHORUS.

Glory to the bleeding Lamb, He has made me what I am; Oh, how great His love for me; Hallelujah! grace is free.

2 Helpless at the cross I lay,
  All my hope had wellnigh fled,
  Jesus took my sins away,
  Jesus raised my drooping head.
3 Then I heard a voice divine
  Gently bid me look and live;
  Oh, what rapture now is mine!
  Joy the world can never give.
4 Saviour, with my latest breath
  Pardoning grace my theme shall be,
  Till I cross the waves of death,
  Till I anchor safe with Thee.
    ANON.

227 7s.

1 SAVIOUR! teach me, day by day,
  Love's sweet lesson to obey;
  Sweeter lesson cannot be,
  Loving Him who first loved me.
2 Teach me all Thy steps to trace,
  Strong to follow in Thy grace;
  Learning how to love from Thee,
  Loving Him who first loved me.
3 Love in loving finds employ—
  In obedience all her joy;
  Ever new that joy will be,
  Loving Him who first loved me.
    Miss JANE E. LEESON, 1842. Abbr.

228 RATHBUN. 8s, 7s. ITHAMAR CONKEY, 1850.

1 In the cross of Christ I glory Tow'ring o'er the wrecks of time; All the light of sacred story Gathers round its head sublime.

2 When the woes of life o'ertake me,
  Hopes deceive, and fears annoy,
  Never shall the cross forsake me:
  Lo! it glows with peace and joy.
3 When the sun of bliss is beaming
  Light and love upon my way,
  From the cross the radiance, streaming,
  Adds more lustre to the day.
4 Bane and blessing, pain and pleasure,
  By the cross are sanctified;
  Peace is there, that knows no measure,
  Joys that through all time abide.
    SIR JOHN BOWRING, 1825.

229 8s, 7s.

1 LIKE the eagle, upward, onward,
  Let my soul in faith be borne:
  Calmly gazing, skyward, sunward,
  Let my eye unshrinking turn!
2 Where the cross, God's love revealing,
  Sets the fettered spirit free,
  Where it sheds its wondrous healing,
  There, my soul, my rest shall be!
3 O may I, no longer dreaming,
  Idly waste my golden day,
  But, each precious hour redeeming,
  Upward, onward press my way!
    HORATIUS BONAR.

230 FORWARD! THE WATCHWORD. 6s, 5s.

From Francis J. Haydn, 1797.

1 Forward! be our watchword, Steps and voices joined; Seek the things before us, Not a look behind; Burns the fiery pillar, At our army's head; Who shall dream of shrinking, By our Captain led?

REFRAIN.
Forward! in the conflict, Through the toil and flight Foes must fall before us, God will speed the right.

2 Forward! out of error,
　Leave behind the night;
Forward through the darkness,
　Forward into light!
Glories upon glories
　Hath our God prepared,
By the souls that love Him,
　One day to be shared!

3 Far o'er yon horizon
　Rise the city towers,
Where our God abideth;
　That fair home is ours!
Thither, onward thither,
　In the Spirit's might,
Lovers of your country,
　Forward into light!'

Henry Alford, 1865. Abbr.

231 6s, 5s.

1 Sons of freemen! ever
　Strive for liberty.
In the Spirit's freedom,
　Be then, truly free!
Daily, in the conflict
　Between right and wrong,
Drive all evil from you,
　Dwell with God alone!

REFRAIN.
Upward, onward, heav'nward,
　Eager press along;
Only 'neath God's banner
　Sing the victor's song!

2 Patiently possessing
　Love and godliness,
Peace and joy within you,
　Bring to you success.
Then, whate'er your lot is —
　Storm, or sunshine bright —
Hope will lead you forward
　Into heavenly light.

Wm. A. May, 1898.

GENERAL PRAISE.

232 THE LORD IS WITH THEE. 7s, 6s. WM. A. MAY.

1 Take courage, O ye ser-vants Who labor for the Lord, Your work of love shall bring you A sure and sweet reward.

REFRAIN.

For "I, the Lord, am with thee;" O be thou not dismayed! I will not fail nor leave thee; Cheer up, be not a-fraid!

Copyright, 1888, by WM. A. MAY.

2 Cheer up, ye heavy laden,
　Your Lord will help to bear
　The weighty cross that grieves you,
　And will your burden share.

3 Stand firm, ye tried and tempted,
　Take courage and be strong;
　Your sorrow and your weeping
　Shall end in victory's song.

LOUISA E. LITZSINGER, 1888.

233 NORWOOD. S. M. Arr. from Swiss Melody.

1 Give to the winds thy fears; Hope, and be undismayed; God hears thy sighs and counts thy tears; God shall lift up thy head.

2 Through waves, and clouds, and storms,
　He gently clears thy way;
　Wait thou His time; so shall this night
　Soon end in joyous day.

3 What though Thou rulest not!
　Yet heaven, and earth, and hell

Proclaim, God sitteth on the throne,
　And ruleth all things well.

4 Far, far above thy thought
　His counsel shall appear,
　When fully He the work has wrought,
　That caused thy needless fear.

PAUL GERHARDT, 1656. Tr. by JOHN WESLEY, 1739.

234 DOXOLOGY. S. M.

　　To God, the Father, Son,
　　　And Spirit, glory be,
　　As was, and is, and shall remain
　　　Through all eternity.

JOHN WESLEY, 1741.

THE PRAISE HYMNARY.

235 NUN DANKET. P. M.   JOHANN CRÜGER, 1649.

1. Now thank we all our God, With heart, and hands, and voices;
Who won-drous things hath done, In whom the world re-joices;
Who from our mother's arms Hath blessed us on our way,
With countless gifts of love, And still is ours to-day.

2. Oh, may this bounteous God
Through all our life be near us,
With ever joyful hearts
And blessèd peace to cheer us;
And keep us in His grace,
And guide us when perplexed,
And free us from all ills
In this world and the next.

3. All praise and thanks to God
The Father, now be given,
The Son and Him who reigns
With them, in highest heaven!
The one Eternal God,
Whom earth and heaven adore;
For thus it was, is now,
And shall be evermore.

                         MARTIN RINKART, 1644.
                         tr. CATHERINE WINKWORTH, 1858.

GENERAL PRAISE.

236 TAPPAN. C. M. 5l.   GEORGE KINGSLEY, 1838.

1 Go, tune thy voice to sacred song, Exert thy noblest powers; Go, mingle with the choral throng, The Saviour's praises to prolong, Amid life's fleeting hours.

2 Hast found the pearl of price unknown,
   That cost a Saviour's blood?
   Heir of a bright celestial crown,
   That sparkles near the eternal throne,
   Oh, sing the praise of God!

3 Sing of the Lamb that once was slain
   That man might be forgiven;
   Sing how He broke death's bars in twain,
   Ascending high in bliss to reign,
   The God of earth and heaven!
                            THOMAS HASTINGS.

237 C. M. 5l.

1 O GOD! we praise Thee, and confess
   That Thou the only Lord
   And everlasting Father art,
   And everlasting Father art,
   By all the earth adored.

2 To Thee all angels cry aloud;
   To Thee the powers on high,
   Both cherubim and seraphim,
   Both cherubim and seraphim,
   Continually do cry: —

3 O holy, holy, holy Lord,
   Whom heavenly hosts obey,
   The world is with the glory filled
   The world is with the glory filled
   Of Thy majestic sway!

4 The apostles' glorious company,
   And prophets crowned with light,
   With all the martyrs' noble host,
   With all the martyrs' noble host,
   Thy constant praise recite.

5 The holy church throughout the world,
   O Lord, confesses Thee,
   That Thou the eternal Father art,
   That Thou the eternal Father art,
   Of boundless majesty.
                        Tr. by NAHUM TATE, 1703.

THE PRAISE HYMNARY.

238 CEPHAS. C. M.
Alexander R. Reinagle, 1826.

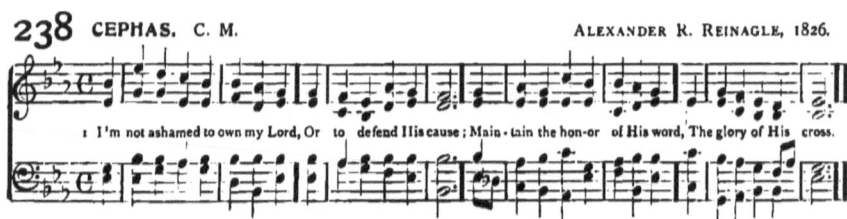

1 I'm not ashamed to own my Lord, Or to defend His cause; Maintain the honor of His word, The glory of His cross.

2 Jesus, my God! — I know His name —
His name is all my trust;
Nor will He put my soul to shame,
Nor let my hope be lost.

3 Firm as His throne His promise stands,
And He can well secure
What I've committed to His hands
Till the decisive hour.

4 Then will He own my worthless name
Before His Father's face,
And in the new Jerusalem
Appoint my soul a place.   Isaac Watts, 1709.

239 C. M.

1 In every trouble, sharp and strong,
My soul to Jesus flies;
My anchor-hold is firm in Him
When swelling billows rise.

2 His comforts bear my spirit up;
I trust a faithful God;
The sure foundation of my hope
Is in a Saviour's blood.

3 Loud hallelujahs sing, my soul,
To Thy Redeemer's name!
In joy and sorrow, life and death,
His love is still the same.
   John Killinghall, 1741.

240 WOODWORTH. L. M.
William B. Bradbury, 1849.

1 Jesus, and shall it ever be — A mortal man ashamed of Thee? Ashamed of Thee, whom angels praise, Whose glories shine through endless days?

2 Ashamed of Jesus! — that dear Friend
On whom my hopes of heaven depend!
No; when I blush, be this my shame,
That I no more revere His name.

3 Ashamed of Jesus! — yes, I may,
When I've no guilt to wash away;
No tears to wipe, no good to crave,
No fears to quell, no soul to save.

4 Till then, — nor is my boasting vain, —
Till then I boast a Saviour slain;
And Oh, may this my glory be,
That Christ is not ashamed of me.
   Joseph Grigg, 1765.   Alt. by Benj. Francis, 1787.

241 L. M.

1 No change of time shall ever shock
My firm affection, Lord, to Thee;
For Thou hast always been my rock,
A fortress and defence to me.

2 Thou my deliverer art, my God!
My trust is in Thy mighty power;
Thou art my shield from foes abroad —
At home my safeguard and my tower.

3 To Thee I will address my prayer,
To whom all praise I justly owe;
So shall I, by Thy watchful care,
Be guarded from my treacherous foe.
   Tate and Brady, 1796.

GENERAL PRAISE.

242 RUSSIA. 10 s.
ALEXIS THEODORE LWOFF, 1833.

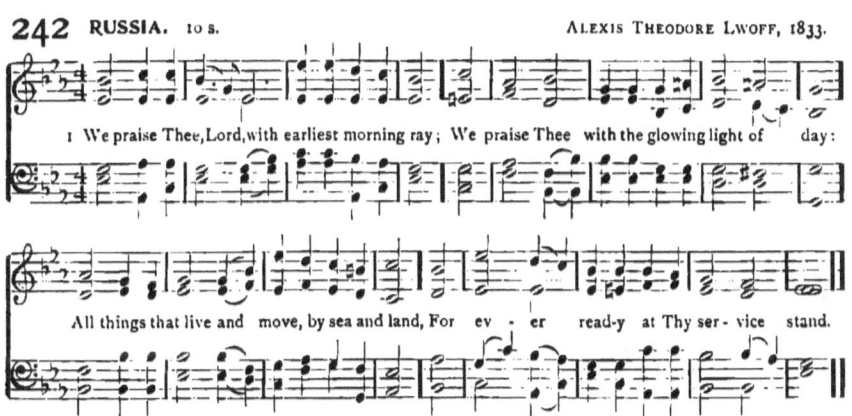

1 We praise Thee, Lord, with earliest morning ray; We praise Thee with the glowing light of day: All things that live and move, by sea and land, For ev-er read-y at Thy ser-vice stand.

2 Thy Christendom is singing night and day,
"Glory to Him, the mighty God, for aye,
By whom, through whom, in whom, all beings are!"
Grant us to echo on the song afar.

3 Thy name supreme, Thy kingdom, in us dwell,
Thy will constrain and feed and guide us well:
Guard us, redeem us in the evil hour;
For Thine the glory, Lord, and Thine the power!
JOHANN FRANCK, Abbr.

243 HOLY CROSS. C. M.
FELIX MENDELSSOHN-BARTHOLDY.

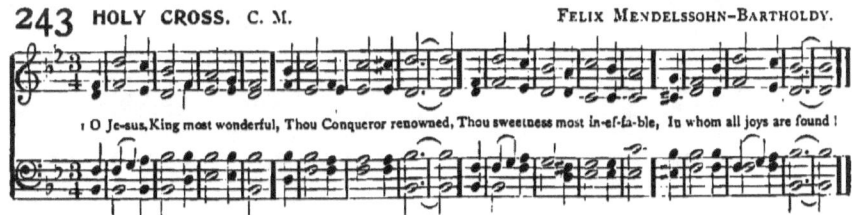

1 O Je-sus, King most wonderful, Thou Conqueror renowned, Thou sweetness most in-ef-fa-ble, In whom all joys are found!

2 When once Thou visitest the heart,
Then truth begins to shine,
Then earthly vanities depart,
Then kindles love divine.

3 O Jesus, Light of all below,
Thou Fount of living fire,
Surpassing all the joys we know,
And all we can desire.

4 Jesus, may all confess Thy name,
Thy wondrous love adore;
And, seeking Thee, themselves inflame
To seek Thee more and more.

5 Thee, Jesus, may our voices bless;
Thee may we love alone;
And ever in our lives express
The image of Thine own.
BERNARD OF CLAIRVAUX, 1153.
Tr. by E. CASWALL, 1849.

244 C. M.
1 OH for a shout of sacred joy
To God, the sovereign King!
Let every land their tongues employ,
And hymns of triumph sing.

2 Jesus, our God, ascends on high;
His heavenly guards around
Attend Him rising through the sky,
With trumpets' joyful sound.

3 While angels shout and praise their King,
Let mortals learn their strains;
Let all the earth His honor sing;
O'er all the earth He reigns.
ISAAC WATTS, 1719. Abbr.

245 DOXOLOGY. C. M.
1 To Father, Son, and Holy Ghost,
One God, whom we adore,
Be glory as it was, is now,
And shall be evermore!
TATE AND BRADY, 1696.

THE PRAISE HYMNARY.

246 LENOX. H. M.
Lewis Edson, 1781.

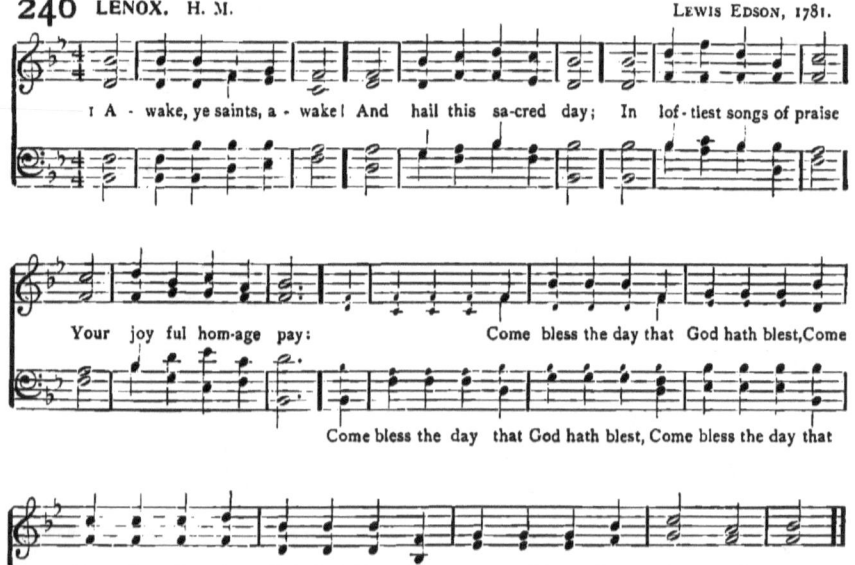

1 Awake, ye saints, awake! And hail this sacred day; In loftiest songs of praise Your joyful homage pay: Come bless the day that God hath blest, Come bless the day that God hath blest, The type of heaven's eternal rest.

2 On this auspicious morn
　The Lord of life arose ;
He burst the bars of death,
　And vanquished all our foes ;
And now He pleads our cause above,
And reaps the fruit of all His love.

3 All hail, triumphant Lord !
　Heaven with hosannas rings,
And earth in humbler strains
　Thy praise responsive sings :
Worthy the Lamb that once was slain,
Through endless years to live and reign !
　　　　　　Elizabeth Scott, 1756.
　　　　　Thomas Cotterill, 1810. Abbr.

247 DOXOLOGY. H. M.
O God, for ever blest,
　To Thee all praise be given ;
Thy Name Triune confest
　By all in earth and heaven ;
As heretofore it was, is now,
And shall be so for evermore.
　　　　Edward H. Bickersteth, 1870.

248 H. M.

1 Welcome, delightful morn,
　Thou day of sacred rest !
I hail thy kind return ; —
　Lord, make these moments blest :
From the low train of mortal toys,
I soar to reach immortal joys.

2 Now may the King descend
　And fill His throne of grace ;
Thy sceptre, Lord, extend,
　While saints address Thy face :
Let sinners feel Thy quickening word,
And learn to know and fear the Lord.

3 Descend, celestial Dove,
　With all Thy quickening powers ;
Disclose a Saviour's love,
　And bless the sacred hours :
Then shall my soul new life obtain,
Nor Sabbaths be enjoyed in vain.
　　　　　　　　Hayward, 1806.

THE LORD'S DAY.

249 DAY OF REST. 7s. 6s. D. Rev. T. S. WYNKOOP, 1898.

1 O day of rest and gladness, O day of joy and light, O balm of care and sadness, Most beautiful, most bright; On Thee, the high and lowly, Bending before the throne, Sing, Holy, Holy, Holy, To the Great Three in One.

Used by per.

2 On Thee, at the creation,
 The light first had its birth:
On Thee, for our salvation
 Christ rose from depths of earth;
On Thee, our Lord, victorious,
 The Spirit sent from Heaven,
And thus on Thee, most glorious
 A triple light was given.

3 To-day on weary nations
 The heavenly manna falls;
To holy convocations
 The silver trumpet calls,
Where gospel light is glowing
 With pure and radiant beams,
And living water flowing
 With soul-refreshing streams.

4 New graces ever gaining
 From this our day of rest,
We reach the rest remaining
 To spirits of the blest:

To Holy Ghost be praises,
 To Father and to Son;
The Church her voice upraises
 To Thee, blest Three in One.
   CHRISTOPHER WORDSWORTH, 1862.

250 7s, 6s. D.

1 THY holy day's returning
 Our hearts exult to see;
And with devotion burning,
 Ascend, O God, to Thee!
To-day with purest pleasure,
 Our thoughts from earth withdraw;
We search for heavenly treasure,
 We learn Thy holy law.

2 We join to sing Thy praises,
 Lord of the Sabbath day;
Each voice in gladness raises
 Its loudest, sweetest lay!
Thy richest mercies sharing,
 Inspire us with Thy love,
By grace our souls preparing
 For nobler praise above.
   RAY PALMER, 1834.

251 ERNAN. 10s.
Lowell Mason, 1850.

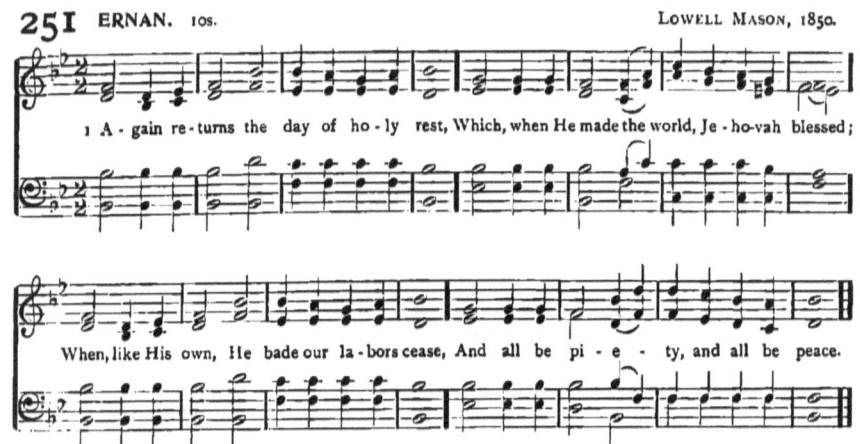

1 Again returns the day of holy rest, Which, when He made the world, Jehovah blessed;
When, like His own, He bade our labors cease, And all be piety, and all be peace.

2 Let us devote this consecrated day
To learn His will, and all we learn obey;
So shall He hear, when fervently we raise
Our supplications and our songs of praise.

3 Father of heaven! in whom our hopes confide,
Whose power defends us, and whose precepts guide,
In life our Guardian, and in death our Friend,
Glory supreme be Thine, till time shall end.
WILLIAM MASON, 1796.

252 MORNINGTON. S. M.
G. W. Mornington.

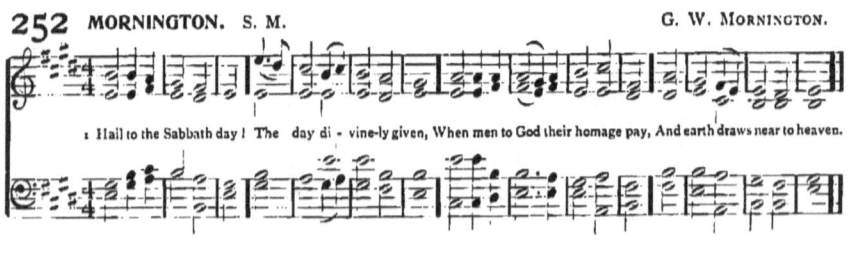

1 Hail to the Sabbath day! The day divinely given, When men to God their homage pay, And earth draws near to heaven.

2 Lord, in this sacred hour
Within Thy courts we bend,
And bless Thy love, and own Thy power,
Our Father and our Friend.

3 Thy temple is the arch
Of yon unmeasured sky;
Thy Sabbath, the stupendous march
Of grand eternity.

4 Lord, may that holier day
Dawn on Thy servants' sight;
And purer worship may we pay
In heaven's unclouded light.
STEPHEN G. BULFINCH, 1832. Abbr.

253 S. M.

1 Sweet is the task, O Lord,
Thy glorious acts to sing,
To praise Thy name, and hear Thy word,
And grateful offerings bring.

2 Sweet, at the dawning hour,
Thy boundless love to tell;
And, when the night wind shuts the flower,
Still on the theme to dwell.

3 Sweet, on this day of rest,
To join, in heart and voice,
With those who love and serve Thee best,
And in Thy name rejoice.
HARRIET AUBER, 1829. Abbr.

THE LORD'S DAY.

254 BLEST DAY. C. M.
J. LEMPRIERE HAMMOND, 1898.

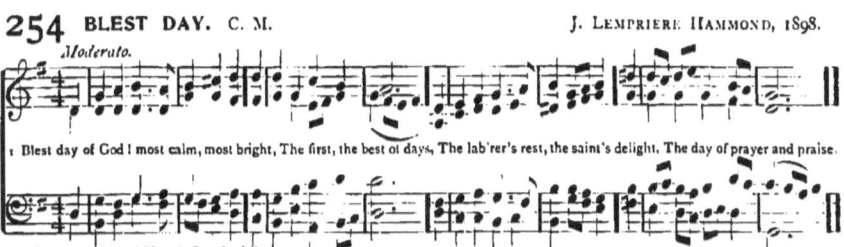

1 Blest day of God! most calm, most bright, The first, the best of days, The lab'rer's rest, the saint's delight, The day of prayer and praise.

Courtesy of the "Church Standard."

2 My Saviour's face made thee to shine;
His rising thee did raise,
And made thee heavenly and divine
Beyond all other days.

3 The first-fruits oft a blessing prove
To all the sheaves behind;
And they the day of Christ who love,
A happy week shall find.

4 This day I must with God appear;
For, Lord, the day is Thine;
Help me to spend it in Thy fear,
And thus to make it mine.

JOHN MASON, 1683.

255 C. M.

1 WHEN, as returns this solemn day,
Man comes to meet his God.
What rites, what honors shall he pay?
How spread His praise abroad?

2 From marble domes and gilded spires
Shall clouds of incense rise?
And gems, and gold, and garlands deck
The costly sacrifice?

3 Vain, sinful man! creation's Lord
Thy offerings well may spare;
But give thy heart, and thou shalt find
Thy God will hear thy prayer.

Mrs. ANNA L. BARBAULD, 1773.

256 DESIRE. L. M.
ANON.

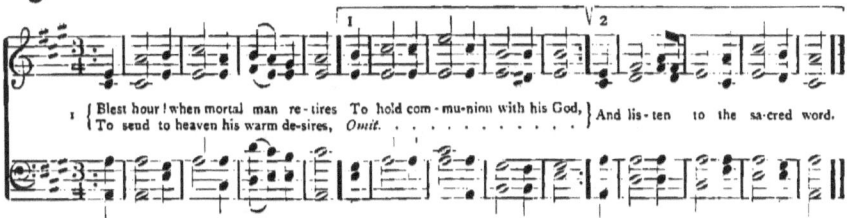

1 { Blest hour! when mortal man re-tires To hold com-mu-nion with his God, }
  { To send to heaven his warm de-sires, Omit. . . . . } And lis-ten to the sa-cred word.

2 Blest hour! when earthly cares resign
Their empire o'er his anxious breast,
While all around the calm divine
Proclaims the holy day of rest.

3 Blest hour! when God Himself draws nigh,
Well pleased His people's voice to hear,
To hush the penitential sigh,
And wipe away the mourner's tear.

4 Blest hour! for where the Lord resorts —
Foretastes of future bliss are given;
And mortals find His earthly courts
The house of God, the gate of Heaven!

THOMAS RAFFLES, 1828.

257 C. M.

1 AND now another week begins,
This day we call the Lord's;
This day He rose, who bore our sins,
For so His word records.

2 Hark, how the angels sweetly sing!
Their voices fill the sky;
They hail their great, victorious King,
And welcome Him on high.

3 Hail! mighty Saviour! Thee we hail,
Who fillest the throne above!
Till heart and flesh together fail,
We'll sing Thy matchless love.

THOMAS KELLY, 1809. Abbr.

258 MORNING PRAISE. 11s. 10s. Arr. from LICHNER.

1 Now when the dusk-y shades of night re-treat-ing, Be-fore the sun's red ban-ner swift-ly flee; . . . Now, when the ter-rors of the dark are flee-ing, O, Lord, we lift our thank-ful hearts to Thee. . .

2 To Thee, whose word the fount of life unsealing,
   When hill and dale in thickest darkness lay,
Awoke bright rays across the dim earth stealing,
   And bade the eve and morn complete the day.

3 Look from the height of heaven, and send to cheer us
   Thy light and truth, and guide us onward still;
Still let Thy mercy, as of old, be near us,
   And lead us safely to Thy Holy Hill.

4 So, when that morn of endless light is waking,
   And shades of evil from its splendors flee,
Safe may we rise, this earth's dark vale forsaking,
   Through all the long bright day to dwell with Thee.

5 Be this by Thee, O God Thrice Holy, granted,
   O Father, Son, and Spirit, ever blest;
Whose glory by the heaven and earth is chanted,
   Whose Name by men and angels is confest.

ENGLISH HYMNARY, 1853.

259 GLORIA PATRI.

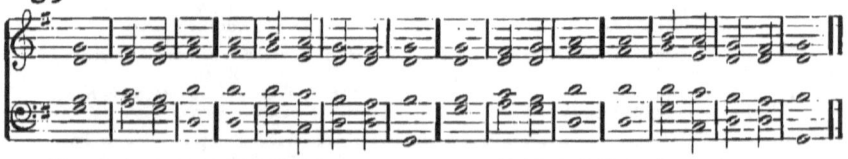

Glory be to the Father, and | to the | Son, ‖ and | to the | Holy | Ghost. ‖
As it was in the beginning, is now, and | ever | shall be, ‖ world | without | end, A- | men.

MORNING AND EVENING.

260 NICÆA. P. M.   JOHN B. DYKES, 1861.

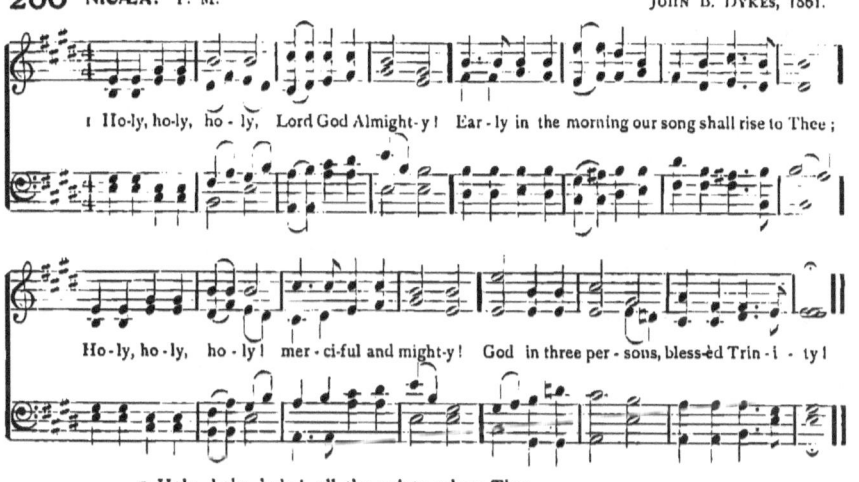

1 Holy, holy, holy, Lord God Almighty! Early in the morning our song shall rise to Thee;
Holy, holy, holy! merciful and mighty! God in three persons, blessèd Trinity!

2 Holy, holy, holy! all the saints adore Thee,
   Casting down their golden crowns around the glassy sea;
Cherubim and seraphim falling down before Thee,
   Which wert and art and evermore shalt be.

3 Holy, holy, holy! though the darkness hide Thee,
   Though the eye of sinful man Thy glory may not see;
Only Thou art holy; there is none beside Thee,
   Perfect in power, in love, and purity.

4 Holy, holy, holy! Lord God Almighty!
   All Thy works shall praise Thy name, in earth and sky and sea;
Holy, holy, holy, merciful and mighty;
   God in three persons, blessèd Trinity!
REGINALD HEBER, 1827. Abbr.

261 HEBRON. L. M.   LOWELL MASON, 1830.

1 Now with creation's morning song Let us, as children of the day, With wakened heart and purpose strong, The works of darkness cast away.

2 Oh, may the morn so pure, so clear,
   Its own sweet calm in us instill!
A guileless mind, a heart sincere,
   Simplicity of word and will.

3 And ever, as the day glides by,
   May we the busy senses rein ;

Keep guard upon the hand and eye,
   Nor let the conscience suffer stain.

4 Grant us, O God, in love to Thee,
   Clear eyes to measure things below;
Faith, the invisible to see;
   And wisdom, Thee in all to know.
Roman Breviary. Tr. EDWARD CASWALL, 1848.

THE PRAISE HYMNARY.

262 DUDLEY. L. M.   WM. A. MAY.

1 O Lord, go with me through this day, Keep me in all I think or say; Oh, may my eyes no e-vil see, My list-'ning ears hear on-ly Thee.

Copyright, 1898, by SILVER, BURDETT & COMPANY.

2 May my slow feet be quick to move,
In paths of righteousness and love ;
Thy peace my heart's sole comfort be,
Because Thy servant trusts in Thee.

3 If Thou shalt call me, Lord, to share
Thy cross, its agony and fear,
With grace upborne, and cloth'd with light,
I shall not falter in the fight.

4 At even-time, my day's work done,
Its battles fought, its vict'ry won,
May I look up Thy face to see,
And catch Thy beaming smile on me.
JAMES H. DUDLEY, 1896.

263 L. M.

1 MY God! how endless is Thy love!
Thy gifts are every evening new,
And morning mercies from above
Gently distill like early dew.

2 Thou spread'st the curtain of the night,
Great Guardian of my sleeping hours!
Thy sovereign word restores the light,
And quickens all my drowsy powers.

3 I yield my powers to Thy command,
To Thee I consecrate my days ;
Perpetual blessings from Thy hand
Demand perpetual songs of praise.
ISAAC WATTS, 1707.

264 NAVARRE. 7s.   Attributed to THIBAULT, King of Navarre.

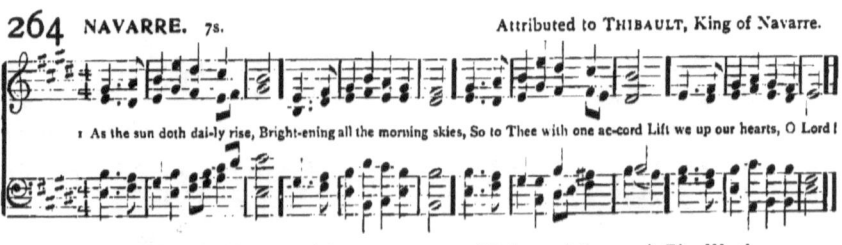

1 As the sun doth dai-ly rise, Bright-ening all the morning skies, So to Thee with one ac-cord Lift we up our hearts, O Lord!

2 Thou, by whom all things are fed,
Give us for the day our bread ;
Strength unto our souls afford
From the Bread of heaven, O Lord !

3 Be our guard in sin and strife ;
Be the leader of our life ;

While we daily search Thy Word,
Wisdom true impart, O Lord !

4 When the hours are dark and drear,
When the tempter lurketh near,
By Thy strengthening grace out-poured
Save the tempted ones, O Lord !
KING ALFRED, tr. EARL NELSON, 1864

MORNING AND EVENING.

265 KELSO. 7s. 6 l. EDWARD J. HOPKINS, 1872.

1 Ev-ery morn-ing mer-cies new Fall as fresh as ear-ly dew; Ev-ery morn-ing let us pay Trib-ute with the ear-ly day; For Thy mer-cies, Lord, are sure: Thy com-pas-sion doth en-dure.

2 Still the greatness of Thy love
Daily doth our sins remove;
Daily, far as east to west,
Lifts the burden from the breast;
Gives unbought to those who pray
Strength to stand in evil day.

3 Let our prayers each morn prevail,
That these gifts may never fail:
And, as we confess the sin
And the tempter's power within,
Feed us with the bread of life;
Fit us for our daily strife.

4 As the morning light returns,
As the sun with splendor burns,
Teach us still to turn to Thee,
Ever-blessèd Trinity,
With our hands our hearts to raise,
In unfailing prayer and praise.

HORATIUS BONAR, 1868.

266 7s. 6 l.

1 CHRIST, whose glory fills the skies,
Christ, the true, the only light,
Sun of Righteousness, arise,
Triumph o'er the shades of night;
Day-spring from on high, be near,
Day-star in my heart appear.

2 Dark and cheerless is the morn,
If Thy light is hid from me;
Joyless is the day's return,
Till Thy mercy's beams I see;
Till they inward light impart,
Warmth and gladness to my heart.

3 Visit, then, this soul of mine,
Pierce the gloom of sin and grief;
Fill me, radiant Sun divine!
Scatter all my unbelief;
More and more Thyself display,
Shining to the perfect day.

CHARLES WESLEY, 1740.

267 THE LORD'S PRAYER. ANON.

1 Our Father, who art in heaven, | hallowed | be Thy | name; ‖ Thy kingdom come: Thy will be done on | earth, as it | is in | heaven.
2 Give us this | day our | daily | bread; ‖ and forgive us our trespasses as we forgive them that | trespass · · a- | gainst — | us.
3 And lead us not into temptation, but de- | liver | us from | evil; ‖ for Thine is the kingdom, and the power, and the glory, for- | ever. | A- — | men.

268 GERMANY. L. M.
LUDWIG VON BEETHOVEN.

1 In sleep's serene oblivion laid, I safely passed the silent night;
Again I see the breaking shade, I drink again the morning light.

2 New-born, I bless the waking hour;
Once more, with awe, rejoice to be;
My conscious soul resumes her power,
And springs, my guardian God, to Thee.

3 O guide me through the various maze
My doubtful feet are doomed to tread;
And spread Thy shield's protecting blaze,
When dangers press around my head.

4 A deeper shade will soon impend,
A deeper sleep mine eyes oppress;
Yet then Thy strength shall still defend,
Thy goodness still delight to bless.

5 That deeper shade shall break away,
That deeper sleep shall leave mine eyes;
Thy light shall give eternal day,
Thy love, the rapture of the skies.

JOHN HAWKESWORTH, 1773.

269 L. M.

1 AWAKE, my soul, and with the sun
Thy daily stage of duty run;
Shake off dull sloth, and joyful rise
To pay thy morning sacrifice.

2 Awake, lift up thyself, my heart,
And with the angels bear thy part,
Who all night long unwearied sing
High praises to the eternal King.

3 Glory to Thee, who safe hast kept,
And hast refreshed me when I slept;
Grant, Lord, when I from death shall wake,
I may of endless life partake.

4 Direct, control, suggest, this day,
All I design, or do or say;
That all my powers, with all their might,
In Thy sole glory may unite.

THOMAS KEN, 1697. Abbr.

270 SEELYE. 8s. 7s.
ANON.

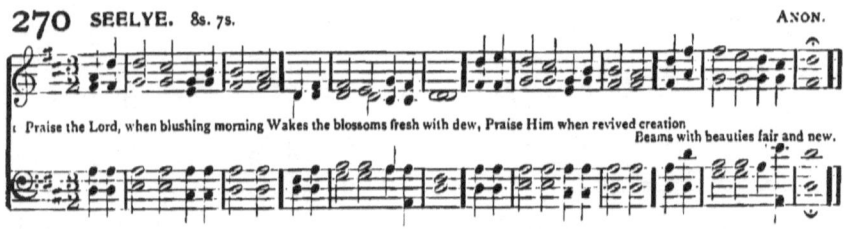

1 Praise the Lord, when blushing morning Wakes the blossoms fresh with dew, Praise Him when revived creation Beams with beauties fair and new.

2 Praise the Lord, when early breezes
Come so fragrant from the flowers;
Praise, thou willow, by the brook-side,
Praise, ye birds, among the bowers.

3 Praise the Lord, and may His blessing
Guide us in the way of truth;
Keep our feet from paths of error,
Make us holy in our youth.

JOHANN S. PATZKE, 1780.
Tr. ANON., 1844.

MORNING AND EVENING.

271 EVENTIDE. 10 s.   Arr. fr. German, WILLIAM H. MONK, 1861.

1 A-bide with me; fast falls the e-ven-tide; The darkness deep-ens; Lord, with me a-bide!
When oth-er help-ers fail, and comforts flee, Help of the helpless, oh, a-bide with me!

2 Not a brief glance I beg, a passing word,
But as Thou dwell'st with Thy disciples, Lord,
Familiar, condescending, patient, free,
Come, not to sojourn, but abide with me.

3 I need Thy presence every passing hour:
What but Thy grace can foil the tempter's power?

Who like Thyself my guide and stay can be?
Thro' cloud and sunshine, oh, abide with me!

4 Swift to its close ebbs out life's little day;
Earth's joys grow dim, its glories pass away;
Change and decay in all around I see;
O Thou, who changest not, abide with me!

HENRY F. LYTE, 1847. Abbr.

272 HURSLEY. L. M.   Arr. by WILLIAM H. MONK, 1861.

1 Sun of my soul, Thou Saviour dear, It is not night if Thou be near; Oh, may no earth-born cloud arise
To hide Thee from Thy servant's eyes.

2 When the soft dews of kindly sleep
My wearied eyelids gently steep,
Be my last thought how sweet to rest
Forever on my Saviour's breast.

3 Abide with me from morn till eve,
For without Thee I cannot live;
Abide with me when night is nigh,
For without Thee I dare not die.

4 Be near to bless me when I wake
Ere through the world my way I take;
Till in the ocean of Thy love
I lose myself in heaven above.

JOHN KEBLE, 1827. Abbr.

273 L. M.

1 THUS far the Lord has led me on,
Thus far His power prolongs my days;
And every evening shall make known
Some fresh memorial of His grace.

2 I lay my body down to sleep;
Peace is the pillow for my head,
While well-appointed angels keep
Their watchful stations round my bed.

3 Faith in His Name forbids my fear;
O may Thy presence ne'er depart;
And, in the morning, make me hear
The love and kindness of Thy heart.

ISAAC WATTS, 1709. Abbr.

THE PRAISE HYMNARY.

274 EVENING HYMN. L. M.   THOMAS TALLIS, 1560.

1 Glory to Thee, my God, this night, For all the blessings of the light: Keep me, oh, keep me, King of kings! Beneath Thine own Almighty wings.

2 Forgive me, Lord, for Thy dear Son,
The ill which I this day have done;
That with the world, myself, and Thee,
I, ere I sleep, at peace may be.

3 Teach me to live, that I may dread
The grave as little as my bed:
Teach me to die, that so I may
Rise glorious at the judgment-day.

4 Oh, let my soul on Thee repose,
And may sweet sleep mine eyelids close!
Sleep, which shall me more vigorous make,
To serve my God when I awake.
           THOMAS KEN, 1697. Abbr.

275   L. M.

1 GREAT GOD! to Thee my evening song
With humble gratitude I raise;
Oh, let Thy mercy tune my tongue,
And fill my heart with lively praise.

2 My days unclouded as they pass,
And every gentle, rolling hour,
Are monuments of wondrous grace,
And witness to Thy love and power.

3 Seal my forgiveness in the blood
Of Jesus; His dear name alone
I plead for pardon, gracious God!
And kind acceptance at Thy throne.
           ANNE STEELE, 1760.

276 STOCKWELL. 8s. 7s.   DARIUS E. JONES, 1847.

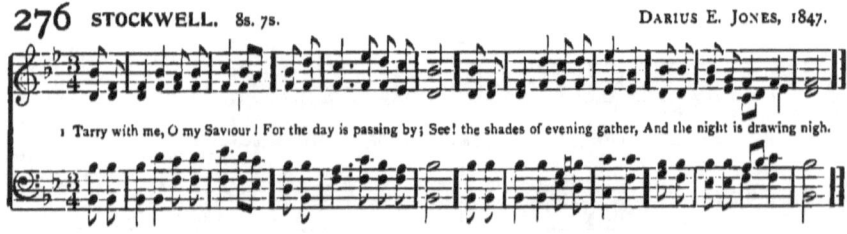

1 Tarry with me, O my Saviour! For the day is passing by; See! the shades of evening gather, And the night is drawing nigh.

2 Deeper, deeper grow the shadows,
Paler now the glowing west,
Swift the night of death advances;
Shall it be the night of rest?

3 Feeble, trembling, fainting, dying,
Lord, I cast myself on Thee;
Tarry with me through the darkness;
While I sleep, still watch by me.

4 Tarry with me, O my Saviour!
Lay my head upon Thy breast;
Till the morning; then awake me—
Morning of eternal rest!
           Mrs. CAROLINE S. SMITH, 1856. Abbr.

277   8s, 7s.

1 SAVIOUR! breathe an evening blessing,
Ere repose our eyelids seal;
Sin and want we come confessing;
Thou canst save, and Thou canst heal.

2 Though the night be dark and dreary,
Darkness cannot hide from Thee;
Thou art He who, never weary,
Watcheth where Thy people be.

3 Should swift death this night o'ertake us,
And our couch become our tomb,
May the morn in heaven awake us,
Clad in bright and deathless bloom.
           JAMES EDMESTON, 1820. Abbr.

MORNING AND EVENING.

278 HOLLEY. 7s.   GEORGE HEWS, 1835.

1 Soft-ly now the light of day Fades upon my sight away; Free from care, from labor free, Lord, I would commune with Thee.

2 Thou, whose all-pervading eye
Naught escapes, without, within,
Pardon each infirmity,
Open fault, and secret sin.

3 Soon, for me, the light of day
Shall forever pass away:
Then, from sin and sorrow free,
Take me, Lord, to dwell with Thee.

4 Thou who, sinless, yet hast known
All of man's infirmity;
Then, from Thine eternal throne,
Jesus, look with pitying eye.
         GEORGE W. DOANE, 1824.

279 7s.

1 STEALING from the world away,
We are come to seek Thy face;
Kindly meet us, Lord, we pray;
Grant us Thy reviving grace.

2 Yonder stars that gild the sky
Shine but with a borrowed light;
We, unless Thy light be nigh,
Wander, wrapt in gloomy night.

3 Sun of righteousness, dispel
All our darkness, doubts, and fears;
May Thy light within us dwell
Till eternal day appears.
         RAY PALMER, 1834.

280 BRADEN. S. M.   WILLIAM B. BRADBURY, 1844.

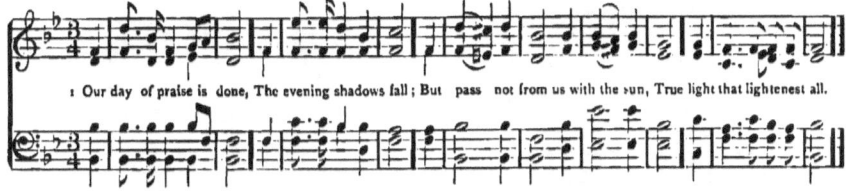

1 Our day of praise is done, The evening shadows fall; But pass not from us with the sun, True light that lightenest all.

2 Around the throne on high,
Where night can never be,
The white-robed harpers of the sky
Bring ceaseless hymns to Thee.

3 Too faint our anthems here,
Too soon of praise we tire;
But, oh, the strains how full and clear
Of that eternal choir!

4 Yet, Lord, to Thy dear will
If Thou attune the heart,
We in Thine angels' music still
May bear our lower part.
         JOHN ELLERTON, 1867. Abbr.

281 S. M.

1 THE day, O Lord, is spent;
Abide with us, and rest;
Our hearts' desires are fully bent
On making Thee our guest.

2 We have not reached that land,
That happy land, as yet,
Where holy angels round Thee stand,
Whose sun can never set.

3 Our sun is sinking now,
Our day is almost o'er;
O Sun of Righteousness, do Thou
Shine on us evermore!
         JOHN M. NEALE, 1844

282 BETHLEHEM! P. M.

George A. Burdett.

1 O little town of Bethlehem! How still we see thee lie;
Above thy deep and dreamless sleep The silent stars go by;
Yet in thy dark streets shineth The everlasting light;
The hopes and fears of all the years Are met in thee to-night.

Copyright, 1895, by Silver, Burdett & Company.

2 For Christ is born of Mary,
   And gathered all above,
While mortals sleep, the angels keep
   Their watch of wondering love.
O morning stars, together
   Proclaim the holy birth!
And praises sing to God the King,
   And peace to men on earth.

3 How silently, how silently,
   The wondrous gift is given!
So God imparts to human hearts
   The blessings of His heaven.

No ear may know His coming,
   But in this world of sin,
Where meek souls will receive Him still,
   The dear Christ enters in.

4 O holy Child of Bethlehem!
   Descend to us, we pray;
Cast out our sin, and enter in,
   Be born in us to-day.
We hear the Christmas angels
   The great glad tidings tell;
O come to us, abide with us,
   Our Lord Emmanuel!

Phillips Brooks.

THE BIRTH OF CHRIST.

283 7s. D.

1 He has come! the Christ of God
Left for us His glad abode;
Stooping from His throne of bliss,
To this darksome wilderness.
He has come! the Prince of Peace;
Come to bid our sorrows cease;
Come to scatter with His light
All the shadows of our night.

2 He the mighty King has come!
Making this poor earth His home;
Come to bear our sin's sad load;
Son of David, Son of God!

He has come, whose name of grace
Speaks deliverance to our race;
Left for us His glad abode;
Son of Mary, Son of God!

3 Unto us a child is born!
Ne'er has earth beheld a morn,
Among all the morns of time,
Half so glorious in its prime.
Unto us a Son is given!
He has come from God's own heaven,
Bringing with Him from above
Holy peace and holy love.

HORATIUS BONAR, 1857.

284 HERALD ANGELS. 7s. D.   FELIX MENDELSSOHN-BARTHOLDY, 1846.

1 Hark! the her-ald an-gels sing "Glo-ry to the new-born King; Peace on earth, and mercy mild, God and sin-ners rec-on-ciled!" { Joyful, all ye nations, rise, / Join the triumph of the skies; } With the angelic host proclaim, "Christ is born in Beth-lehem!" With the an-gel-ic host proclaim, "Christ is born in Beth-le-hem!"

2 Christ, by highest heaven adored;
Christ, the everlasting Lord:
Late in time behold Him come,
Offspring of the Virgin's womb:
Vailed in flesh the Godhead see;
Hail the incarnate Deity,
Pleased as man with men to dwell;
Jesus, our Immanuel!

3 Hail! the heaven-born Prince of Peace!
Hail the Sun of Righteousness!
Light and life to all He brings
Risen with healing in His wings:
Mild He lays His glory by,
Born that man no more may die;
Born to raise the sons of earth,
Born to give them second birth.

CHARLES WESLEY, 1739

THE PRAISE HYMNARY.

285 CAROL. C. M. D.   RICHARD S. WILLIS, 1849.

1. It came up-on the mid-night clear, That glo-rious song of old, From an-gels bend-ing near the earth, To touch their harps of gold; "Peace on the earth, good-will to men, From Heaven's all-gra-cious King;" The world in sol-emn still-ness lay To hear the an-gels sing!

2. Still through the cloven skies they come,
    With peaceful wings unfurled;
   And still their heavenly music floats
    O'er all the weary world;
   Above its sad and lowly plains
    They bend on hovering wing,
   And ever o'er its babel sounds
    The blessed angels sing!

3. And ye beneath life's crushing load
    Whose forms are bending low,
   Who toil along the climbing way
    With painful steps and slow,—

   Look now; for glad and golden hours
    Come swiftly on the wing;
   Oh rest beside the weary road,
    And hear the angels sing!

4. For, lo, the days are hastening on,
    By prophet bards foretold,
   When with the ever circling years
    Comes round the age of gold;
   When Peace shall over all the earth
    Its ancient splendors fling,
   And the whole world give back the song
    Which now the angels sing!

EDMUND H. SEARS, 1850.

THE BIRTH OF CHRIST.

286 ANTIOCH. C. M.   Arr. from HANDEL, by LOWELL MASON, 1836.

Joy to the world, the Lord is come! Let earth receive her King; Let ev-'ry heart pre-pare Him room, And heaven and nature sing, And heaven and nature sing, And heaven, And heaven and nature sing.

2 Joy to the world, the Saviour reigns;
Let men their songs employ;
While fields and floods, rocks, hills, and plains
Repeat the sounding joy.

3 No more let sin and sorrow grow,
Nor thorns infest the ground;
He comes to make His blessings flow
Far as the curse is found.

4 He rules the world with truth and grace,
And makes the nations prove
The glories of His righteousness,
And wonders of His love.
ISAAC WATTS, 1719

287 C. M.

1 MORTALS, awake, with angels join
And chant the solemn lay;
Joy, love, and gratitude combine
To hail the auspicious day.

2 In heaven the rapturous song began,
And sweet seraphic fire
Through all the shining legions ran,
And strung and tuned the lyre.

3 With joy the chorus we'll repeat, —
"Glory to God on high!
Good-will and peace are now complete;
Jesus was born to die!"

4 Hail, Prince of life, forever hail!
Redeemer, Brother, Friend!
Though earth, and time, and life shall fail,
Thy praise shall never end!
SAMUEL MEDLEY, 1782. Abbr.

288 DIX. 7s. 6l.   CONRAD KOCHER, arr. by WILLIAM H. MONK, 1868.

1 { As with gladness men of old Did the guiding star be-hold;
    As with joy they hailed its light, Leading onward, beaming bright; } So, most gracious Lord, may we Evermore be led to Thee.

2 As with joyful steps they sped
To that lowly manger-bed,
There to bend the knee before
Him whom heaven and earth adore;
So may we with willing feet
Ever seek the Mercy-seat.

3 As they offered gifts most rare
At that manger rude and bare;
So may we with holy joy,
Pure, and free from sin's alloy,
All our costliest treasures bring,
Christ, to Thee, our heavenly King.
WILLIAM C. DIX, 1859.

289 HOLY VOICES. 8s. 7s. D.
HENRY SMART, 1860.

1 Hark! what mean those ho-ly voic-es, Sweet-ly sound-ing through the skies? Lo! the an-gel-ic host re-joic-es, Heavenly al-le-lu-ias rise. Lis-ten to the wondrous sto-ry Which they chant in hymns of joy:—"Glo-ry in the high-est, glo-ry! Glo-ry be to God Most High!"

2 "Peace on earth, good will from heaven,
Reaching far as man is found;
Souls redeemed and sins forgiven;—
Loud our golden harps shall sound.
Christ is born, the great Anointed;
Heaven and earth His praises sing!
O receive Whom God appointed
For your Prophet, Priest, and King!"

3 "Hasten, mortals, to adore Him;
Learn His Name, and taste His joy:
Till in heaven ye sing before Him,
Glory be to God Most High!"
Let us learn the wondrous story
Of our great Redeemer's birth;
Spread the brightness of His glory
Till it cover all the earth.

JOHN CAWOOD, 1819.

290 GLORY BE TO GOD.
GREGORIAN.

Glory be to God on high, And on earth peace, good-will to men. A-MEN.

We praise Thee, we bless Thee, we worship Thee, we | glorify | Thee, ||
We give thanks to | Thee · for | Thy · great | glory. AMEN.

THE BIRTH OF CHRIST.

291　GLORY TO GOD. P. M.　　　　　　　　　　Arr. from LOHENGRIN.

1 "Glo-ry to God! peace on the earth! Good-will to men!" sang the an-gels a-bove;
Glo-ry to God! peace on the earth! Good-will to men! — sound the chorus of love!
D. S. Come let us sing — sing of His grace, Grateful thanksgiving shall (Omit.) ut-ter His praise.

Bright dawns the morning, when heav'n is so near; Sweet be our an-them, for Je-sus is here,

2 Praise ye the Lord! lift to His name
High hallelujahs from each happy voice;
Strike the loud chord! praise ye the Lord!
Let every soul in His glory rejoice!
Oh, for a strain such as angels repeat,
When the redeem'd cast their crowns at His feet;
"Worthy the Lamb! once He was slain,
Now on His throne He is reigning again!"

3 O Christ of God! risen and crowned!
Come with Thy presence, Thy Spirit impart!
Come with Thy love! come with Thy power!
Breathe on our souls, and enrich every heart!
Sad were Thy sufferings, shameful Thy cross,
Sharing our punishment, bearing our loss;
Now, Lord of all, Thee we adore!
Bring we our souls to be Thine evermore!
　　　　　　　　　　　CHARLES S. ROBINSON.

292　P. M.

1 O STARRY night, thy silver light
Doth o'er the world its rare radiance shed;
Just as of old, when, we are told.
Men to the babe in a manger were led.
As through the ages cometh thy sweet song,
First given to earth by celestial throng;
So, for all men, still shines thy bright star,
And to all men speeds thy story afar.

2 Peace among men! sing it again!
Hark to the chorus now girdling the earth!
Good will to all! It is God's call.
Telling the nations of Christ's glorious birth.
Peace and good will to all men, let us sing,
Glory to God! let the chiming bells ring!
Heaven and earth with joy now resound —
Hope, Love and Grace for all men, now abound.
　　　　　　　　　　　WM. A. MAY, 1898.

THE PRAISE HYMNARY.

293 CRUCIFIX. 7s. 6s.   Greek Melody. Arr. by HASLAM.

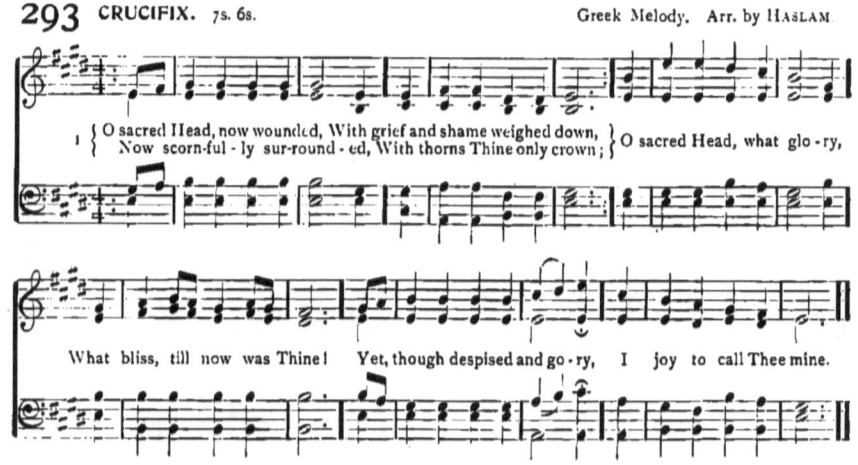

1. O sacred Head, now wounded, With grief and shame weighed down,
Now scornfully surrounded, With thorns Thine only crown;
O sacred Head, what glory,
What bliss, till now was Thine!
Yet, though despised and gory,
I joy to call Thee mine.

2. What Thou, my Lord, hast suffered
Was all for sinners' gain;
Mine, mine was the transgression,
But Thine the deadly pain:
Lo, here I fall, my Saviour!
'T is I deserve Thy place;
Look on me with Thy favor,
Vouchsafe to me Thy grace.

3. What language shall I borrow
To thank Thee, dearest Friend,
For this Thy dying sorrow,
Thy pity without end?

O make me Thine forever;
And, should I fainting be,
Lord, let me never, never,
Outlive my love to Thee!

4. Be near me when I 'm dying,
O show Thy cross to me!
And for some succor flying,
Come, Lord, and set me free!
These eyes, new faith receiving,
From Jesus shall not move;
For he who dies believing,
Dies safely through Thy love.

BERNARD OF CLAIRVAUX, 1153,
Tr. by J. W. ALEXANDER, 1849.

294 LITLINGTON TOWER. L. M.   JOSEPH BARNBY, 1862.

1. Lord Jesus, when we stand afar, And gaze upon Thy holy cross, In love of Thee and scorn of self, O, may we count the world as loss.

2. When we behold Thy bleeding wounds,
And the rough way that Thou hast trod,
Make us to hate the load of sin
That lay so heavy on our God.

3. O Holy Lord! uplifted high
With outstretched arms, in mortal woe,

Embracing in Thy wondrous love
The sinful world that lies below,—

4. Give us an ever-living faith
To gaze beyond the things we see;
And in the mystery of Thy death
Draw us and all men unto Thee.

WILLIAM W. HOW, 1854.

THE SUFFERINGS OF CHRIST.

295 WONDROUS CROSS.   W. L. MASON.

1 When I sur-vey the wondrous cross, On which the Prince of Glo-ry died, My rich-est gain I count but loss, And pour contempt on all my pride. In the cross of Christ I glo-ry, Towering o'er ... the wrecks of time; All the light of sa-cred sto-ry Gathers round its head sub-lime.

CHORUS. cross of Christ I glo-ry, Towering o'er the wrecks of time.

Copyright by GOODENOUGH & WOGLOM CO. Used by per.

2 Forbid it, Lord, that I should boast,
Save in the death of Christ, my God:
All the vain things that charm me most,
I sacrifice them to His blood.

3 See, from His head, His hands, His feet,
Sorrow and love flow mingled down:

Did e'er such love and sorrow meet,
Or thorns compose so rich a crown?

4 Were the whole realm of nature mine,
That were a present far too small;
Love so amazing, so divine,
Demands my soul, my life, my all.

                                           ISAAC WATTS, 1707. Abbr.

DONCASTER. L. M.   EDWARD MILLER, 1787.

1 When I survey the wondrous cross, On which the Prince of Glory died, My richest gain I count but loss, And pour contempt on all my pride.

111

2 Was it for crimes that I have done,
He groaned upon the tree?
Amazing pity, grace unknown,
And love beyond degree!

3 But drops of grief can ne'er repay
The debt of love I owe;
Here, Lord, I give myself away,
'T is all that I can do!

Isaac Watts, 1707.

THE SUFFERINGS OF CHRIST.

297 WAVERTREE. L. M. 6l.   WILLIAM SHORE, 1840.

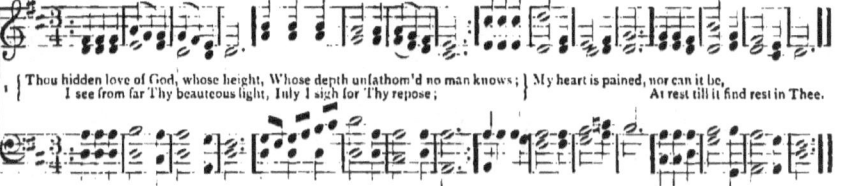

1 { Thou hidden love of God, whose height, Whose depth unfathom'd no man knows; } { My heart is pained, nor can it be,
  I see from far Thy beauteous light, July I sigh for Thy repose; At rest till it find rest in Thee.

2 Is there a thing beneath the sun
   That strives with Thee my heart to share?
   Ah! tear it thence, and reign alone,
   The Lord of every motion there.
   Then shall my heart from earth be free,
   When it hath found repose in Thee.

3 Oh, hide this self from me, that I
   No more, but Christ in me, may live;
   My vile affections crucify,
   Nor let one darling lust survive;
   In all things nothing may I see,
   Nothing desire, or seek, but Thee.

4 Each moment draw from earth away
   My heart that lowly waits Thy call;
   Speak to my inmost soul, and say,
   I am thy love, thy God, thy all:
   To feel Thy power, to hear Thy voice,
   To taste Thy love, be all my choice.
                    GERARD TERSTEEGEN, 1731.
                    Tr. by JOHN WESLEY, 1739.

298 FOUNTAIN. C. M.   Western Melody. Arr. LOWELL MASON, 1830.

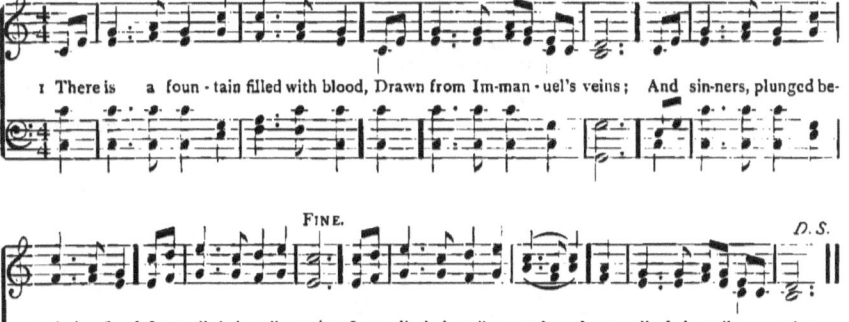

1 There is a foun-tain filled with blood, Drawn from Im-man-uel's veins; And sin-ners, plunged be-neath that flood, Lose all their guilty stains, Lose all their guilty stains, Lose all their guilty stains.

2 The dying thief rejoiced to see
   That fountain in his day;
   And there may I, though vile as he,
   Wash all my sins away.

3 Thou dying Lamb, Thy precious blood
   Shall never lose its power,
   Till all the ransomed church of God
   Be saved to sin no more.

4 E'er since, by faith, I saw the stream
   Thy flowing wounds supply,
   Redeeming love has been my theme,
   And shall be till I die.

5 And when this feeble, faltering tongue
   Lies silent in the grave,
   Then, in a nobler, sweeter song,
   I'll sing Thy power to save.
                    WILLIAM COWPER, 1779.

THE PRAISE HYMNARY.

299 ESSEX. 7s. 5l. THOMAS CLARK.

1 Christ the Lord is risen again, Christ hath broken every chain; Hark! angelic voices cry, Singing evermore on high, Hallelujah! Praise the Lord!

2 He who bore all pain and loss,
Comfortless, upon the cross,
Lives in glory now on high,
Pleads for us, and hears our cry:
Hallelujah! Praise the Lord!

3 He who slumbered in the grave
Is exalted now to save;
Now through Christendom it rings
That the Lamb is King of kings:
Hallelujah! Praise the Lord!

4 Now He bids us tell abroad
How the lost may be restored,
How the penitent forgiven,
How we, too, may enter heaven:
Hallelujah! Praise the Lord!

Bohemian Easter Hymn, 1831. C. WINKWORTH, tr. 1858.

300 ST. ALBINUS. 7s, 8s. HENRY J. GAUNTLETT, 1872.

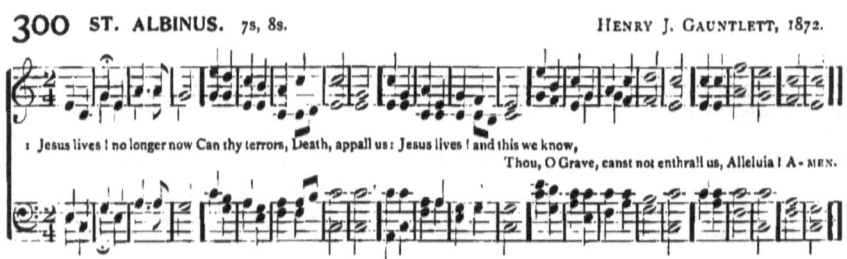

1 Jesus lives! no longer now Can thy terrors, Death, appall us: Jesus lives! and this we know, Thou, O Grave, canst not enthrall us, Alleluia! A-MEN.

2 Jesus lives: henceforth is death
But the gate of life immortal;
This shall calm our trembling breath,
When we pass its gloomy portal.

3 Jesus lives: our hearts know well
Naught from us His love shall sever;
Life, nor death, nor powers of hell
Tear us from His keeping ever.

4 Jesus lives: to Him the throne
Over all the world is given:
May we go where He is gone,
Rest and reign with Him in heaven.

CHRISTIAN F. GELLERT, 1757.
FRANCES E. COX, tr. 1841. Abbr.

THE RESURRECTION OF CHRIST.

301 CONQUEROR. P. M.   Arr. fr. PALESTRINA.

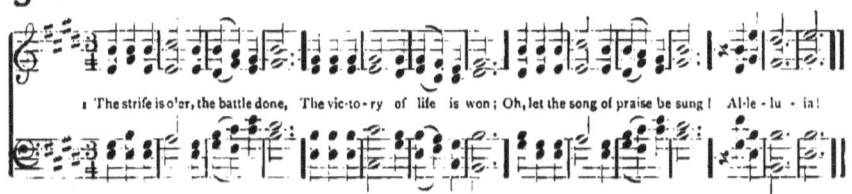

1 The strife is o'er, the battle done, The vic-to-ry of life is won; Oh, let the song of praise be sung! Al-le-lu-ia!

2 The powers of death have done their worst,
But Christ their legions hath dispersed;
Let shout of holy joy outburst:
    Alleluia!

3 The three sad days are quickly sped;
He rises glorious from the dead:
All glory to our risen Head!
    Alleluia!

4 Lord, by the stripes which wounded Thee,
From death's dread sting Thy servants free,
That we may live and sing to Thee,
    Alleluia!
        Tr. FRANCIS POTT, 1860.

302 P. M.

1 THE rosy morn has robed the sky;
The Lord has risen with victory:
Let earth be glad, and raise the cry:
    Alleluia.

2 The Prince of Life with death has striven,
To cleanse the earth His blood has given,
Has rent the vail, and opened heaven:
    Alleluia.

3 And he, dear Lord, that with Thee dies,
And fleshly passions crucifies,
In body, like to Thine, shall rise:
    Alleluia.
        WILLIAM COOK. Abbr.

303 FERRIER. 7s.   JOHN B. DYKES, 1861.

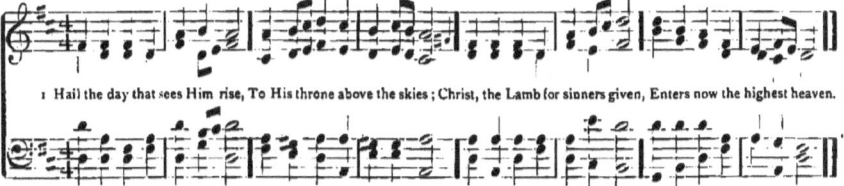

1 Hail the day that sees Him rise, To His throne above the skies; Christ, the Lamb for sinners given, Enters now the highest heaven.

2 There for Him high triumph waits;
Lift your heads, eternal gates!
He hath conquered death and sin,
Take the King of Glory in.

3 Lo, the heaven its Lord receives!
Yet He loves the earth He leaves;
Though returning to His throne,
Still He calls mankind His own.

4 Lord, though parted from our sight
Far above the starry height,
Grant our hearts may thither rise,
Seeking Thee above the skies.
        CHARLES WESLEY, 1739. Abbr.

304 7s.

1 CHRIST to heaven is gone before
In the body here He wore;
He that as our Brother died,
Is our Brother glorified.

2 All the angels wondering own,
'Tis our nature on the throne;
"How He lovèd them, behold!"
Trembles on the harps of gold.

3 Fear not, ye of little faith,
For He hath abolished death;
And no longer now we die,
We but follow Christ on high.

4 As our Shepherd He is there,
With the comfort of His care;
Fear no evil, doubt no more,
Christ to heaven is gone before.
        GEORGE RAWSON, 1857. Abbr.

305 DIADEMATA. S. M. D. GEORGE J. ELVEY, 1868.

1 Crown Him with many crowns, The Lamb upon His throne; Hark! how the heavenly anthem drowns All music but its own! Awake, my soul, and sing Of Him who died for thee; And hail Him as thy matchless King Thro' all eternity.

2 Crown Him, the Lord of love!
  Behold His hands and side, —
  Rich wounds, yet visible above
  In beauty glorified:
No angel in the sky
  Can fully bear that sight,
But downward bends his wondering eye
  At mysteries so bright.

3 Crown Him, the Lord of life!
  Who triumphed o'er the grave;
  Who rose victorious to the strife
  For those He came to save;
His glories now we sing,
  Who died and rose on high,
Who died eternal life to bring,
  And lives that death may die.

4 Crown Him, the Lord of heaven,
  One with the Father known,
  One with the Spirit through Him given
  From yonder glorious throne!
To Thee be endless praise,
  For Thou for us hast died;
Be Thou, O Lord, through endless days
  Adored and magnified.
    MATHEW BRIDGES, 1848.

306 S. M. D.

1 THOU art gone up on high
  To mansions in the skies,
And round Thy throne unceasingly
  The songs of praise arise.
But we are lingering here
  With sin and care oppressed:
Lord! send Thy promised Comforter,
  And lead us to Thy rest!

2 Thou art gone up on high:
  But Thou didst first come down,
Through earth's most bitter misery
  To pass unto Thy crown.
And girt with griefs and fears
  Our onward course must be;
But only let that path of tears
  Lead us at last to Thee!

3 Thou art gone up on high:
  But Thou shalt come again
With all the bright ones of the sky
  Attendant in Thy train.
Oh, by Thy saving power
  So make us live and die,
That we may stand in that dread hour
  At Thy right hand on high!
    Mrs. E. L. TOKE, 1851.

THE ENTHRONEMENT OF CHRIST.

307 TAMWORTH. 8s, 7s, 4s.   Scotch. Arr. by CHARLES LOCKHART, 1790.

Look, ye saints, the sight is glorious ; See the Man of sorrows now
From the fight returned victorious ! Every knee to Him shall bow :
Crown Him ! crown Him ! Crown Him ! crown Him !
Crowns become the Victor's brow.

2 Crown the Saviour, angels, crown Him!
Rich the trophies Jesus brings;
In the seat of power enthrone Him,
While the vault of heaven rings;
‖ Crown Him! crown Him! ‖
Crown the Saviour King of kings!

3 Sinners in derision crowned Him,
Mocking thus the Saviour's claim;
Saints and angels, crowd around Him!
Own His title, praise His name!
‖ Crown Him! crown Him! ‖
Spread abroad the Victor's fame.

4 Hark, those bursts of acclamation!
Hark, those loud, triumphant chords!
Jesus takes the highest station;
Oh, what joy the sight affords!
‖ Crown Him! crown Him! ‖
King of kings and Lord of lords!

THOMAS KELLY, 1806.

308 C. M.

1 YE choirs of new Jerusalem,
Your sweetest notes employ,
The Paschal victory to hymn
In strains of holy joy:

2 How Judah's Lion burst His chains,
And bruised the serpent's head;
And cried aloud, through death's domains,
To wake the imprisoned dead.

3 From hell's devouring jaws the prey
Alone our Leader bore;
His ransomed hosts pursue the way
Where He hath gone before.

4 Right gloriously He triumphs now;
To Him all power is given;
To Him in one communion bow
All saints in earth and heaven.

FULBERT, tr. by ROBERT CAMPBELL, 1850. Abbr.

309 ST. AGNES. C. M.   JOHN B. DYKES, 1858.

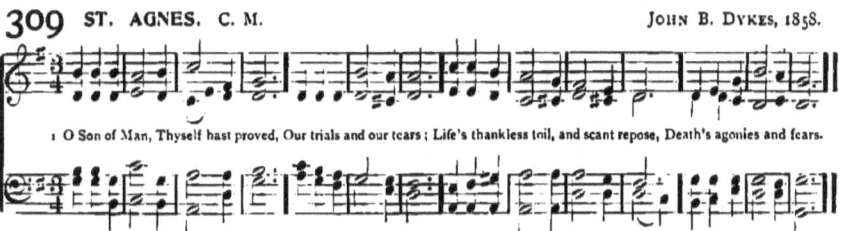

1 O Son of Man, Thyself hast proved, Our trials and our tears ; Life's thankless toil, and scant repose, Death's agonies and fears.

2 O Son of God, in glory raised,
Thou sittest on Thy throne :
There by Thy pleadings and Thy grace
Still succoring Thine own.

3 In all things like Thy brethren Thou
Wast made, yet free from sin ;
Yet how unlike to us, O Lord ;
Replies the voice within.

JOSEPH ANSTICE, 1835. Abbr.

310 CATON. L. M.
EDWARD MILLER, 1790.

1 Come, gracious spirit, heavenly Dove, With light and comfort from above; Be Thou our Guardian, Thou our Guide; O'er ev'ry thought and step preside.

2 To us the light of truth display,
And make us know and choose Thy way;
Plant holy fear in every heart,
That we from God may ne'er depart.

3 Lead us to holiness, the road
That we must take to dwell with God;
Lead us to Christ, the living way,
Nor let us from His precepts stray.

4 Lead us to God, our final rest,
To be with Him forever blest;
Lead us to Heaven, that we may share
Fulness of joy forever there.

SIMON BROWNE, 1720.

311 L. M.

1 COME, sacred Spirit, from above,
And fill the coldest heart with love:
Oh, turn to flesh the flinty stone,
And let Thy sovereign power be known.

2 Speak Thou, and from the haughtiest eyes
Shall floods of contrite sorrow rise;
While all their glowing souls are borne
To seek that grace which now they scorn.

3 Oh, let a holy flock await
In crowds around Thy temple-gate!
Each pressing on with zeal to be
A living sacrifice to Thee.

PHILIP DODDRIDGE, 1755. Abbr.

312 ELYRIA. 7s.
MARIA LUIGI CHERUBINI.

1 Gracious Spirit, Love divine! Let Thy light within me shine; All my guilty fears remove, Fill me with Thy heavenly love.

2 Speak Thy pardoning grace to me,
Set the burdened sinner free;
Lead me to the Lamb of God,
Wash me in His precious blood.

3 Life and peace to me impart,
Seal salvation on my heart;

Breathe Thyself into my breast,
Earnest of immortal rest.

4 Let me never from Thee stray,
Keep me in the narrow way;
Fill my soul with joy divine,
Keep me, Lord, forever Thine.

JOHN STOCKER, 1776.

THE HOLY SPIRIT.

313 ECHO HYMN. 6s. 4s.   BRAUN, 1675.

1 Come, Holy One, in love, Descending, like the dove, Shed on us from above Thine own bright ray! Divinely good Thou art; Thy sacred gifts impart, To gladden each sad heart; Oh, come to-day!

2 Come, tenderest Friend and best,
Our most delightful Guest,
Enter each longing breast
  With soothing power;
Rest, which the weary know,
Shade, 'mid the noon-tide glow,
Peace, when deep griefs o'erflow,
  Cheer us, this hour!

3 Come, Light serene and still,
Brightening our every ill,
Our inmost bosoms fill,
  Dwell in each breast.
We know no dawn but Thine;
Send forth Thy beams divine,
On our dark souls now shine,
  And make us blest!

From the Latin of KING ROBERT of France, 1031. Abbr.

314 GOULD. C. M.   JOHN E. GOULD, 1846.

1 Our blest Redeemer, ere He breathed His tender, last farewell, A Guide, a Comforter bequeathed, With us on earth to dwell.

2 He came, sweet influence to impart,
  A gracious, willing Guest,
While He can find one humble heart
  Wherein to fix His rest.

3 And every virtue we possess,
  And every victory won,
And every thought of holiness,
  Is His and His alone.

4 Spirit of purity and grace!
  Our weakness pitying see;
Oh, make our hearts Thy dwelling-place,
  Purer and worthier Thee!

HARRIET AUBER, 1829.

315 C. M.

1 SPIRIT of peace! Celestial Dove!
  How excellent Thy praise!
No richer gift than Christian love
  Thy gracious power displays.

2 Sweet as the dew on herb and flower
  That silently distills,
At evening's soft and balmy hour,
  On Zion's fruitful hills,—

3 So, with mild influence from above
  Shall promised grace descend,
Till universal peace and love
  O'er all the earth extend!

HENRY F. LYTE, 1834.

316 CECILIA. 8s. 7s.
JOHN B. DYKES, 1868.

1 The King of love my Shepherd is, Whose goodness faileth never; I nothing lack, if I am His, And He is mine forever.

2 Where streams of living water flow,
My ransomed soul He leadeth,
And, where the verdant pastures grow,
With food celestial feedeth.

3 In death's dark vale I fear no ill
With Thee, dear Lord, beside me;
Thy rod and staff my comfort still,
Thy cross before to guide me.

4 And so, through all the coming days,
Thy love shall fail me never,
And be the theme of all my praise
Within Thy house forever.

Sir HENRY W. BAKER, 1868. Abbr.

317 CANONBURY. L. M.
ROBERT SCHUMANN, 1839.

1 Jesus, Thou Joy of loving hearts! Thou Fount of Life! Thou Light of men! From the best bliss that earth imparts, We turn unfilled to Thee again.

2 Thy truth unchanged hath ever stood;
Thou savest those that on Thee call;
To them that seek Thee, Thou art good, —
To them that find Thee, All in all!

3 Our restless spirits yearn for Thee,
Where'er our changeful lot is cast;
Glad, when Thy gracious smile we see, —
Blest, when our faith can hold Thee fast.

4 O Jesus, ever with us stay!
Make all our moments calm and bright!
Chase the dark night of sin away,
Shed o'er the world Thy holy Light!

BERNARD OF CLAIRVAUX.
Tr. RAY PALMER, 1858. Abbr.

318 L. M.

1 JESUS! — the very thought is sweet;
In that dear name all heart-joys meet;
But sweeter than sweet honey far
The glimpses of His presence are.

2 No word is sung more sweet than this:
No name is heard more full of bliss;
No thought brings sweeter comfort nigh,
Than Jesus, Son of God most high.

3 Jesus, Thou sweetness, pure, and blest,
Truth's fountain, Light of souls distress'd,
Surpassing all that heart requires,
Exceeding all that soul desires!

4 No tongue of mortal can express,
No letters write, its blessedness:
Alone who hath Thee in his heart
Knows, love of Jesus, what Thou art.

5 We follow Jesus now, and raise
The voice of prayer, the hymn of praise,
That He at last may make us meet
With Him to gain the heavenly seat.

Tr. by J. M. NEALE, 1842.

TRUST IN CHRIST.

319 6s. 4s.

1 Now I have found a Friend;
  Jesus is mine; —
His love shall never end;
  Jesus is mine;
Though earthly joys decrease,
Though earthly friendships cease,
Now I have lasting peace:
  Jesus is mine.

2 When earth shall pass away, —
  Jesus is mine, —
In the great judgment day, —
  Jesus is mine, —
Oh! what a glorious thing,
Then to behold my King,
On tuneful harp to sing,
  Jesus is mine.

3 Father! Thy name I bless;
  Jesus is mine;
Thine was the sovereign grace;
  Praise shall be Thine;
Spirit of holiness!
Sealing the Father's grace,
Thou mad'st my soul embrace
  Jesus, as mine.

HENRY J. McK. HOPE, 1852. Abbr.

320 OLIVET. 6s. 4s. LOWELL MASON, 1831.

1 My faith looks up to Thee, Thou Lamb of Cal-va-ry, Sav-iour di-vine! Now hear me while I pray, Take all my guilt a-way, Oh, let me from this day Be whol-ly Thine!

2 May Thy rich grace impart
Strength to my fainting heart;
  My zeal inspire;
As Thou hast died for me,
Oh, may my love to Thee
Pure, warm, and changeless be,
  A living fire!

3 While life's dark maze I tread,
And griefs around me spread,
  Be Thou my guide;
Bid darkness turn to day,
Wipe sorrow's tears away,
Nor let me ever stray
  From Thee aside.

4 When ends life's transient dream,
When death's cold, sullen stream
  Shall o'er me roll,
Blest Saviour! then, in love,
Fear and distrust remove;
Oh, bear me safe above,
  A ransomed soul!

RAY PALMER, 1830.

321 6s. 4s.

1 JESUS, Thy name I love,
All other names above,
  Jesus, my Lord!
Oh, Thou art all to me!
Nothing to please I see,
Nothing apart from Thee,
  Jesus, my Lord!

2 Thou, blessèd son of God,
Hast bought me with Thy blood,
  Jesus, my Lord!
Oh, how great is Thy love,
All other loves above,
Love that I daily prove,
  Jesus, my Lord!

3 When unto Thee I flee,
Thou wilt my refuge be,
  Jesus, my Lord!
What need I now to fear?
What earthly grief or care,
Since Thou art ever near,
  Jesus, my Lord!

JAMES G. DECK, 1851. Abbr.

322 C. P. M.

1 My God! Thy boundless love I praise;
How bright on high its glories blaze!
How sweetly bloom below!
It streams from Thine eternal throne,
Through heaven its joys forever run.
And o'er the earth they flow.

2 'T is in Thy Word I see love shine
With grace and glory all divine,
Proclaiming sins forgiven;
There, faith, bright cherub, points the way
To realms of everlasting day,
And opens all her heaven.

3 Then let the love that makes me blest
With cheerful praise inspire my breast,
And ardent gratitude;
And all my thoughts and passions tend
To Thee, my Father and my Friend,
My soul's eternal good!

HENRY MOORE, 1810. Abbr.

323 ARIEL. C. P. M.   Arr. fr. MOZART, by LOWELL MASON, 1836.

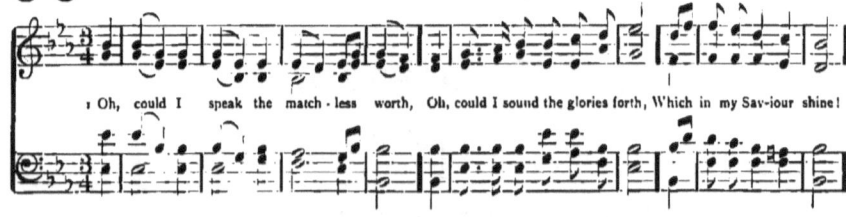

1 Oh, could I speak the match-less worth, Oh, could I sound the glories forth, Which in my Sav-iour shine!

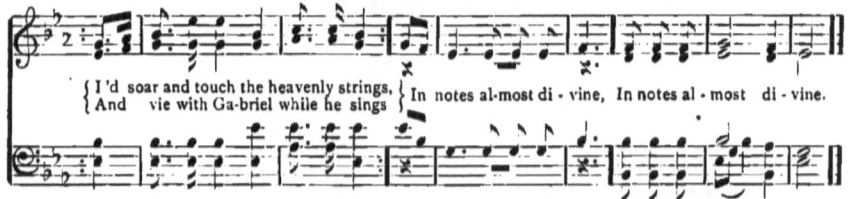

I 'd soar and touch the heavenly strings,
And vie with Ga-briel while he sings
In notes al-most di-vine, In notes al-most di-vine.

2 I 'd sing the precious blood He spilt,
My ransom from the dreadful guilt
Of sin and wrath divine!
I 'd sing His glorious rightcousness,
In which all-perfect heavenly dress
My soul shall ever shine.

3 I 'd sing the characters He bears,
And all the forms of love He wears,
Exalted on His throne:
In loftiest songs of sweetest praise,
I would to everlasting days
Make all His glories known.

4 Well — the delightful day will come,
When my dear Lord will bring me home,
And I shall see His face:
Then with my Saviour, Brother, Friend,
A blest eternity I 'll spend,
Triumphant in His grace.

SAMUEL MEDLEY, 1789.

TRUST IN CHRIST.

324 FLEMMING. 8s. 6s.   FRIEDRICH F. FLEMMING, 1810.

1 O Holy Saviour! Friend unseen,
Since on Thine arm thou bid'st me lean,
Help me, throughout life's changing scene,
By faith to cling to Thee!

2 Without a murmur I dismiss
My former dreams of earthly bliss;
My joy, my recompense be this,
Each hour to cling to Thee!

3 What though the world deceitful prove,
And earthly friends and hopes remove;
With patient, uncomplaining love,
Still would I cling to Thee.

4 Though oft I seem to tread alone
Life's dreary waste, with thorns o'ergrown,
Thy voice of love, in gentlest tone,
Still whispers, "Cling to me!"

5 Though faith and hope are often tried,
I ask not, need not, aught beside;
So safe, so calm, so satisfied,
The soul that clings to Thee!

CHARLOTTE ELLIOTT, 1834.

325 8s. 6s.

1 DRAWN to the cross, which Thou hast blest
With healing gifts for souls distressed,
To find in Thee my life, my rest,
Christ crucified, I come.

2 Thou knowest all my griefs and fears,
Thy grace abused, my misspent years,
Yet now to Thee, with contrite tears,
Christ crucified, I come.

3 Wash me and take away each stain,
Let nothing of my sin remain;
For cleansing, though it be through pain,
Christ crucified, I come.

4 And then for work to do for Thee
Which shall so sweet a service be
That angels might well envy me,
Christ crucified, I come.

Miss G. M. IRONS, 1880.

326 CONSOLATION. 5s. 9s.   Arr.

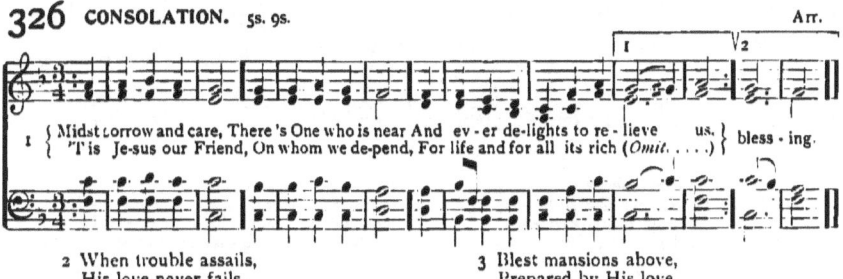

1 { Midst sorrow and care, There's One who is near And ever delights to relieve us,
   'Tis Jesus our Friend, On whom we depend, For life and for all its rich (*Omit....*) } blessing.

2 When trouble assails,
His love never fails,
He meets us with sweet consolation.
His bounties are free,
He hears every plea,
And welcomes the cry of the needy.

3 Blest mansions above,
Prepared by His love,
Are waiting, at last to receive us.
Oh, Saviour and Friend,
On whom we depend,
Our hearts shall forever adore Thee!

ANON.

THE PRAISE HYMNARY.

327 L. M.

1 God calling yet! shall I not hear?
Earth's pleasures shall I still hold dear?
Shall life's swift passing years all fly,
And still my soul in slumber lie?

2 God calling yet! shall I not rise?
Can I His loving voice despise,
And basely His kind care repay?
He calls me still; can I delay?

3 God calling yet! and shall I give
No heed, but still in bondage live?
I wait, but He does not forsake;
He calls me still; my heart, awake!

4 God calling yet! I cannot stay;
My heart I yield without delay;
Vain world, farewell! from thee I part;
The voice of God hath reached my heart.

GERHARD TERSTEEGEN, 1735.
Tr. SARAH B. FINDLATER, 1855.

328 BERA. L. M.   JOHN E. GOULD, 1849.

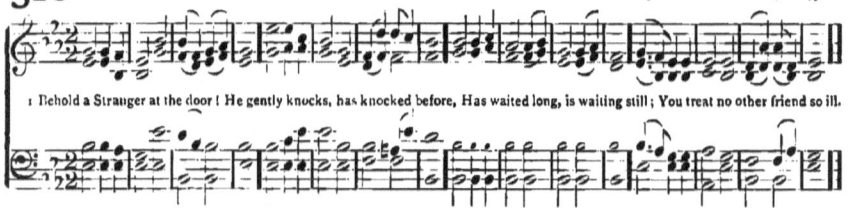

1 Behold a Stranger at the door! He gently knocks, has knocked before, Has waited long, is waiting still; You treat no other friend so ill.

2 Oh, lovely attitude! He stands
With melting heart and laden hands;
Oh, matchless kindness! and He shows
This matchless kindness to His foes.

3 But will He prove a friend indeed?
He will, the very friend you need —
The Friend of sinners; yes, 'tis He,
With garments dyed on Calvary.

4 Rise, touched with gratitude divine,
Turn out His enemy and thine,
That soul-destroying monster sin,
And let the heavenly Stranger in.

JOSEPH GRIGG, 1765.

329 ASHWELL. L. M.   LOWELL MASON, 1842.

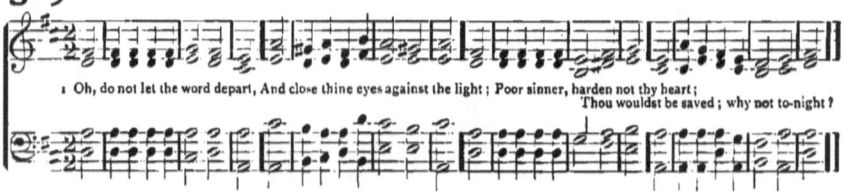

1 Oh, do not let the word depart, And close thine eyes against the light; Poor sinner, harden not thy heart;
Thou wouldst be saved; why not to-night?

2 To-morrow's sun may never rise
To bless thy long-deluded sight;
This is the time; oh, then be wise!
Thou wouldst be saved; why not to-night?

3 Our God in pity lingers still;
And wilt thou thus His love requite?
Renounce at length thy stubborn will;
Thou wouldst be saved; why not to-night?

4 Our blessèd Lord refuses none
Who would to Him their souls unite;
Then be the work of grace begun:
Thou wouldst be saved; why not to-night?

Mrs. ELIZABETH REED, 1825.

INVITATION.

330 OFFERED MERCY. P. M.
Wm. A. May.

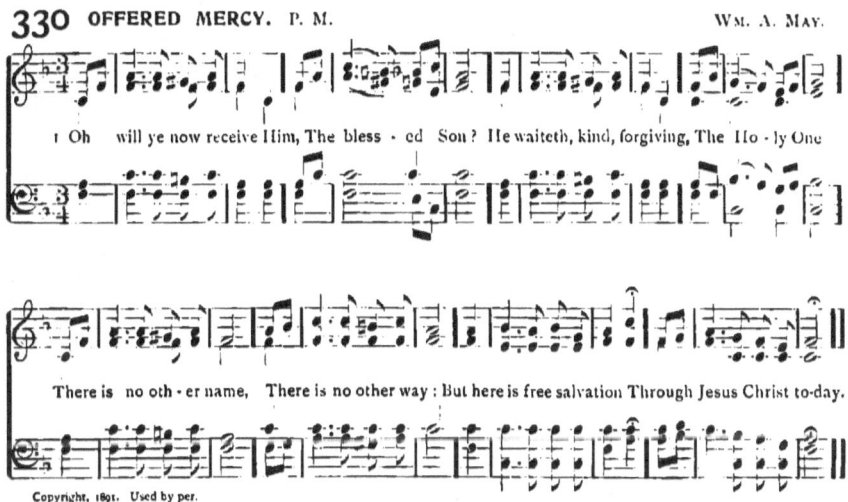

Copyright, 1891. Used by per.

2 The crimson tide is flowing
   Down from Calvary ;
   A precious fountain opened,
   Sinner, for thee !
   There is no other name,
   There is no other way :
   Accept the proffered mercy
   While it is called to-day.

3 Unto " His own " He cometh,
   Sinner, receive
   The gift of grace and pardon :
   Only believe !
   There is no other name,
   There is no other way :
   With loving voice entreating,
   The Saviour calls to-day.

   Mrs. Ellen Woolfolk, 1889.

331 COME UNTO ME.
Anon.

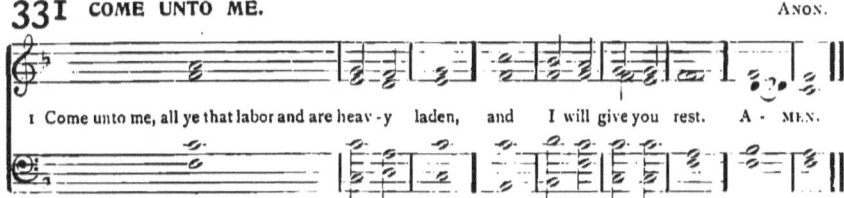

2 Take my yoke upon you, and learn of me ; for I am meek and | lowly · · in | heart : ‖ and ye shall find | rest · · un | to your | souls.
3 For my yoke is easy, and my | burden · · is | light, ‖ for my yoke is easy, | and my | burden · · is | light.
4 And the Spirit and the Bride say, Come. And let him that | heareth · · say, | Come. ‖ And let him that is athirst come ; and whosoever will, let him take the | waters · · of | life free | ly. | A- | men.

THE PRAISE HYMNARY.

332 COME UNTO ME. 7s. 6s. D. JOHN B. DYKES, 1874.

1 "Come un-to Me, ye wea-ry, And I will give you rest." O bless-ed voice of Je - sus, Which comes to hearts op - prest! It tells of ben - e - dic - tion, Of par-don, grace, and peace, Of joy that hath no end - ing, Of love which can - not cease.

2 "Come unto Me, ye wanderers,
　And I will give you light."
O loving voice of Jesus,
　Which comes to cheer the night!
Our hearts were filled with sadness,
　And we had lost our way,
But Thou hast brought us gladness,
　And songs at break of day.

3 "Come unto Me, ye fainting,
　And I will give you life."
O cheering voice of Jesus,
　Which comes to aid our strife!
The foe is stern and eager,
　The fight is fierce and long;
But Thou hast made us mighty,
　And stronger than the strong.

4 "And whosoever cometh,
　I will not cast him out."
O welcome voice of Jesus,
　Which drives away our doubt,
Which calls us, very sinners,
　Unworthy though we be
Of love so free and boundless,
　To come, dear Lord, to Thee!
　　　　　WILLIAM C. DIX, 1864.

333 7s. 6s. D.

1 O JESUS, our salvation,
　Low at Thy cross we lie;
Lord, in Thy great compassion,
　Hear our bewailing cry.
We come to Thee with mourning,
　We come to Thee in woe;
With contrite hearts returning,
　And tears that overflow.

2 O gracious Intercessor,
　O Priest within the vail,
Plead, for each lost transgressor,
　The blood that cannot fail.
We spread our sins before Thee,
　We tell them one by one;
Oh, for Thy name's great glory,
　Forgive all we have done.

3 Oh, by Thy cross and passion,
　Thy tears and agony,
And crown of cruel fashion,
　And death on Calvary;
By all that untold suffering,
　Endured by Thee alone;
O Priest, O spotless offering,
　Plead for us, and atone!
　　　　　JAMES HAMILTON, 1865. Abbr.

INVITATION.

334 STEPHANOS. P. M.   Henry W. Baker, 1861.

1 Art thou weary, art thou languid, Art thou sore distressed? "Come to Me," saith One, "and coming, Be at rest."

2 Hath He marks to lead me to Him,
   If He be my guide?
"In His feet and hands are wound-prints,
   And His side."

3 Is there diadem, as monarch,
   That His brow adorns?
"Yes, a crown in very surety,
   But of thorns!"

4 If I find Him, if I follow,
   What His future here?

5 "Many a sorrow, many a labor,
   Many a tear."

5 If I still hold closely to Him,
   What hath He at last?
"Sorrow vanquished, labor ended,
   Jordan past."

6 If I ask Him to receive me,
   Will He say me nay?
"Not till earth and not till heaven
   Pass away."

              Stephen the Sabaite, 8th Cent.
              Tr. John M. Neale, 1851.

335 TO-DAY. 6s. 4s.   Lowell Mason, 1831.

1 To-day the Saviour calls, Ye wanderers, come; O, ye benighted souls, Why longer roam?

2 To-day the Saviour calls,
   Oh, hear Him now;
Within these sacred walls
   To Jesus bow.

3 The Spirit calls to-day:
   Yield to His power:
Oh, grieve Him not away;
   'Tis mercy's hour.

              Samuel F. Smith, 1831. Abbr.

336 INVITATION. P. M.   J. Courtnay.

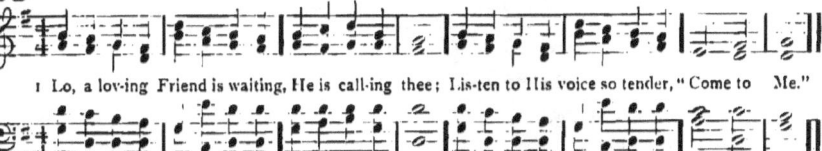

1 Lo, a loving Friend is waiting, He is calling thee; Listen to His voice so tender, "Come to Me."

2 "On the cross for thee I suffered,
   Death I bore for thee;
Canst thou still refuse My mercy?
   Trust in Me."

3 "Long hast thou been Satan's captive,
   I will set thee free:
Then, rejoicing in thy freedom,
   Follow Me."

4 Many times hath Jesus spoken,
   Now He speaks again;
Shall thy Saviour's invitation
   Be in vain?

5 Soon that voice will cease its calling,
   Wilt thou still delay?
Wait no longer, sin grows stronger,
   Yield to-day.

              John M. Wigner, 1882.

THE PRAISE HYMNARY.

337 PASS ME NOT.
W. H. DOANE.

1 Pass me not, O gentle Saviour, Hear my humble cry;
While on others Thou art smiling, Do not pass me by.

CHORUS.
Saviour, Saviour, Hear my humble cry,
While on others Thou art calling, Do not pass me by.

Used by permission of W. H. Doane, owner of copyright.

2 Let me at a throne of mercy
   Find a sweet relief;
   Kneeling there in deep contrition,
   Help my unbelief.

3 Trusting only in Thy merit,
   Would I seek Thy face;
   Heal my wounded, broken spirit,
   Save me by Thy grace.

4 Thou the Spring of all my comfort,
   More than life to me;
   Whom have I on earth beside Thee,
   Whom in heaven but Thee.

FANNY J. CROSBY, 1868.

REPENTANCE.

338 FREEMAN. 8s. 6s.   EDWARD A. FREEMAN, 1895.

1 Just as I am, without one plea, But that Thy blood was shed for me, And that Thou bidd'st me come to Thee, O Lamb of God, I come!

Used by per.

2 Just as I am, and waiting not
To rid my soul of one dark blot,
To Thee, whose blood can cleanse each spot,
    O Lamb of God, I come!

3 Just as I am,—poor, wretched, blind;
Sight, riches, healing of the mind,
Yea, all I need, in Thee to find,
    O Lamb of God, I come!

4 Just as I am,—Thou wilt receive,
Wilt welcome, pardon, cleanse, relieve;
Because Thy promise I believe,
    O Lamb of God, I come!

5 Just as I am,—Thy love unknown
Hath broken every barrier down;
Now to be Thine, yea, Thine alone,
    O Lamb of God, I come!
        CHARLOTTE ELLIOTT, 1836. Abbr.

339 8s. 6s.

1 JUST as Thou art; to me, a child
Self banished and unreconciled,
To win through patient mercy mild,
    Come, Father, unto me.

2 Just as Thou art; without delay,
Although to rescue me Thy way
Grows dark with Calvary's bloody day,
    Come, Jesus, unto me.

3 Just as Thou art; my guilty soul,
Beyond my struggling will's control,
To cleanse from sin and make me whole,
    Come, Spirit, unto me.

4 Just as Thou art; blest Three in One,
Accepting, as it were my own,
The praise of what is Thine alone;
    Come, Father, Spirit, Son.
      ADDISON BALLARD, sl. alt. Circ. 1895.

340 HAYNES. 7s. 3l.   HORACE L. BAKER, 1898.

1 Heal me, O my Saviour, heal; Heal me as I suppliant kneel; Heal me, and my pardon seal.

Used by per.

2 Fresh the wounds that sin hath made;
Hear the prayers I oft have prayed,
And in mercy send me aid.

3 Thou the true Physician art;
Thou, O Christ, canst health impart,
Binding up the bleeding heart.

4 Other comforters are gone;
Thou canst heal, and Thou alone,
Thou for all my sin atone.
    GODFREY THRING, 1866. Abbr.

341 7s. 3l.

1 LORD, in this Thy mercy's day,
Ere from us it pass away,
On our knees we fall and pray.

2 Holy Jesus, grant us tears,
Fill us with heart-searching fears,
Ere that awful doom appears.

3 Lord, on us Thy Spirit pour,
Kneeling lowly at Thy door,
Ere it close for evermore.
    ISAAC WILLIAMS, 1844.

342 BENEDICTUS. S. M.
J. Baptiste Calkin.

1 Breathe on me, Breath of God, Fill me with life a-new, That I may love what Thou dost love, And do what Thou wouldst do.

2 Breathe on me, Breath of God,
　Until my heart is pure,
　Until with Thee I will one will,
　To do or to endure.

3 Breathe on me, Breath of God,
　Till I am wholly Thine,
　Till all this earthly part of me
　Glows with Thy fire divine.

4 Breathe on me, Breath of God,
　So shall I never die,
　But live with Thee the perfect life
　Of Thine eternity.

Edwin Hatch.

343 AULÉ. 7s, 6s.
Arr. from Old Melody.

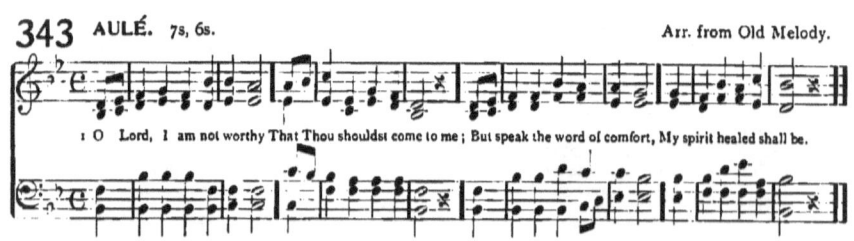

1 O Lord, I am not worthy That Thou shouldst come to me; But speak the word of comfort, My spirit healed shall be.

2 O Lord, I am not worthy
　That Thou shouldst dwell with me;
　But, Saviour, I now open
　My contrite heart to Thee.

3 And humbly I'll receive Thee,
　The Bridegroom of my soul,
　No more by sin to grieve Thee,
　Or fly Thy sweet control.

Anon.

344 WEARINESS. 7s.
Anon.

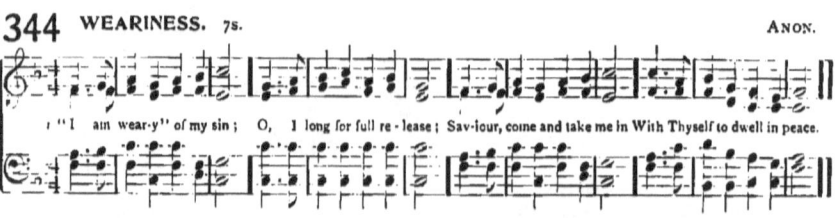

1 "I am wear-y" of my sin; O, I long for full re-lease; Sav-iour, come and take me in With Thyself to dwell in peace.

2 "I am weary" of my pains;
　Bring me, Lord, with Thee to rest;
　Change my groans to joyful strains
　'Mid the concert of the blest.

3 "I am weary" of the earth,
　Where the wicked spurn Thy love;
　With Thy sons of heavenly birth
　Let me worship Thee above.

Anon.

REPENTANCE.

345 OLD, OLD STORY. 7s. 6s. D.   W. H. DOANE.

1 Tell me the old, old story Of unseen things above, Of Jesus and His glory, Of Jesus and His love. Tell me the story simply, As to a little child, For I am weak and weary, And helpless and defiled. *Refrain.* Tell me the old, old story, Tell me the old, old story, Of Jesus and His love.

Used by per.

2 Tell me the story slowly,
   That I may take it in —
That wonderful redemption,
   God's remedy for sin !
Tell me the story often,
   For I forget so soon !
The "early dew" of morning
   Has passed away at noon !

3 Tell me the story softly,
   With earnest tones and grave ;
Remember ! I 'm the sinner
   Whom Jesus came to save.

Tell me that story always,
   If you would really be,
In any time of trouble,
   A comforter to me.

4 Tell me the same old story,
   When you have cause to fear
That this world's empty glory
   Is costing me too dear.
O yes, and when its glory
   Is drawing on my soul,
Tell me the old, old story :
   "Christ Jesus makes thee whole."

                    CATHERINE HANKEY, 1865.

346 IRENE. P. M.
Arr. fr. SCHOLEFIELD.

1 Jesus, heed me, lost and dying, Unto Thee for shelter flying, Hear, oh, hear my heart's sore crying: Heed me, or I die!

2 All my sin and sorrow feeling,
Come I, as the leper, kneeling;
Come to Thee for help and healing,
Heal me, or I die!

3 Not my tears of deep contrition
Can secure one sin's remission,
Helpless, hopeless my condition:
Help me, or I die!

4 Far away my dead works flinging,
Nothing owning, nothing bringing,
Only to Thy mercy clinging:
Bless me, or I die!

5 By the cross, where hope is beaming,
By its crimson fountain streaming,
Flowing for the world's redeeming:
Cleanse me, or I die!

ROBERT M. OFFORD, 1883.

347 ST. CRISPIN. L. M.
GEORGE J. ELVEY, 1859.

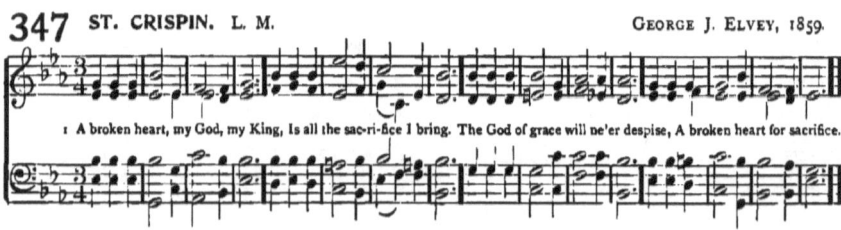

1 A broken heart, my God, my King, Is all the sacrifice I bring. The God of grace will ne'er despise, A broken heart for sacrifice.

2 Now will I teach the world Thy ways;
Sinners shall learn Thy sovereign grace;
I'll lead them to my Saviour's blood,
And they shall praise a pardoning God.

3 O may Thy love inspire my tongue!
Salvation shall be all my song;
And all my powers shall join to bless
The Lord, my strength and righteousness.

ISAAC WATTS, 1719. Abbr.

348 MONSELL. S. M.
JOSEPH BARNBY, 1866.

1 Sweet is Thy mercy, Lord! Before Thy mercy-seat My soul, adoring, pleads Thy word, And owns Thy mercy sweet.

2 Light Thou my weary way,
Lead Thou my wandering feet,
That while I stay on earth I may
Still find Thy mercy sweet.

3 Thus shall the heavenly host
Hear all my songs repeat,
To Father, Son, and Holy Ghost,
My joy, Thy mercy sweet.

JOHN S. B. MONSELL, 1862. Abbr.

REPENTANCE.

349 AURELIA. 7s. 6s. D. SAMUEL S. WESLEY. Circ. 1868.

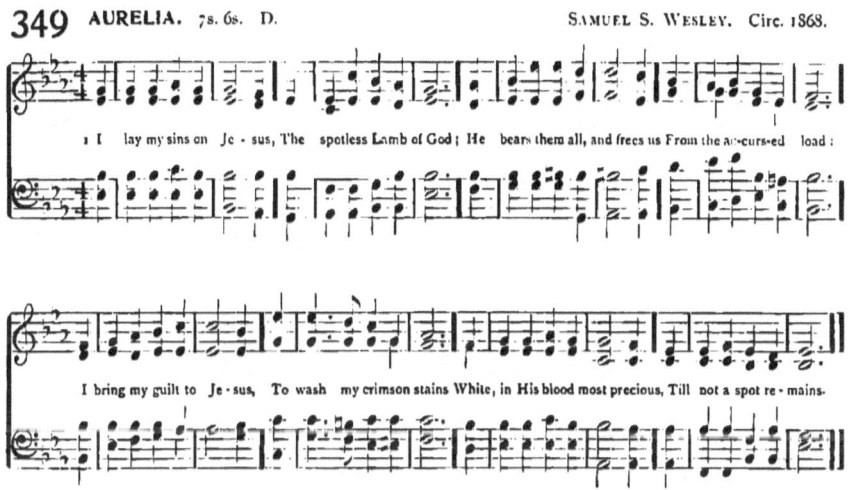

1 I lay my sins on Jesus, The spotless Lamb of God; He bears them all, and frees us From the accursed load:
I bring my guilt to Jesus, To wash my crimson stains White, in His blood most precious, Till not a spot remains.

2 I lay my wants on Jesus,
All fullness dwells in Him;
He heals all my diseases,
He doth my soul redeem:
I lay my griefs on Jesus,
My burdens and my cares;
He from them all releases,
He all my sorrows shares.

3 I rest my soul on Jesus,
This weary soul of mine;
His right hand me embraces,
I on His breast recline:
I love the name of Jesus,
Immanuel, Christ the Lord;
Like fragrance on the breezes,
His name abroad is poured.

4 I long to be like Jesus, —
Meek, loving, lowly, mild;
I long to be like Jesus,
The Father's holy child;
I long to be with Jesus,
Amid the heavenly throng,
To sing, with saints, His praises,
To learn the angels' song.

HORATIUS BONAR, 1845.

350 7s. 6s.

1 I NEED Thee, precious Jesus,
For I am full of sin;
My soul is dark and guilty,
My heart is dead within;
I need the cleansing fountain
Where I can always flee,
The blood of Christ most precious,
The sinner's perfect plea.

2 I need Thee, precious Jesus,
For I am very poor;
A stranger and a pilgrim,
I have no earthly store;
I need the love of Jesus
To cheer me on my way,
To guide my doubting footsteps,
To be my strength and stay.

3 I need Thee, precious Jesus,
And hope to see Thee soon,
Encircled with the rainbow,
And seated on Thy throne:
There, with Thy blood-bought children,
My joy shall ever be,
To sing Thy praises, Jesus,
To gaze, my Lord, on Thee.

FREDERICK WHITFIELD, 1855.

THE PRAISE HYMNARY.

351 MORE LIKE JESUS. 7s. D. W. H. DOANE.

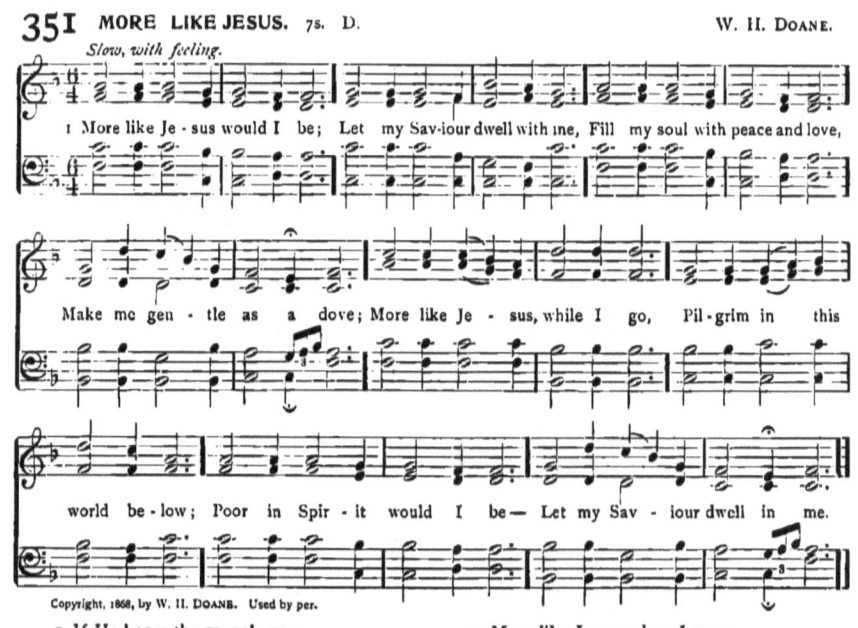

Copyright, 1868, by W. H. DOANE. Used by per.

2 If He hears the raven's cry;
If His ever watchful eye
Marks the sparrows when they fall,
Surely He will hear my call,
He will teach me how to live,
All my sinful thoughts forgive;
Pure in heart I still would be—
Let my Saviour dwell in me.

3 More like Jesus, when I pray,
More like Jesus day by day,
May I rest me by His side,
Where the tranquil waters glide;
Born of Him, through grace renewed,
By His love my will subdued,
Rich in faith I still would be,—
Let my Saviour dwell in me.

FANNIE J. CROSBY.

352 VAUGHAN. C. M. JOHN B. DYKES, 1867.

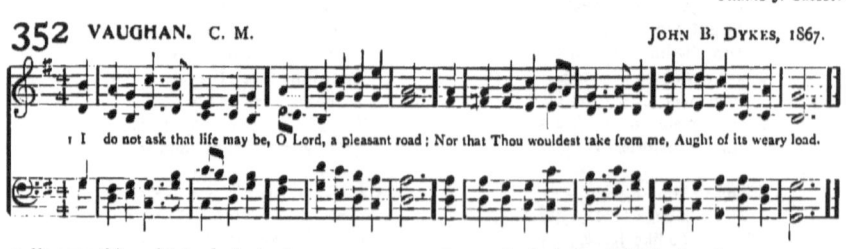

2 For one thing chiefly do I plead,
  Dear Lord, lead me aright :
Though strength should fail, and heart should
    bleed,
  Lead me through peace to light.

3 I do not ask to understand
  My cross, my way to see;

Let me in darkness feel Thy hand,
  And simply follow Thee.

4 Joy is like day, but peace divine
  May rule the quiet night :
Lead me, till perfect day shall shine,
  O Lord, through peace to light.

ADELAIDE A. PROCTER, 1862.

CONSECRATION.

353 ATTITUDE. 7s. 6s. D.   JUSTIN H. KNECHT, 1799, and EDWARD HUSBAND, 1871.

1 O Jesus, Thou art standing
Outside the fast-closed door,
In lowly patience waiting
To pass the threshold o'er:
Shame on us, Christian brethren,
His name and sign who bear;
O shame, thrice shame upon us,
To keep Him standing there!

2 O Jesus, Thou art knocking;
And lo, that hand is scarred,
And thorns Thy brow encircle,
And tears Thy face have marred.
O love that passeth knowledge,
So patiently to wait!
O sin that hath no equal,
So fast to bar the gate!

3 O Jesus, Thou art pleading
In accents meek and low:
"I died for you, My children,
And will ye treat me so?"
O Lord, with shame and sorrow,
We open now the door:
Dear Saviour, enter, enter,
And leave us nevermore.

WILLIAM W. HOW, 1867.

354 LEAVE IT WITH GOD.

R. DeWitt Mallary.

Copyright, 1894, by Rankin and Mallary. Used by per.

2 Leave it with God, who feedeth the sparrow,
Chooseth for thee, the path that is narrow;
Heareth the prayer, unuttered, unspoken;
Healeth with balm the heart that is broken;
Leave it with God, leave it with God,
Leave it with God, to Him tell thy sorrow.

3 Leave it with God, for He is still near thee,
Tell Him thy grief, He's waiting to hear thee,
Taker of gifts, as well as the giver;
Leave it with God, sure He will deliver,
Leave it with God, leave it with God,
Leave it with God, to Him tell thy sorrow.

4 Leave it with God: thy losses, thou 'lt gain them;
Things that perplex thee, He will explain them,
He is a Father, watchful and tender;
He is a Father; make full surrender.
Leave it with God, leave it with God,
Leave it with God, to Him tell thy sorrow.

J. E. Rankin.

CONSECRATION.

355 ABERHONDDU. 7s. 6s. D.   OLD WELSH HYMNAL.

1 O Jesus, I have promised To serve Thee to the end;
  Be Thou for ev-er near me, My Master and my Friend;
  I shall not fear the battle If Thou art by my side, Nor wander from the path-way If Thou wilt be my guide.

2 Oh, let me feel Thee near me;
  The world is ever near;
  I see the sights that dazzle,
  The tempting sounds I hear;
  My foes are ever near me,
  Around me and within;
  But, Jesus, draw Thou nearer,
  And shield my soul from sin.

3 O Jesus, Thou hast promised
  To all who follow Thee,
  That where Thou art in glory
  There shall Thy servant be;
  And, Jesus, I have promised
  To serve Thee to the end;
  Oh, give me grace to follow,
  My Master and my Friend.
  JOHN E. BODE, 1869. Abbr.

356  7s. 6s. D.

1 WHEN human hopes all wither,
  And friends no aid supply,
  Then whither, Lord, ah! whither
  Can turn my straining eye?
  'Mid storms of grief still rougher,
  'Midst darker, deadlier shade,
  That cross where Thou didst suffer,
  On Calvary was displayed.

2 On that my gaze I fasten,
  My refuge that I make;
  Though sorely Thou mayst chasten,
  Thou never canst forsake;
  Thou, on that cross didst languish,
  Ere glory crowned Thy head!
  And I, through death and anguish,
  Must be to glory led.
  CHARLOTTE ELLIOTT.

357 I'LL LIVE FOR HIM.   C. R. DUNBAR, 1882.
D. C.

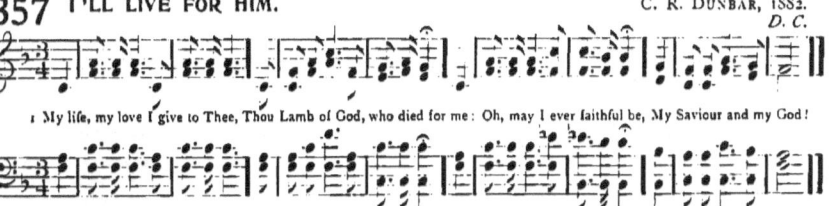

1 My life, my love I give to Thee, Thou Lamb of God, who died for me: Oh, may I ever faithful be, My Saviour and my God!

CHO.—I'll live for Him who died for me, How happy then my life shall be! I'll live for Him who died for me, My Saviour and my God!
Copyright, R. E. HUDSON. By per.

2 I now believe Thou dost receive,
  For Thou hast died that I might live;
  And now henceforth I'll trust in Thee,
  My Saviour and my God!

3 Oh, Thou who died on Calvary,
  To save my soul and make it free,
  I consecrate my life to Thee,
  My Saviour and my God!
  R. E. HUDSON, 1882.

THE PRAISE HYMNARY.

358 OAK. 6s. 4s.   LOWELL MASON, 1854.

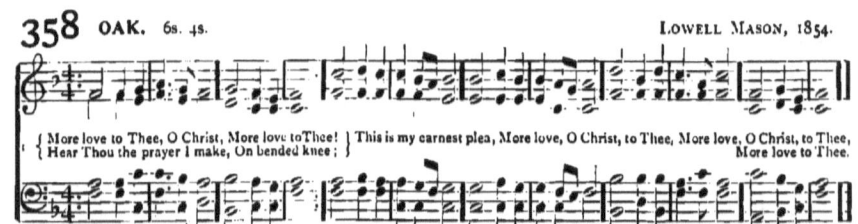

{ More love to Thee, O Christ, More love to Thee! } This is my earnest plea, More love, O Christ, to Thee, More love, O Christ, to Thee,
{ Hear Thou the prayer I make, On bended knee; }   More love to Thee.

2 Once earthly joy I craved,
   Sought peace and rest;
Now Thee alone I seek,
   Give what is best:
This all my prayer shall be,
More love, O Christ, to Thee,
   More love to Thee!

3 Let sorrow do its work,
   Send grief and pain;
Sweet are Thy messengers,
   Sweet their refrain,
When they can sing with me,
More love, O Christ, to Thee,
   More love to Thee!

4 Then shall my latest breath
   Whisper Thy praise;
This be the parting cry
   My heart shall raise,
This still its prayer shall be,
More love, O Christ, to Thee,
   More love to Thee!

                Mrs. ELIZABETH P. PRENTISS, 1850.

359 6s. 4s.

1 NEARER, my God, to Thee,
   Nearer to Thee;
E'en though it be a cross
   That raiseth me;
Still all my song shall be,
Nearer, my God, to Thee,
   Nearer to Thee.

2 Though like the wanderer,
   The sun gone down,
Darkness be over me,
   My rest a stone;
Yet in my dreams I'd be
Nearer, my God, to Thee,
   Nearer to Thee.

3 There let the way appear
   Steps unto Heaven;
All that Thou sendest me,
   In mercy given;
Angels to beckon me
Nearer, my God, to Thee,
   Nearer to Thee.

4 Then, with my waking thoughts
   Bright with Thy praise,
Out of my stony griefs
   Bethel I'll raise;
So by my woes to be
Nearer, my God, to Thee,
   Nearer to Thee.

           Mrs. SARAH F. ADAMS, 1840. Abbr.

360 8s. 7s. D. Sing to "Ellesdie," No. 177.

1 JESUS, I my cross have taken,
   All to leave, and follow Thee;
Naked, poor, despised, forsaken,
   Thou from hence my all shall be.
Perish every fond ambition,
   All I've sought and hoped and known;
Yet how rich is my condition,
   God and heaven are still my own.

2 Let the world despise and leave me,
   They have left my Saviour, too;
Human hearts and looks deceive me;
   Thou art not, like man, untrue;
And, while Thou shalt smile upon me,
   God of wisdom, love, and might,
Foes may hate, and friends may shun me;
   Show Thy face, and all is bright.

3 Man may trouble and distress me;
   'T will but drive me to Thy breast:
Life with trials hard may press me;
   Heaven will bring me sweeter rest.
O 't is not in grief to harm me,
   While Thy love is left to me;
O 't were not in joy to charm me,
   Were that joy unmixed with Thee.

4 Go, then, earthly fame and treasure!
   Come, disaster, scorn, and pain!
In Thy service pain is pleasure;
   With Thy favor, loss is gain.
I have called Thee, "Abba, Father;"
   I have stayed my heart on Thee:
Storms may howl, and clouds may gather,
   All must work for good to me.

                   HENRY F. LYTE, 1827.

CONSECRATION.

361 ALL FOR CHRIST. 7s.   From MOZART.

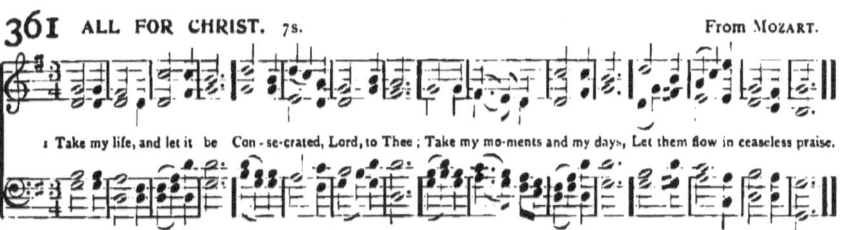

1 Take my life, and let it be Con-se-crated, Lord, to Thee; Take my mo-ments and my days, Let them flow in ceaseless praise.

2 Take my hands, and let them move
At the impulse of Thy love;
Take my feet, and let them be
Swift and beautiful for Thee.

3 Take my voice, and let me sing
Always, only, for my King;
Take my lips, and let them be
Filled with messages from Thee.

4 Take my silver and my gold,
Not a mite would I withhold;

Take my intellect, and use
Every power as Thou shalt choose.

5 Take my will, and make it Thine,
It shall be no longer mine;
Take my heart, it is Thine own,
It shall be Thy royal throne.

6 Take my love, my Lord, I pour
At Thy feet its treasure store;
Take myself, and I will be,
Ever, only, all for Thee.
              FRANCES R. HAVERGAL, 1858.

362 AZMON. C. M.   CARL G. GLÄSER. Arr. 1839.

1 "Thine, Thine forever"—blessed bond That knits us, Lord, to Thee; May voice, and heart, and soul respond Amen, so let it be.

2 When this world strikes its dulcet harp,
And earth our heaven appears,
Be "Thine forever," clear and sharp,
God's trumpet in our ears.

3 When sin in pleasure's soft disguise
Would work us deadliest harm,
May "Thine forever" from the skies
Steal down and break the charm.

4 When Satan flings his fiery darts
Against our weary shield,
May "Thine forever" in our hearts
Forbid us faint or yield.

5 Thine all along the flowery spring,
Along the summer prime,
Till autumn fades in welcoming
The silver frost of time.

6 "Thine, Thine forever,"—body, soul,
Henceforth devote to Thee,
While everlasting ages roll:
Amen, so let it be.
          EDWARD H. BICKERSTETH, 1877.

363 C. M.

1 O JESUS CHRIST, grow Thou in me,
And all things else recede;
My heart be daily nearer Thee,
From sin be daily freed.

2 Each day, let Thy supporting might
My weakness still embrace;
My darkness vanish in Thy light;
Thy life my death efface.

3 In Thy bright beams, which on me fall,
Fade every evil thought;
That I am nothing, Thou art all,
I would be daily taught.

4 Make this poor self grow less and less,
Be Thou my life and aim;
O, make me daily, through Thy grace,
More worthy of Thy Name.

5 Let faith in Thee and in Thy might
My every motive move;
Be Thou alone my soul's delight,
My passion and my love.
          JOHANN C. LAVATER, 1780.

THE PRAISE HYMNARY.

364 ANYWHERE WITH JESUS. D. B. TOWNER.

1 Anywhere with Jesus I can safely go, Anywhere He leads me in this world below. Anywhere without Him, dearest joys would fade, Anywhere with Jesus I am not afraid.

CHORUS.
Anywhere! anywhere! Fear I cannot know, Anywhere with Jesus I can safely go.

Copyright, 1887, by D. B. TOWNER. Used by per.

2 Anywhere with Jesus I am not alone,
  Other friends may fail me, He is still my own.
  Though His hand may lead me over drearest ways,
  Anywhere with Jesus is a house of praise.

3 Anywhere with Jesus I can go to sleep,
  When the darkling shadows round about me creep;
  Knowing I shall waken never more to roam,
  Anywhere with Jesus will be home, sweet home.
  JESSIE H. BROWN.

FAITH AND TRUST.

365 SAFE IN THE ARMS OF JESUS. W. H. Doane

Used by per.

   2 Safe in the arms of Jesus,
      Safe from corroding care,
     Safe from the world's temptations,
      Sin cannot harm me there.
     Free from the blight of sorrow,
      Free from my doubts and fears ;
     Only a few more trials,
      Only a few more tears.

   3 Jesus, my heart's dear refuge,
      Jesus has died for me ;
     Firm on the Rock of Ages
      Ever my trust shall be.
     Here let me wait with patience,
      Wait till the night is o'er :
     Wait till I see the morning
      Break on the golden shore.
                    FANNIE J. CROSBY.

THE PRAISE HYMNARY.

366 LEBANON. S. M. D.   JOHN ZUNDEL, 1855.

1 I was a wand'ring sheep, I did not love the fold; I did not love my Shepherd's voice,
D.S. I did not love my Fa-ther's voice,
I would not be con-trolled; I was a way-ward child, I did not love my home,
I loved a-far to roam.

2 The Shepherd sought His sheep,
   The Father sought His child,
They followed me o'er vale and hill,
   O'er deserts waste and wild:
They found me nigh to death,
   Famished, and faint, and lone;
They bound me with the bands of love;
   They saved the wandering one.

3 Jesus my Shepherd is,
   'T was He that loved my soul,
'T was He that washed me in His blood,
   'T was He that made me whole;

   'T was He that sought the lost,
That found the wandering sheep,
   'T was He that brought me to the fold,
'T is He that still doth keep.

4 No more a wandering sheep,
   I love to be controlled;
I love my tender Shepherd's voice,
   I love the peaceful fold:
No more a wayward child,
   I seek no more to roam;
I love my heavenly Father's voice,
   I love, I love His home!
               HORATIUS BONAR, 1845.

367 GEER. C. M.   HENRY W. GREATOREX, 1849.

1 There is a fold whence none can stray, And pastures ev-er green, Where sul-try sun or storm-y day, Or night is nev-er seen.

2 Far up the everlasting hills,
   In God's own light it lies;
His smile its vast dimension fills
   With joy that never dies.

3 One narrow vale, one darksome wave,
   Divides that land from this:
I have a Shepherd pledged to save
   And bear me home to bliss.

4 Soon at His feet my soul will lie
   In life's last struggling breath;
But I shall only seem to die,
   I shall not taste of death.
          JOHN EAST, 1836. Abbr.

368 C. M.

1 THE bird let loose in eastern skies,
   When hastening fondly home,
Ne'er stoops to earth her wing, nor flies
   Where idle warblers roam.

2 So grant me, Lord, from every care
   And stain of passion free,
Aloft, through virtue's purer air,
   To hold my course to Thee.

3 No sin to cloud, no lure to stay
   My soul, as home she springs;
Thy sunshine on her joyful way,
   Thy freedom in her wings.
          THOMAS MOORE, 1816. Abbr.

FAITH AND TRUST.

369 ZION. 8s. 7s. 4s. THOMAS HASTINGS, 1830.

1. Guide me, O Thou great Jehovah,
   Pilgrim through this barren land;
   I am weak, but Thou art mighty;
   Hold me with Thy powerful hand;
   ‖ Bread of heaven, Feed me till I want no more. ‖

2. Open Thou the crystal fountain
   Whence the healing streams do flow;
   Let the fiery, cloudy pillar
   Lead me all my journey through;
   ‖ Strong Deliverer,
   Be Thou still my Strength and Shield. ‖

3. When I tread the verge of Jordan,
   Bid my anxious fears subside;
   Death of death! and hell's destruction!
   Land me safe on Canaan's side;
   ‖ Songs of praises
   I will ever give to Thee. ‖

   WILLIAM WILLIAMS, 1773.

370 8s. 7s. 4s.

1. I would love Thee, God and Father,
   My Redeemer and my King!
   I would love Thee: for without Thee
   Life is but a bitter thing.
   ‖ I would love Thee;
   Ever guide me with Thine eye. ‖

2. I would love Thee — I have vowed it;
   On Thy love my heart is set;
   While I love Thee, I will never
   My Redeemer's love forget!
   ‖ I would love Thee;
   Ever guide me with Thine eye. ‖

   Fr. Mme. JEANNE B. DE LA M. GUYON, 1710.

371 NAOMI. C. M. LOWELL MASON, 1836.

1. Father, whate'er of earthly bliss, Thy sovereign hand denies, Accepted at Thy throne of grace, Let this petition rise:

2. Give me a calm, a thankful heart,
   From every murmur free;
   The blessings of Thy grace impart,
   And let me live to Thee.

3. Let the sweet hope that Thou art mine,
   My path of life attend;
   Thy presence through my journey shine,
   And bless its happy end.

   ANNE STEELE, 1760.

THE PRAISE HYMNARY.

372 WHERE HE LEADS I'D FOLLOW. W. A. Ogden.

1 Sweet are the promis-es, kind is the word, Dear-er far than an-y message man ev-er heard; Pure was the mind of Christ, sin-less I see; He the great ex-am-ple is, and pat-tern for me.

CHORUS.
Where ...... He leads I'd fol ... low, Where He leads I'd fol-low,
Where He leads I'd fol-low, Where He leads I'd fol-low,
Fol ... low all the way, Fol-low Je-sus ev-ery day.
Fol-low all the way, yes, fol-low all the way.

Copyright, 1885, by W. A. OGDEN. Used by per.

2 Sweet is the tender love Jesus hath shown,
   Sweeter far than any love that mortals have known;
   Kind to the erring one, faithful is He;
   He the great example is, and pattern for me.

3 List to His loving words, "Come unto me,
   Weary, heavy laden, there is sweet rest for thee;"
   Trust in His promises, faithful and sure;
   Lean upon the Saviour, and thy soul is secure.
                               W. A. Ogden.

FAITH AND TRUST.

373 RUTHERFORD. P. M. Chrétien D'Urhan, 1834. Har. by E. F. Rimbault, 1845.

The sands of time are sink-ing, The dawn of heav-en breaks,
The sum-mer morn I've sighed for, The fair, sweet morn a-wakes.
O, dark hath been the mid-night, But day-spring is at hand,
And glo-ry, glo-ry dwell-eth In Em-man-uel's land.

2 O Christ, He is the fountain,
  The deep, sweet well of love!
The streams of earth I've tasted;
  More deep I'll drink above.
There to an ocean fullness
  His mercy doth expand,
And glory, glory dwelleth
  In Emmanuel's land.

3 With mercy and with judgment
  My web of time He wove,
And aye the dews of sorrow
  Were lustred with His love:

I'll bless the hand that guided,
  I'll bless the heart that planned,
When throned where glory dwelleth
  In Emmanuel's land.

4 Oh! I am my Belovèd's
  And my Belovèd's mine,
He brings a poor, vile sinner,
  Into His house divine.
Upon the Rock of Ages
  My soul redeemed shall stand,
Where glory, glory dwelleth
  In Emmanuel's land.

Annie R. Cousin, 1857

THE PRAISE HYMNARY.

374 LEOMINSTER. S. M. D.   English. Har. by Sir ARTHUR S. SULLIVAN.
Slowly.

1 One sweetly solemn thought
Comes to me o'er and o'er,—
Nearer my home, today, am I
Than e'er I've been before.
Nearer my Father's house,
Where many mansions be;
Nearer today the great, white throne,
Nearer the crystal sea.

2 Nearer the bound of life,
  Where burdens are laid down;
Nearer to leave the heavy cross;
  Nearer to gain the crown.
But, lying dark between,
  Winding down through the night,
There rolls the silent, unknown stream
  That leads at last to light.

3 Even now, perchance, my feet
  Are slipping on the brink,
And I, to-day, am nearer home,—
  Nearer than now I think.
Father, perfect my trust;
  Strengthen my spirit's faith;
Nor let me stand, at last, alone
  Upon the shore of death.

PHOEBE CARY, 1852. Abbr.

375 Sing to "Shining Shore." 8s. 7s.

1 My days are gliding swiftly by,
  And I, a pilgrim stranger,
Would not detain them as they fly,
  Those hours of toil and danger.
    For, oh, we stand on Jordan's strand,
      Our friends are passing over;
    And just before, the Shining Shore
      We may almost discover!

2 We'll gird our loins, my brethren dear,
  Our heavenly home discerning;
Our absent Lord has left us word,
  Let every lamp be burning.
    For, oh, we stand on Jordan's strand,
      Our friends are passing over;
    And just before, the Shining Shore
      We may almost discover!

3 Should coming days be cold and dark,
  We need not cease our singing;
That perfect rest naught can molest,
  Where golden harps are ringing.
    For, oh, we stand on Jordan's strand,
      Our friends are passing over;
    And just before, the Shining Shore
      We may almost discover!

4 Let sorrow's rudest tempest blow,
  Each cord on earth to sever;
Our King says, Come, and there's our home
  Forever, oh, forever!
    For, oh, we stand on Jordan's strand,
      Our friends are passing over;
    And just before, the Shining Shore
      We may almost discover!

DAVID NELSON, 1835. Abbr.

HEAVEN.

376 PILGRIMS. P. M.
HENRY SMART, 1861.

1 Hark, hark, my soul: angelic songs are swelling O'er earth's green fields and ocean's wave-beat shore; How sweet the truth those bless-èd strains are telling Of that new life when sin shall be no more.

REFRAIN.
Angels of gladness, angels of light, Singing to welcome the pilgrims of the night.

2 Onward we go, for still we hear them singing,
   Come, weary souls, for Jesus bids you come;
   And through the dark, its echoes sweetly ringing,
   The music of the gospel leads us home.—REF.

3 Far, far away, like bells at evening pealing,
   The voice of Jesus sounds o'er land and sea;
   And laden souls, by thousands meekly stealing,
   Kind Shepherd, turn their weary steps to Thee.—REF.

4 Angels! sing on, your faithful watches keeping;
   Sing us sweet fragments of the songs above;
   Till morning's joy shall end the night of weeping,
   And life's long shadows break in cloudless love.—REF.

FREDERICK W. FABER, 1854.

THE PRAISE HYMNARY.

377 PARADISE. P. M. JOSEPH BARNBY, 1866.

1 O Paradise! O Paradise! Who doth not crave for rest?
Who would not seek the happy land Where they that loved are blest?

CHORUS.
Where loyal hearts and true Stand ever in the light,
All rapture through and through, In God's most holy sight.

2 O Paradise! O Paradise!
   The world is growing old;
   Who would not be at rest and free,
   Where love is never cold?

3 O Paradise! O Paradise!
   'T is weary waiting here;
   We long to be where Jesus is,
   To feel, to see Him near;

4 O Paradise! O Paradise!
   We long to sin no more;
   We long to be as pure on earth
   As on thy spotless shore;

5 Lord Jesus, King of Paradise,
   Oh, keep us in Thy love,
   And guide us to that happy land
   Of perfect rest above:

FREDERICK W. FABER, 1854.

HEAVEN.

378 ALFORD. P. M. JOHN B. DYKES, 1875.

1 Ten thousand times ten thousand, In sparkling raiment bright,
The armies of the ransomed saints Throng up the steeps of light:
'Tis finished, all is finished, Their fight with death and sin;
Fling open wide the golden gates, and let the victors in.

2 What rush of hallelujahs
  Fills all the earth and sky!
What ringing of a thousand harps
  Bespeaks the triumph nigh!
Oh, day, for which creation
  And all its tribes were made!
Oh, joy for all its former woes
  A thousand fold repaid!

3 Oh, then what raptured greetings
  On Canaan's happy shore!
What knitting severed friendships up,
  Where partings are no more!
Then eyes with joy shall sparkle.
  That brimmed with tears of late;
Orphans no longer fatherless,
  Nor widows desolate.

HENRY ALFORD, 1866.

THE PRAISE HYMNARY.

379 CASKET. C. M.   CHARLES F. ROPER.

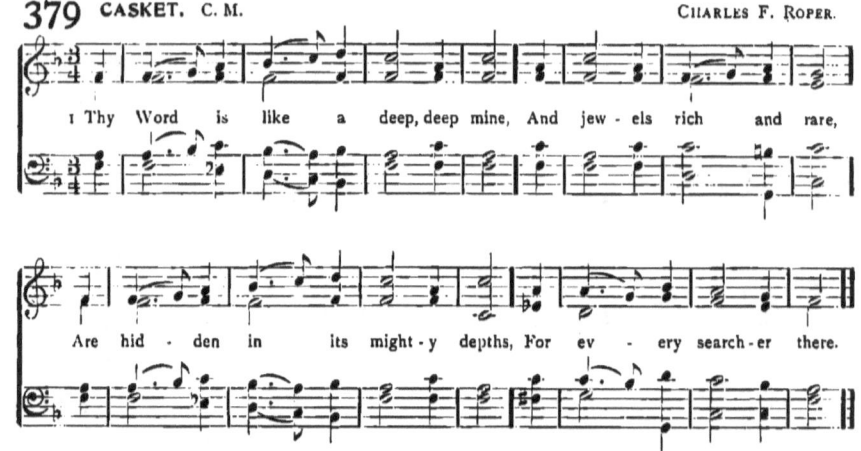

1 Thy Word is like a deep, deep mine, And jewels rich and rare, Are hidden in its mighty depths, For every searcher there.

2 Thy Word is like a starry host,
A thousand rays of light
Are seen to guide the traveler,
And make his pathway bright.

3 Thy Word is like a glorious choir,
And loud its anthems ring,
Though many tongues and parts unite,
It is one song they sing.

4 Thy Word is like an armory,
Where soldiers may repair,
And find for life's long battle-day,
All needful weapons there.
      E. HODDER, 1868.

380 C. M.

1 How precious is the book divine,
By inspiration given!
Bright as a lamp its doctrines shine,
To guide our souls to heaven.

2 It sweetly cheers our drooping hearts,
In this dark vale of tears;
Life, light, and joy it still imparts,
And quells our rising fears.

3 This lamp, through all the tedious night
Of life, shall guide our way,
Till we behold the clearer light
Of an eternal day.
      JOHN FAWCETT, 1782. Abbr.

381 CLYDE. 8s. 4s.   Arr. by EMMELAR.

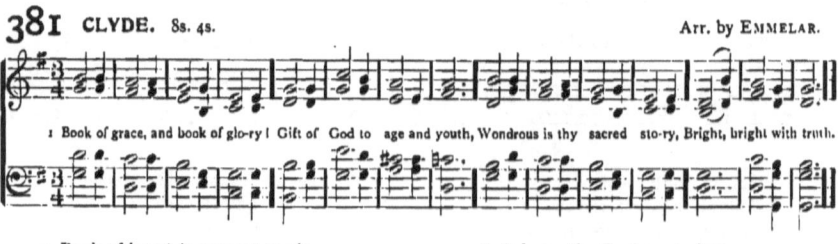

1 Book of grace, and book of glory! Gift of God to age and youth, Wondrous is thy sacred story, Bright, bright with truth.

2 Book of love! in accents tender
Speaking unto such as we;
May it lead us, Lord, to render
All, all to Thee.

3 Book of hope! the spirit, sighing,
Sweetest comfort finds in Thee,

As it hears the Saviour crying,
"Come, come to Me!"

4 Book of life, when we, reposing,
Bid farewell to friends we love,
Give us, for the life then closing,
Life, life above.
      THOMAS MACKELLAR.

THE SCRIPTURES.

382 DUNDEE. C. M.
Arr. fr. Christopher Tye, 1553.

1 A glory gilds the sacred page, Majestic like the sun;
It gives a light to every age; It gives, but borrows none.

2 The Hand that gave it, still supplies
The gracious light and heat;
His truths upon the nations rise,
They rise, but never set.

3 Let everlasting thanks be Thine
For such a bright display
As makes a world of darkness shine
With beams of heavenly day.

4 My soul rejoices to pursue
The steps of Him I love,
Till glory breaks upon my view
In brighter worlds above.
WILLIAM COWPER, 1772.

383 C. M.

1 FATHER of mercies, in Thy word
What endless glory shines!
Forever be Thy name adored
For these celestial lines.

2 'T is here the tree of knowledge grows,
And yields a free repast;
Here purer sweets than nature knows,
Invite the longing taste.

3 'T is here the Saviour's welcome voice
Spreads heavenly peace around,
And life and everlasting joys
Attend the blissful sound.
ANNE STEELE, 1760. Abbr.

384 PETROX. 6s.
W. BOYD.

1 Lord, Thy word abideth, And our foot-steps guideth; Who its truth believeth Light and joy receiveth.

2 When the storms are o'er us,
And dark clouds before us,
Then its light directeth,
And our way protecteth.

3 Word of mercy, giving
Succor to the living;
Word of life supplying
Comfort to the dying!

4 Oh, that we, discerning
Its most holy learning,
Lord, may love and fear Thee,
Evermore be near Thee!
Sir HENRY W. BAKER, 1861.

THE PRAISE HYMNARY.

385 ST. BASIL. 7s. 3l. — German Chorale.

1 Jesus, with Thy church abide, Be her Saviour, Lord, and Guide, While on earth her faith is tried. A-MEN.

2 Keep her life and doctrine pure,
Help her, patient to endure,
Trusting in Thy promise sure:
3 May she guide the poor and blind,
Seek the lost until she find,
And the broken-hearted bind:

4 Save her love from growing cold,
Make her watchmen strong and bold,
Fence her round — Thy peaceful fold.
5 Help her in her time of fast,
Till her toil and woe are past,
And the Bridegroom come at last.

WILLIAM POLLOCK, 1870. Abbr.

386 ST. ANN'S. C. M. — WILLIAM CROFT, 1708.

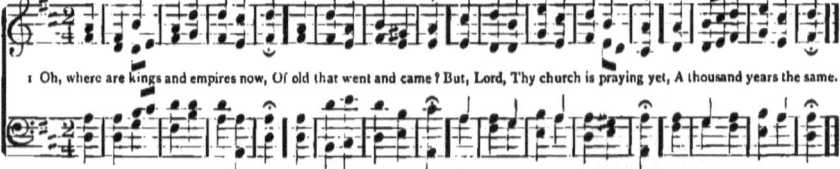

1 Oh, where are kings and empires now, Of old that went and came? But, Lord, Thy church is praying yet, A thousand years the same.

2 We mark her goodly battlements,
And her foundations strong;
We hear within the solemn voice
Of her unending song.

3 For not like kingdoms of the world
Thy holy church, O God!
Though earthquake shocks are threatening her,
And tempests are abroad; —

4 Unshaken as eternal hills,
Immovable she stands,
A mountain that shall fill the earth,
A house not made by hands.

ARTHUR C. COXE, 1839.

387 C. M.

1 How goodly is Thy church, O Lord,
How bright her portals shine;
Her stately battlements declare
Her workmanship divine.

2 Against her storms have fiercely raged
And tempests hurled their might;
But still unhurt she firmly stands;
How glorious is the sight!

3 Nor shall the power of all her foes
Against Thy church prevail;
For Thou shalt smite them with Thy sword,
And cause their schemes to fail.

J. B. THOMPSON, 1897.

388 STATE STREET. S. M. — JONATHAN C. WOODMAN, 1844.

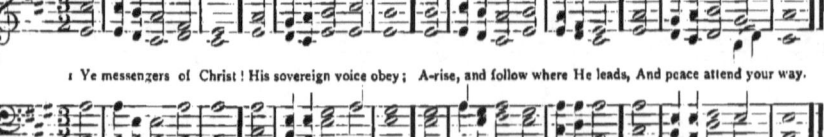

1 Ye messengers of Christ! His sovereign voice obey; A-rise, and follow where He leads, And peace attend your way.

2 The Master, whom you serve,
Will needful strength bestow;
Depending on His promised aid,
With sacred courage go.

3 Mountains shall sink to plains,
And hell in vain oppose;
The cause is God's, and must prevail
In spite of all His foes.

Mrs. VOKES, 1797.

THE CHURCH.

389 WALMER ROAD. C. M. D.   W. L. MASON.

1. How lovely are Thy dwellings fair! O Lord of Hosts, how dear
   The pleasant tabernacles are, (*Omit*. . . . .) Where Thou dost dwell so near!
   My soul doth long and almost die Thy courts, O Lord, to see;
   My heart and flesh aloud do cry, O living God, for Thee.

Copyright, 1891, by THE GOODENOUGH & WOGLOM CO. Used by per.

2 There even the sparrow, freed from wrong,
   Hath found a house of rest;
  The swallow there, to lay her young,
   Hath built her brooding nest;
  Even by Thy altars, Lord of Hosts,
   They find their safe abode;
  And home they fly, from round the coasts
   Toward Thee, my King, my God.

3 Happy, who in Thy house reside,
   Where Thee they ever praise!
  Happy, whose strength in Thee doth bide,
   And in their hearts Thy ways!
  For God, the Lord, both sun and shield,
   Gives grace and glory bright;
  No good from them shall be withheld
   Whose ways are just and right.

                                                          JOHN MILTON.

390 ST. THOMAS. S. M.   WILLIAM TANSUR, 1768.

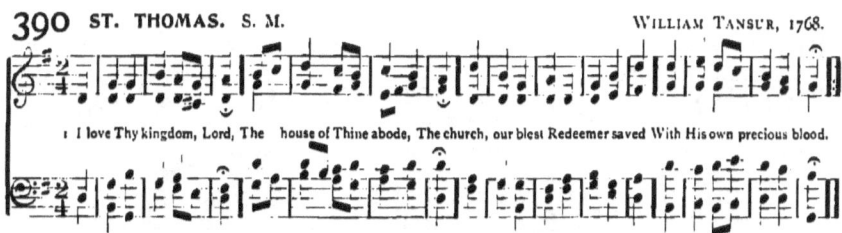

1 I love Thy kingdom, Lord, The house of Thine abode, The church, our blest Redeemer saved With His own precious blood.

2 I love Thy church, O God!
   Her walls before Thee stand,
  Dear as the apple of Thine eye,
   And graven on Thy hand.
3 For her my tears shall fall,
   For her my prayers ascend;
  To her my cares and toils be given,
   Till toils and cares shall end.
4 Beyond my highest joy
   I prize her heavenly ways,

  Her sweet communion, solemn vows,
   Her hymns of love and praise.
5 Jesus, Thou Friend divine,
   Our Saviour and our King!
  Thy hand, from every snare and foe
   Shall great deliverance bring.
6 Sure as Thy truth shall last,
   To Zion shall be given
  The brightest glories earth can yield,
   And brighter bliss of heaven.
                        TIMOTHY DWIGHT, 1800.

THE PRAISE HYMNARY.

391 NATIVITY. C. M.   HENRY LAHEE, 1855.

1 Thou ever-living Corner Stone, E-ter-nal Son of Man, Look down from heaven in love, and own The work our builders plan.

2 Not unto us — to Thy great name
  Be wall and headstone raised.
  Here may the Lord Jehovah's fame
  By all our tribes be praised.

3 O Thou who saidst, Let there be light!
  And light from chaos sprung,
  Shine hence to men in darkest night,
  Of distant clime and tongue.

4 Nor less for this fair land we pray,
  Whose banner here shall wave;
  Forth from Thy throne send, day by day,
  The streams that heal and save.

5 Thy parting prayer, O Lord, fulfill!
  And make Thy people one;
  Yea, whosoever doth His will —
  Our brother, as God's son.
            W. H. COBB, 1897.

392 C. M.

1 O THOU, whose own vast temple stands,
  Built over earth and sea,
  Accept the walls that human hands
  Have raised to worship Thee.

2 Lord, from Thine inmost glory send,
  Within these courts to bide,
  The peace that dwelleth without end,
  Serenely by Thy side!

3 May erring minds that worship here
  Be taught the better way;
  And they who mourn, and they who fear,
  Be strengthened as they pray.

4 May faith grow firm, and love grow warm,
  And pure devotion rise,
  While round these hallowed walls the storm
  Of earth-born passion dies.
            WILLIAM C. BRYANT, 1835.

393 SEYMOUR. 7s.   From VON WEBER, 1825, arr. by HENRY W. GREATOREX, 1849.

1 Lord of hosts! to Thee we raise Here a house of prayer and praise: Thou Thy people's hearts prepare, Here to meet for praise and prayer.

2 Let the living here be fed
  With Thy Word, the Heavenly Bread:
  Here, in hope of glory blest,
  May the dead be laid to rest:

3 Here to Thee a temple stand,
  While the sea shall gird the land:
  Here reveal Thy mercy sure,
  While the sun and moon endure.

4 Hallelujah! — earth and sky
  To the joyful sound reply:
  Hallelujah! hence ascend
  Prayer and praise till time shall end.
            JAMES MONTGOMERY, 1825.

DEDICATION.

394 MORGAN PARK. C. M. D.

Wm. A. May.

1. We ded-i-cate this house to Thee, O triune God our Lord,
Ac-cept and sanc-ti-fy the gift, (Omit . . . .) We pray with one accord. Within these hallowed walls e-rect Thy throne of power and love; Let glo-ry fill these earthly courts, A glo-ry from a-bove.

Copyright, 1898, by SILVER, BURDETT & COMPANY.

2 Here let Thy messengers unfold
  The truths from Book Divine,
To cheer the heart, illume the soul,
  And cause the face to shine.
From souls devout and flushed with joy,
  Let worship here arise;
May faith and hope, and love and peace,
  Dwell here as in the skies.

3 Let age find here a haven sweet,
  And youth, a refuge strong;
The widow and the fatherless
  Pour out their hearts in song.
Here let the burdened saint find rest,
  The sinner be forgiven;
And every sad, or bitter heart,
  Be soothed by thoughts of heaven.

4 Accept our gift, bestow Thine own,
  And fill this house with grace,
Where thronging multitudes shall come
  To meet Thee face to face.
Here let Thy name be glorified
  While decades onward run;
Here every cause of man be helped
  And all Thy will be done.
    THOMAS J. MORGAN, 1892.

395 C. M. D.

1 O Thou to whom a thousand years
  Are as the passing day,
Who guidest us, through joy and tears,
  Along our homeward way;
This sacred shrine, O God, to Thee
  We and our fathers raised,
And here with prayer and melody
  Thy name we oft have praised.

2 Here saints of God, bowed down with years
  The young to Thee have led,
And here, still smiling through our tears,
  We've laid away our dead.
Memory recalls the faces dear,
  The voices and the words,
Of those who prayed, and witnessed here
  For Thee, our blessed Lord.

3 Our songs, our prayers, with one accord,
  To Thee on high we raise
The matchless grace of Christ the Lord
  Eternally to praise.
And when no more this earthly house
  Our mortal eyes shall see,
Grant us, O Lord, a dwelling-place,
  Eternally with Thee.
    NATHANIEL BUTLER, 1897.

396 6s. 4s. Sing to "Italian Hymn."

1 GREAT God, our Sovereign King,
  To Thee this house we bring;
    Accept, we pray.
  Make this Thy dwelling-place,
  Here show Thy smiling face,
  Display Thy saving grace,
    Now and alway.

2 Thou, Christ, our model art
  For body, mind, and heart;
    Help us to be
  Strong, heavy loads to bear,
  Finding truth everywhere,
  Tender, men's woes to share.
    Saviour, like Thee.

3 Here may our sons grow strong,
  Battling with every wrong,
    Girded with might.
  Here strangers find a home,
  Here rich and poor oft come,
  Here lips that lie be dumb,
    Here speed the right.
    ALEXANDER BLACKBURN, 1897. Abbr.

155

397 ADRIAN. S. M.

JOHN E. GOULD, 1846.

1 With willing hearts we tread The path the Saviour trod;
We love th' example of our Head, The glorious Lamb of God.

2 On Thee, on Thee alone,
Our hope and faith rely,
O Thou who didst for sin atone,
Who didst for sinners die.

3 We trust Thy sacrifice;
To Thy dear cross we flee:
Oh, may we die to sin, and rise
To life and bliss in Thee.
SAMUEL F. SMITH, 1843.

398 S. M.

1 HERE, Saviour, we do come,
In Thine appointed way;
Obedient to Thy high commands,
Our solemn vows we pay.

2 Oh, bless this sacred rite,
To bring us near to Thee!
And may we find that as our day
Our strength shall also be.
BENJAMIN BEDDOME, 1817. Alt. and Abbr.

399 EMMANUEL. C. M.

Arr. from BEETHOVEN.

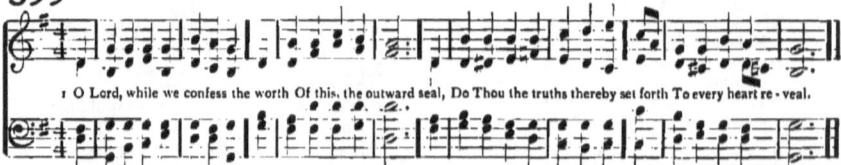

1 O Lord, while we confess the worth Of this, the outward seal, Do Thou the truths thereby set forth To every heart reveal.

2 Death to the world we here avow,
Death to each fleshly lust;
Newness of life our calling now,
A risen Lord our trust.

3 And we, O Lord, who now partake
Of resurrection life,
With every sin, for Thy dear sake,
Would be at constant strife.

4 Baptized into the Father's name,
We'd walk as sons of God;
Baptized in Thine, we own Thy claim
As ransomed by Thy blood.

5 Baptized into the Holy Ghost,
We'd keep His temple pure,
And make Thy grace our only boast
And by Thy strength endure.
MARY BOWLY, 1846.

400 C. M.

1 O FATHER, Son, and Holy Ghost,
One God, in persons Three!
We come in faith to count the cost
And give ourselves to Thee.

2 We seek to serve no other King,
Follow no other Guide,
Nor earth nor any earthly thing
Shall keep us from Thy side.

3 We seek to know no other love,
Save what we love in Thee;
And Thee we choose, all else above,
Our chiefest love to be.

4 Thy blood our only treasure is,
Thy cross our chosen part;
Thy service is our highest bliss,
Our home, within Thy heart.
ANON., 1867. Abbr.

BAPTISM.

401 VALENTIA. C. M.   EBERWEIN. Arr. by GEORGE KINGSLEY, 1853

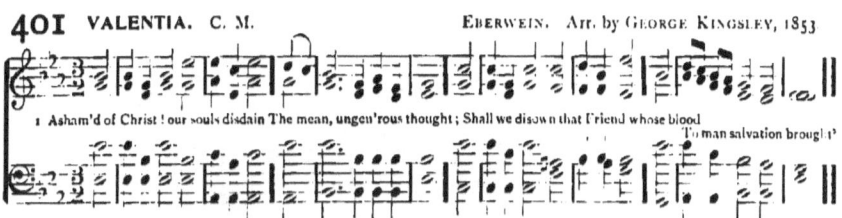

1 Asham'd of Christ! our souls disdain The mean, ungen'rous thought; Shall we disown that Friend whose blood To man salvation brought?

2 With the glad news of love and peace,
   From heaven to earth He came;
   For us endured the painful cross,
   For us despised the shame.

3 To His command let us submit
   Ourselves without delay;
   Our lives — yea, thousand lives of ours —
   His love can ne'er repay.

4 To bear His name — His cross to bear —
   Our highest honor this!
   Who nobly suffers for Him now,
   Shall reign with Him in bliss.
          JOHN NEEDHAM, 1768. Sl. alt.

402 C. M.

1 'T IS God the Father we adore
   In this baptismal sign;
   'T is He whose voice, on Jordan's shore,
   Proclaimed the Son divine.

2 The Father owned Him; let our breath
   In answering praise ascend,
   As in the image of His death
   We own our heavenly Friend.

3 Let earth and heaven our zeal record,
   And future witness bear
   That we to Zion's mighty Lord
   Our full allegiance swear.
        MARIA G. SAFFERY, 1818. Abbr.

403 CAMBRIDGE. C. M.   JOHN RANDALL, 1790.

1 Lord, I am Thine, and in Thy aid I place my firmest trust: How large the price Thy love has paid For vile, po-lut-ed dust! For vile, po-lut-ed dust! For vile, po-lut-ed dust!

2 In Thine assembly now I stand;
   My vows to Thee I bring,
   Obedient to Thy great command,
   My Saviour and my King.

3 I stand before the open fount;
   Thy gracious words invite:
   How poor an offering, O my God,
   I make Thee in this rite!

4 Thine ordinance, great Saviour, bless;
   Support me all my days;
   May I each gospel truth confess,
   And walk in all Thy ways.
          ANON.

404 C. M.

1 WELCOME, O Saviour! to my heart;
   Possess Thine humble throne;
   Bid every rival hence depart,
   And claim me for Thine own.

2 The world and Satan I forsake —
   To Thee, I all resign;
   My longing heart, O Jesus! take,
   And fill with love divine.

3 Oh! may I never turn aside,
   Nor from Thy bosom flee;
   Let nothing here my heart divide —
   I give it all to Thee.
        HUGH BOURNE, 1825.

405 HANFORD. P. M.

Sir Arthur S. Sullivan, 1872.

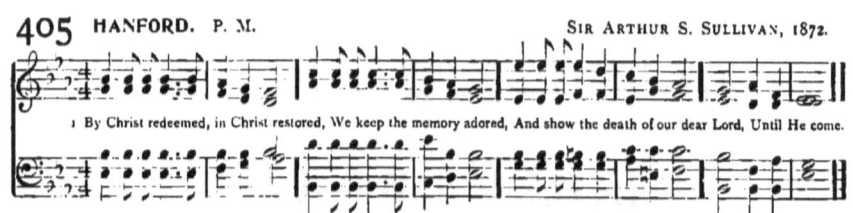

1 By Christ redeemed, in Christ restored, We keep the memory adored, And show the death of our dear Lord, Until He come.

2 His body broken in our stead
Is here, in this memorial bread;
And so our feeble love is fed,
Until He come.

3 His fearful drops of agony,
His life-blood shed for us we see:
The wine shall tell the mystery,
Until He come.

4 And thus that dark betrayal night,
With the last advent we unite —
The shame, the glory, by this rite,
Until He come.

5 Oh, blessèd hope! with this elate,
Let not our hearts be desolate,
But, strong in faith, in patience wait,
Until He come!

George Rawson, 1857. Abbr.

406 DOLOMITE. 6s.

Austrian Melody.

1 I hunger, and I thirst; Je-sus, my manna be; Ye living waters burst Out of the rock for me.

2 Thou bruised and broken Bread,
My life-long wants supply;
As living souls are fed,
O feed me or I die.

3 Thou true Life-giving Vine,
Let me Thy sweetness prove;
Renew my life with Thine,
Refresh my soul with love.

4 Rough paths my feet have trod
Since first their course began:
Feed me, Thou Bread of God;
Help me, Thou Son of Man.

5 For still the desert lies
My thirsting soul before,
O living waters, rise
Within me evermore.

John S. B. Monsell, 1860.

407 BENEDICTION CHANT.

A-MEN.

1 And now we rise: the symbols | disap- | pear! ||
The feast, though not the love, is | past and | gone, ||
The bread and wine remove; but | Thou art | here, ||
Nearer than ever; still our | shield and | sun. ||

2 Feast after feast thus comes and | passes | by, ||
And passing points to the glad | feast a- | bove, ||
Giving sweet foretaste of the | festal | joy, ||
The Lamb's great bridal feast of | bliss and | love. || — A-MEN. ||

Horatius Bonar, 1856.

THE LORD'S SUPPER.

408 OLMUTZ. S. M.   Arr. from Gregorian by LOWELL MASON, 1832.

1 A parting hymn we sing, Around Thy table, Lord, Again our grateful tribute bring, Our solemn vows record.

2 Here have we seen Thy face,
   And felt Thy presence here,
So may the savor of Thy grace
   In word and life appear.

3 The purchase of Thy blood, —
   By sin no longer led, —
The path our dear Redeemer trod,
   May we rejoicing tread.

4 In self-forgetful love
   Be our communion shown,
Until we join the church above
   And know as we are known.
              AARON R. WOLFE, 1821.

409 S. M.

1 BLEST feast of love divine!
   'T is grace that makes us free
To feed upon this bread and wine,
   In memory, Lord, of Thee.

2 That blood which flowed for sin,
   In symbol here we see,
And feel the blessed pledge within
   That we are loved by Thee.

3 O, if this glimpse of love
   Be so divinely sweet,
What will it be, O Lord, above,
   Thy gladdening smile to meet?
              Sir EDWARD DENNY, 1839.

410 DEDHAM. C. M.   WILLIAM GARDINER, 1822.

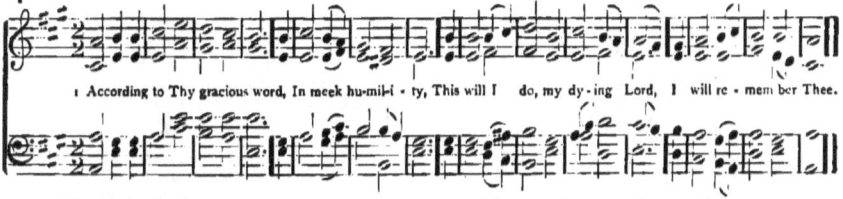

1 According to Thy gracious word, In meek humility, This will I do, my dying Lord, I will remember Thee.

2 Thy body, broken for my sake,
   My bread from heaven shall be;
Thy testamental cup I take,
   And thus remember Thee.

3 Gethsemane can I forget?
   Or there Thy conflict see,
Thine agony and bloody sweat,
   And not remember Thee?

4 When to the cross I turn mine eyes
   And rest on Calvary,
O Lamb of God, my sacrifice!
   I must remember Thee: —

5 Remember Thee, and all Thy pains
   And all Thy love to me;
Yea, while a breath, a pulse remains,
   Will I remember Thee.
              JAMES MONTGOMERY, 1825. Abbr.

411 C. M.

1 PREPARE us, Lord, to view Thy cross,
   Who all our griefs hast borne;
To look on Thee, whom we have pierced —
   To look on Thee and mourn.

2 While thus we mourn, we would rejoice,
   And as Thy cross we see,
Let each exclaim, in faith and hope,
   "The Saviour died for me!"
              THOMAS COTTERILL, 1820.

412 C. M.

1 TOGETHER with these symbols, Lord,
   Thy blessèd self impart;
And let Thy holy flesh and blood
   Feed the believing heart.

2 Come, Holy Ghost, with Jesus' love,
   Prepare us for this feast;
Oh, let us banquet with our Lord,
   And lean upon His breast.
              JOHN CENNICK, 1741. Abbr.

THE PRAISE HYMNARY.

413 ROCKINGHAM. L. M.   LOWELL MASON, 1830.

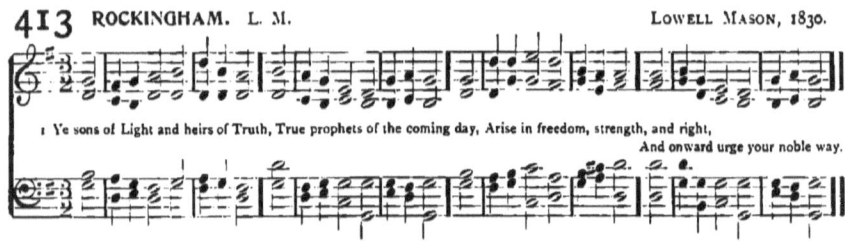

1 Ye sons of Light and heirs of Truth, True prophets of the coming day, Arise in freedom, strength, and right, And onward urge your noble way.

2 The God of ages, Life of all,
   Within your souls enthronèd be,
   Revealing through your life and work
   His children's sacred liberty.

3 Go forth in love to conquer sin,
   In truth to triumph over wrong,
   Till all earth's voices blend with yours
   In hope's immortal, conquering song.

4 On every trusting, seeking soul
   Glow down forever from on high
   The love and beauty of our Lord,
   All lives to bless and sanctify.
               C. E. ORDWAY, 1897. Abbr.

414 L. M.

1 LORD, we would come before Thee here
   Presenting youths and maidens dear,
   And we would ask Thy spirit's power
   To help us in this sacred hour.

2 May knowledge her rich stores unroll,
   May wisdom sanctify each soul;
   And science lay, with reverence meet,
   Her trophies at the Saviour's feet.

3 Whatever work we have to do,
   Whatever purpose we pursue,
   Whatever part in life we play,
   Lord, guide and guard us in the way.
               J. P. HUTCHINSON, 1895. Abbr.

415 8s. 7s. Sing to "Autumn," No. 58.

1 FATHER, now we hear Thee calling
   Us to spend our lives for Thee,
   As our Master did before us,
   In Thy service glad and free.
   In a world of toil and sorrow,
   In a world of sin and shame,
   Thou hast bidden us to labor,
   And Thy saving grace proclaim.

2 Breathe on us Thy Holy Spirit,
   As to service forth we go;
   May He, ever in us dwelling,
   Cause us all Thy will to know.

With a coal from off Thine altar,
Touch our lips with power divine;
Fill our souls with heavenly brightness,
That Thy light through us may shine.

3 As we go Thy truth proclaiming,
   Trusting in Thy might alone,
   Send Thy blessing on our labors,
   All Thy saving power make known.
   May our words and deeds reveal Thee
   As we strive men's souls to win;
   May they free from sorrow's bondage,
   And restrain from paths of sin.
               J. F. JENNESS, 1897. Abbr.

416 H. M. Sing to "Lenox," No. 246.

1 YE saints! your music bring,
   And swell the rapturous sound;
   Strike every trembling string,
   Till earth and heaven resound:
   The triumphs of the cross we sing,
   Awake, ye saints! each joyful string.

2 The cross, the cross alone,
   Subdued the powers of hell;
   Like lightning from his throne

The prince of darkness fell;
The triumphs of the cross we sing,
Awake, ye saints! each joyful string.

3 The cross hath power to save
   From all the foes that rise;
   The cross hath made the grave
   A passage to the skies.
   The triumphs of the cross we sing:
   Awake, ye saints! each joyful string.
               ANDREW REED, 1817.

OCCASIONAL.

417 MISSIONARY CHANT. L. M.   Heinrich C. Zeuner, 1832.

1 Eternal God! we come to Thee, Thy grace and glory to adore, Thy love unfathomed as the sea, Thy mercy promised evermore.

2 How blest the feet of those who bring,
   Glad tidings from Thy glorious throne;
And from the mountain-tops that fling
   The banner of Thy Son alone.

3 Give to Thy servant power and love,
   To speak the wonders of Thy grace,
And send Thy Spirit from above,
   To rest within this holy place.

4 Let the rich gift of souls redeemed,
   Of wanderers won to Christ, our King,
Be like the glories that have streamed
   From Thy blest throne where angels sing.

5 Bless our loved Zion with Thy light!
   Dwell in this temple, Gracious Lord!
Come Thou with power, and grace, and might,
   That here Thy name may be adored.
              Wm. Oland Bourne, circ. 1896.

418 L. M.

1 Bless, Lord, this household and its head,
   With food from heaven may each be fed;
Bless Thou the tie we weave to-night,
   In tender love all hearts unite!

2 Eager for toil Thy servant stands,
   With girded loins and ready hands;
Oh, grant, whate'er his work may be,
   His labor may be blest by Thee!

3 No lot of ease for him we ask,
   But strength to meet his daily task;
Wisdom from Thee aright to see
   And use each opportunity.

4 O heavenly Source of Light and Love,
   Our hearts to reverent worship move,
And in Thy Spirit's unity
   Bind each to each and all to Thee!
              Alice W. Brotherton, 1896.

419 KINGSLEY. L. M.   George Kingsley, circ. 1838?

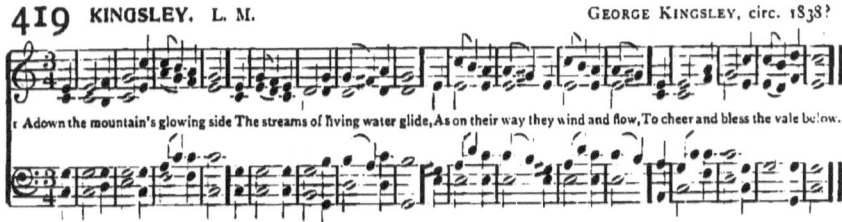

1 Adown the mountain's glowing side The streams of living water glide, As on their way they wind and flow, To cheer and bless the vale below.

2 A mountain vale in Palestine
   Once saw the stream of life divine,
As from the lips of Jesus fell
   The words of life by Jacob's well.

3 The living waters bright and clear
   Still flow the hearts of men to cheer;
While words of life divine shall come
   To truly bless the church and home.

4 In strength and beauty we would grow,
   As here we tread the paths below,
And seek the holy peace and love
   Of friends who live in homes above.
              George Osgood, 1897.

420 L. M.

1 One life to live, just one below,
   Is given once to mortal man,
For work and rest, for weal or woe,
   And all is measured by a span.

2 How and for whom is he to live
   That he may gain the blest reward?
Surrendered life — let all be given
   In faith and love to Christ the Lord.

3 "To live is Christ," was said by Paul;
   I'll gain by dying in the strife;
I consecrate to Him my all,
   My body, mind, heart, soul, and life.
              J. L. Lower, 1897.

THE PRAISE HYMNARY.

421 MISSIONARY HYMN. 7s, 6s. D. LOWELL MASON, 1823.

1 From Greenland's icy mountains, From India's coral strand, Where Afric's sunny fountains Roll down their golden sand: From many an ancient river, From many a palmy plain, They call us to deliver Their land from error's chain.

2 What though the spicy breezes
   Blow soft o'er Ceylon's isle;
Though every prospect pleases,
   And only man is vile?
In vain, with lavish kindness,
   The gifts of God are strown;
The heathen, in his blindness,
   Bows down to wood and stone.

3 Can we, whose souls are lighted
   By wisdom from on high,
Can we to men benighted
   The lamp of life deny?
Salvation! O salvation!
   The joyful sound proclaim,
Till earth's remotest nation
   Has learned Messiah's name.

4 Waft, waft, ye winds, His story
   And you, ye waters, roll,
Till, like a sea of glory,
   It spreads from pole to pole:
Till o'er our ransomed nature
   The Lamb, for sinners slain,
Redeemer, King, Creator,
   In bliss returns to reign.

REGINALD HEBER, 1819.

422 7s, 6s. D.

1 OUR country's voice is pleading,
   Ye men of God, arise!
His providence is leading,
   The land before you lies;
Daygleams are o'er it brightening,
   And promise clothes the soil;
Wide fields for harvest whitening,
   Invite the reaper's toil.

2 Go where the waves are breaking
   On California's shore,
Christ's precious gospel taking,
   More rich than golden ore;
On Allegheny's mountains,
   Through all the western vale,
Beside Missouri's fountains,
   Rehearse the wondrous tale.

3 The love of Christ unfolding,
   Speed on from east to west,
Till all, His cross beholding,
   In Him are fully blest.
Great Author of salvation,
   Haste, haste the glorious day,
When we, a ransomed nation,
   Thy sceptre shall obey.

Mrs. MARIA F. ANDERSON, 1848.

423 L. M. Sing to "Missionary Chant," No. 417.

1 YE Christian heralds, go, proclaim
   Salvation through Immanuel's name;
To distant climes the tidings bear,
   And plant the rose of Sharon there.

2 He'll shield you with a wall of fire,
   With flaming zeal your breasts inspire,
Bid raging winds their fury cease,
   And hush the tempest into peace.

3 And when your labors all are o'er,
   Then we shall meet to part no more;
Meet with the blood-bought throng, to fall,
   And crown our Jesus Lord of all!

BOURNE H. DRAPER, 1803.

MISSIONS.

424 ROTHWELL. L. M.
WILLIAM TANSUR, 1743.

1 Look from Thy sphere of endless day, O God of mercy and of might! In pity look on those who stray, Benighted, in this land of light. Benighted, in this land of light.

2 Send forth Thy heralds, Lord! to call
The thoughtless young, the hardened old,
A scattered, homeless flock, till all
Be gathered to Thy peaceful fold.

3 Send them Thy mighty word to speak,
Till faith shall dawn, and doubt depart,
To awe the bold, to stay the weak,
And bind and heal the broken heart.

4 Then all these wastes, a dreary scene,
That make us sadden as we gaze,
Shall grow with living waters green,
And lift to heaven the voice of praise.
WILLIAM C. BRYANT, 1840. Abbr.

425 L. M.

1 UPLIFT the banner! Let it float
Skyward and seaward, high and wide;
The sun shall light its shining folds,
The cross on which the Saviour died.

2 Uplift the banner! Heathen lands
Shall see from far the glorious sight,
And nations, gathering at the call,
Their spirits kindle in its light.

3 Uplift the banner! Let it float
Skyward and seaward, high and wide;
Our glory only in the cross,
Our only hope the Crucified.
GEORGE W. DOANE, 1824. Abbr.

426 DOVER. S. M.
From AARON WILLIAMS' Coll.

1 Come, kingdom of our God, Sweet reign of light and love! Shed peace, and hope, and joy abroad, And wisdom from above.

2 Over our spirits first
Extend Thy healing reign;
There raise and quench the sacred thirst,
That never pains again.

3 Come, kingdom of our God!
And make the broad earth Thine;
Stretch o'er her lands and isles the rod
That flowers with grace divine.
JOHN JOHNS, 1837. Abbr.

427 S. M.

1 O LORD our God arise,
The cause of truth maintain,
And wide o'er all the peopled world,
Extend her blessed reign.

2 Thou Prince of Life arise,
Nor let Thy glory cease,
Far spread the conquest of Thy grace,
And bless the earth with peace.

3 Thou Holy Ghost, arise,
Expand Thy quickening wing,
And o'er a dark and ruined world,
Let light and order spring.
RALPH WARDLAW, 1803. Abbr.

2 The martyr first, whose eagle eye
   Could pierce beyond the grave;
Who saw his Master in the sky,
   And called on Him to save.
Like Him with pardon on his tongue,
   In midst of mortal pain,
He prayed for them that did the wrong:—
   Who follows in his train?

3 A glorious band, the chosen few,
   On whom the Spirit came;
Twelve valiant saints, their hope they knew,
   And mocked the cross and flame.
They met the tyrant's brandished steel,
   The lion's gory mane;
They bowed their necks the death to feel:—
   Who follows in their train?

4 A noble army, men and boys,
   The matron and the maid,
Around the Saviour's throne rejoice,
   In robes of light arrayed.
They climbed the steep ascent of heaven
   Through peril, toil, and pain:
O God, to us may grace be given
   To follow in their train.

REGINALD HEBER, 1827.

OCCASIONAL.

429 WEBB. 7s, 6s. D.
GEORGE J. WEBB, 1830.

1 Stand up! stand up for Jesus! Ye soldiers of the cross;
Lift high His royal banner,
It must not suffer loss:
From victory unto victory, His army shall He lead,
Till every foe is vanquished,
And Christ is Lord indeed.

2 Stand up! — stand up for Jesus!
The trumpet call obey;
Forth to the mighty conflict,
In this His glorious day:
"Ye that are men, now serve Him,"
Against unnumbered foes;
Your courage rise with danger,
And strength to strength oppose.

3 Stand up! — stand up for Jesus!
Stand in His strength alone;
The arm of flesh will fail you,
Ye dare not trust your own:
Put on the gospel armor,
And, watching unto prayer,
Where duty calls, or danger,
Be never wanting there.

4 Stand up! — stand up for Jesus!
The strife will not be long;
This day the noise of battle,
The next the victor's song:
To him that overcometh,
A crown of life shall be;
He with the King of Glory
Shall reign eternally!

GEORGE DUFFIELD, 1858.

430 7s. 6s. D.

1 THE morning light is breaking;
The darkness disappears;
The sons of earth are waking
To penitential tears;
Each breeze that sweeps the ocean
Brings tidings from afar
Of nations in commotion,
Prepared for Zion's war.

2 Rich dews of grace come o'er us
In many a gentle shower,
And brighter scenes before us
Are opening every hour:
Each cry, to heaven going,
Abundant answers brings,
And heavenly gales are blowing,
With peace upon their wings.

3 See heathen nations bending
Before the God we love,
And thousand hearts ascending
In gratitude above;
While sinners, now confessing,
The gospel call obey,
And seek the Saviour's blessing, —
A nation in a day.

SAMUEL F. SMITH, 1843.

431 RETROSPECT. 7s. 6s. D.
ANON.

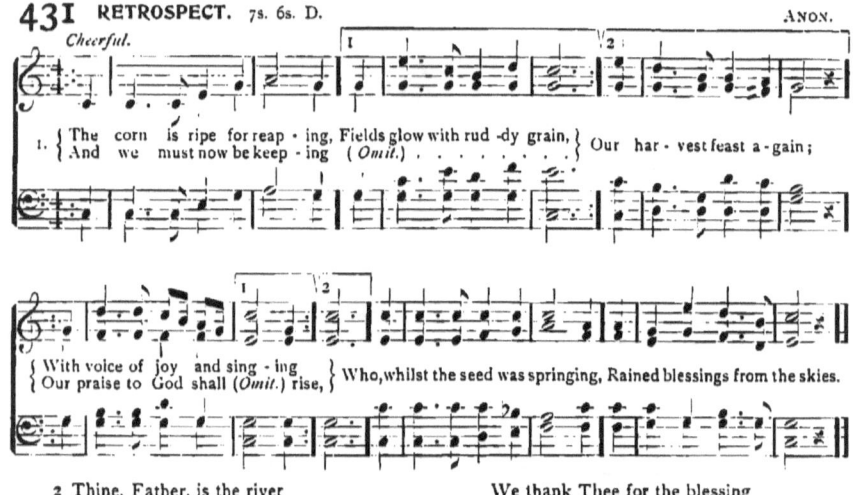

1. The corn is ripe for reaping, Fields glow with ruddy grain,
And we must now be keeping *(Omit.)* . . . . . Our harvest feast again;
With voice of joy and sing-ing
Our praise to God shall *(Omit.)* rise, Who, whilst the seed was springing, Rained blessings from the skies.

2 Thine, Father, is the river
That maketh rich the earth;
Through Thee, O Gracious Giver,
The buried seed had birth:
Thou on the furrows raining,
Didst make them soft with showers,
The thirsty crops maintaining
Through silent summer hours.

3 The year, by Thee anointed,
Is now with goodness crowned;
Robed in the robes appointed,
With gladness girded round.

We thank Thee for the blessing
Which meets us on our way,
And come, Thy love confessing,
With happy hearts to-day.

4 But whilst our lips are praising,
Our lives to Thee belong;
With them we would be raising
A nobler, sweeter song;
One that may sound forever,
Whilst earth's great Harvest speeds,—
A song of high endeavor,
Rung out in earnest deeds.

ANON.

432 NOTTINGHAM. C. M.
JEREMIAH CLARK, 1700.

1 Break, new-born year, on glad eyes break! Melodious voices move! On, rolling Time! Thou canst not make The Father cease to love.

2 Our hearts in tears may oft run o'er;
But, Lord, Thy smile still beams;
Our sins are swelling evermore;
But pardoning grace still streams.

3 Lord, from this year more service win,
More glory, more delight!
O make its hours less sad with sin,
Its days with Thee more bright!

4 Then we may bless its precious things,
If earthly cheer should come:
Or gladsome mount on angel wings,
If Thou wouldst take us home.

5 O golden then the hours must be!
The year must needs be sweet:
Yes, Lord, with happy melody
Thine opening grace we meet.

THOMAS H. GILL, 1855.

THE NEW YEAR.

433 OPENING YEAR. 6s. 5s. 12 l.　　　　　　　　　French Air.

1. Standing at the portal of the opening year, Words of comfort meet us, hushing every fear; Spoken through the silence by our Father's voice, Tender, strong, and faithful, making us rejoice. *Chorus.* Onward then and fear not, children of the day! For His word shall never, never pass away! For His word shall never, never pass away!

2. I, the Lord, am with thee, be thou not afraid,
I will help and strengthen, be thou not dismayed!
Yea, I will uphold thee with My own right hand,
Thou art called and chosen in My sight to stand.

3. For the year before us, oh, what rich supplies!
For the poor and needy living streams shall rise;
For the sad and sinful shall His grace abound;
For the faint and feeble perfect strength be found.

4. He will never fail us, He will not forsake;
His eternal covenant He will never break.
Resting on His promise, what have we to fear?
God is all sufficient for the coming year.

FRANCES R. HAVERGAL, 1873.

THE PRAISE HYMNARY.

434 ELLERS. 10s.   EDWARD J. HOPKINS, 1867.

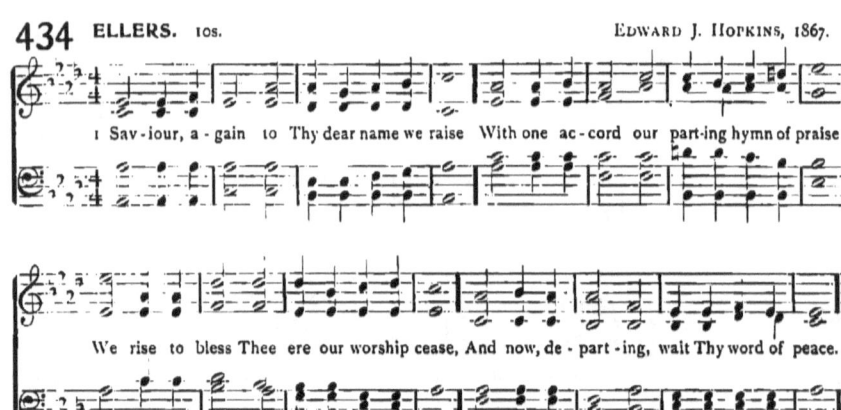

1 Saviour, again to Thy dear name we raise With one accord our parting hymn of praise; We rise to bless Thee ere our worship cease, And now, departing, wait Thy word of peace.

2 Grant us Thy peace upon our homeward way;
With Thee began, with Thee shall end the day;
Guard Thou the lips from sin, the hearts from shame,
That in this house have called upon Thy name.

3 Grant us Thy peace, Lord, through the coming night;
Turn Thou for us its darkness into light;
From harm and danger keep Thy children free,
For dark and light are both alike to Thee.

4 Grant us Thy peace throughout our earthly life,
Our balm in sorrow, and our stay in strife;
Then, when Thy voice shall bid our conflict cease,
Call us, O Lord, to Thine eternal peace.

JOHN ELLERTON, 1866.

435 DOXOLOGY. 10s.

To Father, Son, and Spirit ever blest,
Eternal praise and glory be addressed;
From age to age, ye saints, His name adore,
And spread His fame, till time shall be no more.

SIMON BROWNE, 1720.

436 INVOCATION. 7s.   MICHAEL COSTA, 1855.

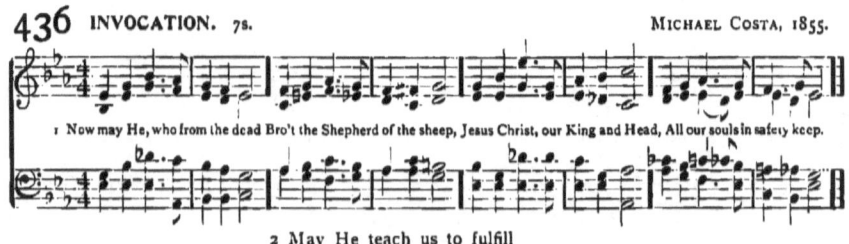

1 Now may He, who from the dead Bro't the Shepherd of the sheep, Jesus Christ, our King and Head, All our souls in safety keep.

2 May He teach us to fulfill
What is pleasing in His sight;
Make us perfect in His will,
And preserve us day and night!

JOHN NEWTON, 1779.

437 8s. 7s. 4s. Sing to "Sicilian Hymn," No. 12.

1 Now in parting, Father, bless us;
Saviour, still Thy peace bestow;
Gracious Comforter, be with us,
As we from Thy presence go:
Bless us, bless us,
Father, Son, and Spirit now.

2 Bless us here, while still as strangers,
Onward to our home we move;
Bless us with eternal blessings,
In our Father's house above:
Ever, ever,
Dwelling in the light of love.

HORATIUS BONAR, 1808.

PARTING HYMNS.

438 GOD BE WITH YOU. W. G. TOMER.

1 God be with you till we meet again;
By His counsels guide, uphold you,
With His sheep securely fold you,
God be with you till we meet again.

CHORUS.
Till we meet, . . . till we meet,
Till we meet at Jesus' feet;
Till we meet, . . . till we meet,
God be with you till we meet again.

Copyright, 1886, by J. E. RANKIN. Used by per.

2 God be with you till we meet again,
'Neath His wings securely hide you;
Daily manna still provide you,
God be with you till we meet again.

3 God be with you till we meet again,
When life's perils thick confound you;
Put His arms unfailing round you,
God be with you till we meet again.

4 God be with you till we meet again,
Keep love's banner floating o'er you;
Smite death's threatening wave before you,
God be with you till we meet again.

J. E. RANKIN.

439   6s. 4s.

1 From everlasting, God,
  To everlasting, God,
    Bend from Thy throne!
  Take Thou our homage free;
  Never to man knelt we,
  Only great King to Thee:
    Shield Thou Thine own.

2 Keep in our hearts, we pray,
  Thoughts of the elder day
    Fresh evermore:
  Works of the fathers dead,
  Words of the fathers said,
  Blood by the fathers shed,
    Birthrights of yore.

3 Forward our banners move;
  Broad lies the land we love;
    Glad songs we sing.
  Proud echoes thrill the air,
  Quick beat the hearts we bear,
  Wreathed on our brows we wear
    Roses of spring.

4 Held by Thy righteous hand,
  Firm our foundations stand,
    Rock-builded, fast.
  While stars shall shine may we
  Wise, just, victorious be,
  Peaceful from sea to sea,
    One till the last.

WILLIAM R. HUNTINGTON, 1861.

440   AMERICA.   6s. 4s.

Adapted by HENRY CAREY, 1740, abt.

1 My country! 't is of thee, Sweet land of liberty, Of thee I sing; Land where my fathers died!
Land of the Pilgrims' pride! From every mountain side Let freedom ring!

2 My native country, thee —
  Land of the noble, free —
    Thy name I love;
  I love Thy rocks and rills,
  Thy woods and templed hills;
  My heart with rapture thrills
    Like that above.

3 Let music swell the breeze,
  And ring from all the trees
    Sweet freedom's song:
  Let mortal tongues awake;
  Let all that breathe partake;
  Let rocks their silence break,
    The sound prolong.

4 Our fathers' God! to Thee,
  Author of liberty,
    To Thee we sing:
  Long may our land be bright
  With freedom's holy light;
  Protect us by Thy might,
    Great God, our King!

SAMUEL F. SMITH, 1832.

441   6s. 4s.

1 God bless our native land!
  Firm may she ever stand,
    Through storm and night;
  When the wild tempests rave,
  Ruler of winds and wave!
  Do Thou our country save,
    By Thy great might.

2 For her our prayer shall rise
  To God above the skies;
    On Him we wait;
  Thou, who art ever nigh,
  Guardian with watchful eye!
  To Thee aloud we cry, —
    God save the state!

CHARLES T. BROOKS, 1835.
JOHN S. DWIGHT, 1844.

442   DOXOLOGY.   6s. 4s.

To God — the Father, Son
And Spirit — Three in One,
  All praise be given!
Crown Him in every song;
To Him your hearts belong;
Let all His praise prolong —
  On earth, in heaven.

EDWIN F. HATFIELD, 1843.

NATIONAL AND PATRIOTIC.

443 GOD OF OUR FATHERS. P. M. Rev. C. O. Arnold, 1897.

1 God of our fa - thers, Bless this our land;
O - cean to o - cean
Own - eth Thy hand. Home of all na - tions From far and near,
Give to u - nite us, Thy faith and fear. God of our fa - thers,
Fail - ing us nev - er, God of our fa - thers, Be ours for ev - er.

2 Lord God of Sa - ba - oth, Might - y in war,
Bound - less and num - ber - less
Thine ar - mies are. Thy right hand con - quer - eth All that op - pose;
Launch forth Thy thun - der - bolts, Smite down our foes; Lord God of Sa - ba - oth,
Fail - ing us nev - er, Lord God of Sa - ba - oth, Fight for us ev - er.

Used by per.

3 Lord God our Saviour,
　Thy love o'erflows,
Making our wilderness
　Bloom as the rose.
Thou with true liberty
　Makest us free,
Knowing no master,
　No king, but Thee;
Lord God our Saviour,
　Failing us never,
Lord God our Saviour,
　Reign Thou forever.

4 Spirit of unity,
　Crown of all kings,
Find us a resting place
　Under Thy wings;
By Thine own presence
　Thy will be done,
Millions of free men
　Banded as one.
Lord God almighty,
　Failing us never,
Thine be the glory,
　Now and forever.

JOHN H. HOPKINS.

THE PRAISE HYMNARY.

444 MENDON. L. M. Arr. by LOWELL MASON, 1832.

O God, beneath Thy guiding hand, Our exiled fathers crossed the sea, And when they trod the wintry strand, With prayer and psalm they worshiped Thee.

2 Thou heardst, well pleased, the song, the prayer,—
Thy blessing came; and still its power
Shall onward through all ages bear
The memory of that holy hour.

3 What change! through pathless wilds no more
The fierce and naked savage roams:
Sweet praise, along the cultured shore,
Breaks from ten thousand happy homes.

4 Laws, freedom, truth, and faith in God
Came with those exiles o'er the waves,
And where their pilgrim feet have trod,
The God they trusted guards their graves.

5 And here Thy name, O God of love,
Their children's children shall adore,
Till these eternal hills remove,
And spring adorns the earth no more.
LEONARD BACON, 1838.

445 L. M.

1 OUR Fathers' God! from ancient days
To everlasting years the same;
The fragrant incense of our praise
We offer to Thy gracious Name.

2 They crossed the trackless, watery sea;
A troubled civic sea we sail:
And as they prayed, we pray to Thee
That chart and compass may not fail.

3 If, kindled by irreverent hand,
Strange fire shall on Thine altars glow,
Oh! then in mercy spare our land,
And turn from us the threatened blow.

4 May all the thrones of civic power
Be loyal unto Truth and Thee;
Thy present aid their constant dower;
Thy word of praise their guerdon be!
GEORGE M. HERRICK, 1898.

446 BEMERTON. C. M. HENRY W. GREATOREX, 1849.

1 O God, who rulest all our days, In whom we live and move, We offer up our humble praise For tokens of Thy love.

2 The watchman waketh but in vain,
Who doth the city keep;
'T is Thou who dost our life sustain
Whene'er we wake or sleep.

3 Through changes of the rolling years,
Through times of joy and pain,
Thy Light has shined, despite our fears,
Through all our loss or gain.

4 Our Fathers' God, our hope and might,
Whose works Thy goodness tell,
May virtue, righteousness, and right
Within our city dwell.

5 For happy homes and prosp'rous days,
For life and health and peace,
With grateful hearts we give Thee praise;
Let not Thy favor cease.
FRANKLIN W. BARTLETT, 1897.

447 C. M.

1 LORD, while for all mankind we pray,
Of every clime and coast,
O hear us for our native land,
The land we love the most.

2 O guard our shores from every foe,
With peace our borders bless;
With prosperous times our cities crown,
Our fields with plenteousness.

3 Unite us in the sacred love
Of knowledge, truth, and Thee;
And let our hills and valleys shout
The songs of liberty.

4 Lord of the nations, thus to Thee
Our country we commend;
Be thou her refuge and her trust,
Her everlasting friend.
JOHN R. WREFORD, 1837. Abbr.

NATIONAL AND PATRIOTIC.

448 BATTLE HYMN OF THE REPUBLIC.
T. BRIGHAM BISHOP, 1858.

2 I have seen Him in the watch-fires of a hundred circling camps;
They have builded Him an altar in the evening dews and damps;
I can read His righteous sentence by the dim and flaring lamps:
His truth is marching on.

3 He has sounded forth the trumpet that shall never call retreat;
He is sifting out the hearts of men before His judgment-seat;
Oh, be swift my soul to answer Him! be jubilant, my feet!
Our God is marching on.

4 In the beauty of the lilies, Christ was born across the sea;
With a glory in His bosom, that transfigures you and me;
As He died to make men holy, let us die to make men free:
While God is marching on.

JULIA WARD HOWE. 1862.

THE PRAISE HYMNARY.

449 VALETE. L. M. 6l.   Sir ARTHUR S. SULLIVAN, 1874

1 God of our fath-ers, known of old; Lord of our far-flung bat-tle line,
De-neath whose aw-ful hand we hold Do-min-ion o-ver palm and pine;
Lord God of Hosts, be with us yet, Lest we for-get — lest we for-get!

2 Far-called our navies melt away;
 On dune and headland sinks the fire;
 Lo, all our pomp of yesterday
 Is one with Nineveh and Tyre!
 Judge of the Nations, spare us yet,
 Lest we forget — lest we forget!

3 If, drunk with sight of power, we loose
 Wild tongues that have not Thee in awe,
 Such boasting as the Gentiles use,
 Or lesser breeds without the law;
 Lord God of Hosts, be with us yet,
 Lest we forget — lest we forget!

4 For heathen heart that puts her trust
 In reeking tube and iron shard,
 All valiant dust that builds on dust,
 And guarding calls not Thee to guard;
 For frantic boast and foolish word,
 Thy mercy on Thy people, Lord.

RUDYARD KIPLING, 1897. Abbr.

NATIONAL AND PATRIOTIC.

450 COMMONWEALTH. P. M.
JOSIAH BOOTH.

When wilt Thou save the people? O God of mercy, when?
Not kings and lords, but nations! Not thrones and crowns, but men!
Flowers of Thy heart, O God, are they; Let them not pass, like weeds, away,
Their her-i-tage, a sun-less day. God save the peo-ple! A-MEN.

2 Shall crime bring crime forever,
   Strength aiding still the strong?
Is it Thy will, O Father,
   That man shall toil for wrong?
No, say Thy mountains; No, Thy skies;
Man's clouded sun shall brightly rise,
And songs ascend, instead of sighs.
   God save the people!

3 When wilt Thou save the people?
   O God of mercy, when?
The people, Lord, the people,
   Not thrones and crowns, but men!
God save the people; Thine they are,
Thy children, as Thine angels fair.
From vice, oppression, and despair,
   God save the people!

EBENEZER ELLIOTT.

NATIONAL AND PATRIOTIC.

THE STAR SPANGLED BANNER. — *Concluded.*

And the rock-ets' red glare, the bombs burst-ing in air,
Now it catch-es the gleam of the morn-ing's first beam,
No ref-uge could save the hire-ling and slave,
Then con-quer we must, for our cause it is just,

Gave proof through the night that our flag was still there.
In full glo-ry re-flect-ed, now shines on the stream;
From the ter-ror of flight, or the gloom of the grave;
And this be our mot-to: "In God is our trust!"

CHORUS. *ff*

Oh, say, does that star-span-gled ban-ner yet wave
'Tis the star-span-gled ban-ner, oh, long may it wave
And the star-span-gled ban-ner in tri-umph doth wave
And the star-span-gled ban-ner in tri-umph shall wave

O'er the land of the free, and the home of the brave?
O'er the land of the free, and the home of the brave!
O'er the land of the free, and the home of the brave!
O'er the land of the free, and the home of the brave!

FRANCIS S. KEY, 1814.

NATIONAL AND PATRIOTIC.

HAIL! COLUMBIA. — *Concluded.*

be our boast, Ev - er mind - ful what it cost,
cere and just, In heaven we place a man - ly trust, That
God like power, He gov - erns in the fear - ful hour Of

Ev - er grate - ful for the prize, Let its al - tar reach the skies.
truth and jus - tice may pre - vail, And ev - ery scheme of bond - age fail!
hor - rid war, or guides with ease, The hap - pier times of hon - est peace.

CHORUS.

Firm, u - nit - ed, let us be, Ral - lying round our lib - er - ty;
Firm, u - nit - ed, let us be, Ral - lying round our lib - er - ty;
Firm, u - nit - ed, let us be, Ral - lying round our lib - er - ty;

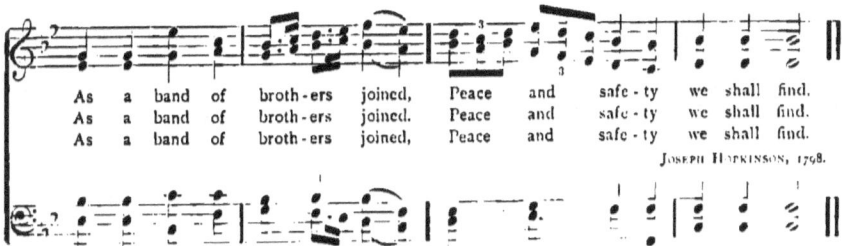

As a band of broth - ers joined, Peace and safe - ty we shall find.
As a band of broth - ers joined, Peace and safe - ty we shall find.
As a band of broth - ers joined, Peace and safe - ty we shall find.

JOSEPH HOPKINSON, 1798.

NATIONAL AND PATRIOTIC.

COLUMBIA, THE GEM OF THE OCEAN. — *Concluded.*

THE PRAISE HYMNARY.

454. PRECIOUS LIVES.
L. B. MARSHALL.

1 Breathe balmy airs, ye fragrant flowers,
O'er every silent sleeper's head;
Ye crystal dews and summer showers,
Dress in fresh green each lowly bed,
Ye crystal dews and summer showers,
Dress in fresh green each lowly bed.

Copyright, 1895, by SILVER, BURDETT & COMPANY.

2 Strew loving offerings o'er the brave,
 Their country's joy, their country's pride;
‖ For us their precious lives they gave;
 For Freedom's sacred cause they died.‖

3 Each cherished name its place shall hold,
 Like stars that gem the azure sky;
‖ Their deeds, on history's page unrolled,
 Are sealed for immortality.‖

4 Long, where on glory's field they fell,
 May Freedom's spotless banner wave;
‖ And fragrant tributes, grateful, tell,
 Where live the free, — where sleep the brave.‖

SAMUEL F. SMITH.

MEMORIAL DAY.

455 TROYTE'S CHANT. W. Hayes. Arr. by A. H. D. Troyte, 1857.

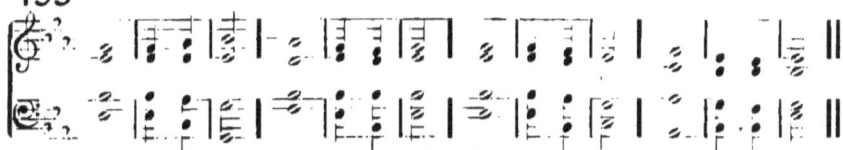

1 With silence only as their | bene- | diction, ‖ God's | angels | come ‖ Where, in the shadow of a great | afflic- | tion, ‖ The | soul sits | dumb. ‖
2 Yet would we say, what every | heart ap- | proveth, — ‖ Our | Father's | will, ‖ Calling to Him the dear ones | whom He | loveth, ‖ Is | mercy | still. ‖
3 Not upon us or ours the | solemn | angel ‖ Hath | evil | wrought; ‖ The funeral anthem is a | glad e- | vangel; ‖ The | good die | not! ‖
4 God calls our loved ones, but we | lose not | wholly ‖ What | He has | given; ‖ They live on earth in thought and | deed, as | truly ‖ As | in His | heaven. ‖

John G. Whittier.

456 BOYLSTON. S. M. Lowell Mason, 1832.

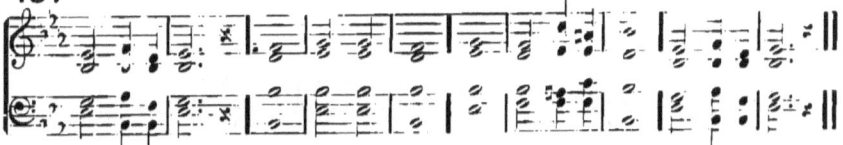

1 Strew all their graves with flowers, They for their coun-try died; And free-ly gave their lives for ours, Their country's hope and pride.

2 Bring flowers to deck each sod
Where rests their sacred dust;
Though gone from earth, they live to God,
Their everlasting trust!

3 Fearless, in freedom's cause
They suffered, toiled and bled;
And died obedient to her laws,
By truth and conscience led.

4 Oft as the year returns,
We o'er their graves shall weep,
And wreathe with flowers their funeral urns,
Their memory dear to keep.

5 Bring flowers of early spring
To deck each soldier's grave;
And summer's fragrant roses bring —
They died our land to save.

Jones Very.

457 THY WILL BE DONE. — Chant. Lowell Mason, 1845.

1 "Thy will be | done!" ‖ In devious way The hurrying stream of | life may run; ‖ Yet still our grateful hearts shall say,] "Thy will be | done."
2 "Thy will be | done!" ‖ If o'er us shine A gladdening and a | prosperous | sun, ‖ This prayer will make it more divine —] "Thy will be | done!"
3 "Thy will be | done!" ‖ Though shrouded o'er Our path with | gloom, ‖ one comfort — one ‖ Is ours: — to breathe, while we adore. | "Thy will be | done."

John Bowring, 1825.

THE PRAISE HYMNARY.

458 CHRISTUS. 8s. 7s. 6 l.   ARTHUR L. BROWN, 1898.

1. Sing, ye faithful, sing with gladness! Wake your noblest, sweetest strain! With the praises of your Saviour

Let His house resound a-gain! Him let all your mus-ic hon-or, And your songs ex-alt His reign!

Used by per.

2 Sing how He came forth from heaven,
  Bowed Himself to Bethlehem's cave
  Stooped to wear the servant's vesture,
  Bore the pain, the cross, the grave,
  Passed within the gates of darkness,
  Thence His banished ones to save!

3 So He tasted death for all men,
  He of all mankind the Head,
  Sinless One among the sinful,
  Prince of life among the dead;
  So He wrought the full redemption,
  And the captor captive led.

4 Now on high, yet ever with us,
  From His Father's throne, the Son
  Rules and guides the world He ransomed,
  Till the appointed work be done,
  Till He see, renewed and perfect,
  All things gathered into one.

5 Day of promised restitution!
  Fruit of all His sorrows past!
  When the crown of His dominion
  He before the throne shall cast,
  And throughout the wide creation
  God be "all in all" at last.
                JOHN ELLERTON, 1870.

459 OLD HUNDRED. L. M.   LOUIS BOURGEOIS, 1551.

Praise God from whom all blessings flow;
  Praise Him, all creatures here below;
Praise Him above, ye heavenly host;
  Praise Fa-ther, Son, and Ho-ly Ghost.
                THOMAS KEN, 1709.

INDEX OF FIRST LINES.

HYMNS.

	Number		Number
A BROKEN heart, my God	347	Come, let us join our cheerful songs	124
A glory gilds the sacred page	382	Come, let us join our songs of praise	96
A mighty fortress is our God	2	Come, O my soul, in sacred lays	111
A parting hymn we sing	408	Come, sacred Spirit, from above	311
A rock in the wilderness welcomed	11	Come, sound His praise abroad	215
Abide with me	271	Come, Thou Almighty King	89
According to Thy gracious word	410	Come, Thou fount of every blessing	158
Adown the mountain's glowing side	419	Come unto Me, ye weary	332
Again returns the day	251	Come we who love the Lord	25
Again the Lord of light and life	105	Come, ye disconsolate	145
Alas! and did my Saviour bleed?	296	Come ye that know and fear	213
All hail the power of Jesus' name!	58	Cross, reproach and tribulation	5
Always with us	179	Crown Him with many crowns	305
Amazing grace, how sweet the sound	196	Crown His head with endless blessing	159
Am I a soldier of the cross?	132		
And now, another week begins	257	DRAWN to the Cross	325
And now we rise, the symbols disappear	407		
Anywhere with Jesus	364	ETERNAL God, we come to Thee	417
Arise, ye people, and adore	16	Eternal Source of life and light	131
Art thou weary?	334	Eternal Spirit, we confess	133
As flows the river, calm and deep	144	Every morning, mercies new	265
Ashamed of Christ! our souls disdain	401	Exalted Prince of life, we own	28
As the sun doth daily rise	264		
As when in silence, vernal showers	136	FATHER, now we hear Thee calling	415
As with gladness, men of old	288	Father of mercies! God of love	162
Awake and sing the song	32	Father of mercies, in Thy word	383
Awake, my soul, and with the sun	269	Father, Thine elect who lovest	109
Awake, my soul, to joyful lays	148	Father, whate'er of earthly bliss	371
Awake, my tongue, thy tribute bring	53	Forever with the Lord	50
Awake, ye saints, awake	246	Forward! be our watchword	230
		For what shall I praise Thee?	66
BE Thou exalted, O my God	112	Friend of sinners! Lord of glory!	76
Begin, my tongue, some heavenly theme	211	From every place below the skies	67
Behold a Stranger at the door	328	From Greenland's icy mountains	421
Behold the glories of the Lamb	94		
Bless, Lord, this household and its head	418	GIVE to the winds thy fears	233
Bless, O my soul, the Living God	98	Glorious things of thee are spoken	6
Blest be the tie that binds	166	Glory be to God the Father	7
Blest be Thou, O God of Israel!	110	Glory, glory everlasting	15
Blest day of God!	254	Glory to God on high	86
Blest feast of love divine!	409	Glory to God! peace on the earth	201
Blest hour! when mortal man	256	Glory to God! Who deigns to bless	163
Book of grace, and book of glory	381	Glory to the Almighty Father	178
Break forth, ye heavens, in song	85	Glory to Thee, my God	274
Break, new-born year	432	Go, tune thy voice to sacred song	236
Breathe on me, Breath of God	342	God Almighty and All-seeing!	223
By Christ redeemed, in Christ restored	405	God be with you till we meet	438
		God calling yet!	327
CENTER of our hopes Thou art	71	God Eternal, Lord of all	21
Children of the Heavenly King	218	God is love, that anthem olden	14
Christ the Lord is risen	299	God is the fountain whence	185
Christ to heaven is gone before	304	God is the refuge of His saints	52
Christ whose glory fills the skies	266	God of my life! thro' all my days	100
Come, all ye saints of God	87	God of our salvation	220
Come, Christians, brethren, ere we part	69	God's glory is a wondrous thing	210
Come, gracious Spirit, Heavenly Dove	310	Gracious Spirit, Love divine	312
Come, Holy One, in love descending	313	Great God, our Sovereign King	396
Come, Jesus, Redeemer!	65	Great God! to Thee my evening song	275
Come, Kingdom of our God	426	Great peace have they who love Thy law	141
Come, let us adore Him!	64	Guide me, O Thou great Jehovah	369

INDEX OF FIRST LINES.

First Line	Number
HAIL the day that sees Him rise	303
Hail, Thou once despisèd Jesus	152
Hail to the Sabbath day!	252
Hallelujah! sing to Jesus	143
Hark, hark my soul!	376
Hark! ten thousand harps	56
Hark! the herald angels sing!	284
Hark! the sound of holy voices	45
Hark! what mean these holy voices?	289
Heal me, O my Saviour	340
Heavenly Shepherd, guide us	154
He has come! the Christ of God	283
He leadeth me!	225
Here, Saviour, do we come	398
Holy and reverend is the name	209
Holy, holy, holy Lord, *for Thy glorious*	78
Holy, holy, holy, Lord God Almighty	260
Hosanna! raise the pealing hymn	36
How blest the heart that knows	202
How firm a foundation	120
How gentle God's commands	198
How goodly is Thy church	387
How lovely are Thy dwellings	389
How precious is the book divine	380
How rich Thy favors, God of grace	17
How sweet, how heavenly is the sight	200
How sweet the name of Jesus sounds	151
How sweet the praise	172
I AM dwelling on the mountain	170
I am weary of my sin	344
I bless the Christ of God	214
I could not do without Thee	206
I do not ask that life may be	352
I heard a voice, the sweetest voice	62
I heard the voice of Jesus say	169
I hunger, and I thirst	406
I lay my sins on Jesus	349
I love Thy kingdom, Lord	390
I love to steal awhile away	205
I need Thee, precious Jesus	350
I was a wandering sheep	366
I worship Thee, sweet will of God	139
I would love Thee, God and Father	370
I 'm not ashamed to own my Lord!	238
In every trouble, sharp and strong	239
In heavenly love abiding	207
In sleep's serene oblivion	1
In the Cross of Christ, I glory	228
It came upon the midnight clear	285
JERUSALEM the golden	127
Jesus, and shall it ever be?	240
Jesus, heed me, lost and dying	346
Jesus, I love Thy charming name	124
Jesus, I my cross have taken	360
Jesus lives! no longer now	300
Jesus, lover of my soul	183
Jesus, Saviour, pilot me	191
Jesus shall reign where'er the sun	26
Jesus, the very thought is sweet	318
Jesus, the very thought of Thee	123
Jesus, Thou Joy of loving hearts	317
Jesus, Thy name I love	321
Jesus, with Thy church abide	385
Joy to the world, the Lord is come!	286
Just as I am	338
Just as Thou art	339
KEEP us, Lord, oh, keep us ever	221
LEAD, kindly light	174
Leave it with God	354
Let children hear the mighty deeds	102
Let every heart and tongue	35
Let saints below in concert sing	197
Let songs of praises fill the sky	103
Let the still air rejoice	90
Let us awake our joys	88
Lift up to God the voice of praise	119
Like the eagle, upward, onward	229
Lo! a loving friend is waiting	336
Look, from Thy sphere of endless day	424
Look, ye saints!	307
Lord, dismiss us, with Thy blessing, Bid us	155
Lord, dismiss us . . . Fill our hearts	222
Lord, I am Thine, and in Thy aid	403
Lord, I perish! save, I cried	226
Lord, in this Thy mercy's day	341
Lord Jesus, when we stand afar	294
Lord of all being; thronèd afar	171
Lord of hosts! to Thee we raise	393
Lord of mercy and of might	73
Lord, Thy glory fills the heavens	4
Lord, Thy word abideth	384
Lord, we would come before Thee	414
Lord, while for all mankind we pray	447
Lord, with glowing heart I 'd praise Thee	57
Love Divine, all love excelling	142
MAJESTIC sweetness sits enthroned	18
May the grace of Christ the Saviour	195
Midst sorrow and care	326
Mine eyes and my desire	38
More like Jesus would I be	351
More love to Thee, O Christ	358
Mortals, awake, with angels join	287
Must Jesus bear the cross alone?	186
My days are gliding swiftly by	375
My faith looks up to Thee	320
My God, how endless is Thy love	263
My God, my King, Thy various praise	81
My God, my boundless love	322
My gracious Redeemer, I love!	173
My hope is built on nothing less	125
My Jesus, as Thou wilt	156
My life, my love, I give to Thee	357
My Saviour, my Almighty Friend	199
My soul complete in Jesus stands	42
My soul, it is thy God	51
My soul shall praise Thee	201
NEARER, my God, to Thee	359
No change of time shall ever shock	241
None but Christ, His merit hides me	44
Not only for one task sublime	37
Now be my heart inspired to sing	31
Now begin the heavenly theme	77
Now I have found a Friend	319
Now I have found the ground	126
Now in a song of grateful praise	40
Now in parting, Father, bless us	437
Now let our souls on wings sublime	83
Now let our voices join	33
Now may He, who from the dead	436
Now thank we all our God	235
Now to the Lord, a noble song	135
Now when the dusky shades of night	258
Now with creation's morning song	261
O DAY of rest and gladness	249
O Father, Son, and Holy Ghost	400
O God, my heart is fully bent	19
O God, we praise Thee and confess	237
O God, who rulest all our days	446
O happy day that fixed my choice	203
O Holy Saviour! Friend unseen	324
O Jesus Christ, grow Thou in me	363

186

INDEX OF FIRST LINES.

First Line	Number
O Jesus, I have promised	355
O Jesus, King most wonderful	243
O Jesus, our salvation	333
O Jesus! the Giver of all we enjoy	121
O Jesus, Thou art standing	353
O little town of Bethlehem!	282
O Lord, go with me thro' this day	262
O Lord, I am not worthy	343
O Lord our God, arise	427
O Lord, while we confess the worth	399
O Love Divine!	224
O Paradise!	377
O sacred head, now wounded	293
O Son of Man, Thyself hast proved	309
O starry night!	292
O Thou, to whom a thousand years	395
O Thou, whose own vast temple stands	392
O worship the King, all glorious	92
O Zion, tune thy voice	108
Of Him who did salvation bring	149
Oh, could I speak the matchless worth	323
Oh, do not let the word depart	329
Oh, for a heart to praise my God	138
Oh, for a shout of sacred joy!	244
Oh, give thanks to Him who made	70
Oh, how happy are they	204
Oh, render thanks to God above	101
Oh, sing amid the storm	106
Oh, sweetly breathe the lyres above	68
Oh, tell me, Thou life and delight	189
Oh! where are kings and empires now?	386
Oh, will ye now receive Him?	330
On Jordan's rugged banks I stand	167
One life to live, just one below	420
One sweetly solemn thought	374
One there is above all others	12
Onward, Christian soldiers	190
Our blest Redeemer, ere He died	314
Our country's voice is pleading	422
Our day of praise is done	280
Pass me not!	337
Pleasant are Thy courts above	8
Praise on Thee, in Zion's gates	23
Praise our glorious King and Lord	79
Praise the Lord, His glories show	1
Praise the Lord, when blushing morning	270
Praise the Lord, ye heavens, adore Him	74
Praise the Saviour, ye who know Him	59
Praise to Thee, Thou great creator	55
Praise ye the Lord, who is King	137
Prepare us, Lord, to view Thy Cross	411
Prince of Peace, control my will	176
Raise your triumphant songs	184
Rejoice, and be glad	147
Rejoice in God, alway	39
Rejoice to-day with one accord	3
Rise, my soul, and stretch thy wings	219
Rock of ages, cleft for me!	122
Safe in the arms of Jesus	365
Saviour, again to Thy dear name	434
Saviour, blessed Saviour	192
Saviour! breathe an evening blessing	277
Saviour, send a blessing to us	13
Saviour, teach me, day by day	227
Saviour, Thy gentle voice	47
Saviour, when in dust to Thee	9
Servants of God! in joyful lays	99
Sing, all ye ransomed of the Lord	117
Sing of Jesus, sing forever	60
Sing the Almighty power of God	48
Sing, ye faithful	458
Softly now the light of day	278
Sons of freemen! ever	231
Spirit of peace! Celestial Dove	315
Standing at the portal	433
Stand up, stand up, for Jesus!	429
Stealing from the world away	279
Sun of my soul	272
Sweet are the promises	372
Sweet is the task, O Lord	253
Sweet is Thy mercy, Lord	348
Sweet the moments, rich in blessing	177
Sweetly sing	161
Swell the anthem, raise the song	20
Take courage, O ye servants	232
Take my life and let it be	361
Take, my soul, thy full salvation	153
Tarry with me, O my Saviour	276
Tell me the old, old story	345
Ten thousand times ten thousand	378
Thank and praise Jehovah's name	24
The bird let loose in eastern skies	368
The corn is ripe for reaping	431
The day, O Lord, is spent	281
The head that once was crowned	61
The heavens declare His glory	128
The King of Love my Shepherd is	316
The Lord is King! lift up thy voice	29
The Lord is my Shepherd	188
The mercies of my God and King	63
The morning light is breaking	430
The rosy morn has robed the sky	302
The sands of time are sinking	372
The Saviour! Oh, what endless charms	95
The Son of God goes forth to war	428
The strife is o'er, the battle done	301
The winds that career o'er the	10
Thee to laud in songs divine	80
Thee we adore, eternal Lord!	30
There is a blessèd home	157
There is a fold whence none can stray	307
There is a fountain filled with blood	298
There is a land of pure delight	168
There is a name I love to hear	150
There is a voice in every gale	82
There is an hour of peaceful rest	217
There's a wideness in God's mercy	180
There's nothing bright, above, below	115
Thine forever, thine forever!	75
Thine, Thine forever	362
Thou art gone up on high	306
Thou dear Redeemer, dying Lamb	187
Thou everliving Corner Stone	391
Thou hidden love of God	297
Thou very present aid	164
Thou, whose almighty Word	91
Three in One, and One in Three	54
Through the heaven new heaven	27
Thus far, the Lord hath led me on	273
Thy holy day's returning	250
Thy Word is like a deep, deep mine	379
'T is God the Father, we adore	402
To God, the great and ever blest	41
To God the only-wise	107
To our Redeemer's glorious name	116
To praise our Shepherd's care	34
To Thee, my Shepherd and my Lord	49
To us the light of truth display	134
To-day the Saviour calls	335
Together with these symbols, Lord	412
Uplift the banner! let it float	425

INDEX OF SUBJECTS.

	Number		Number
Wait, my soul, upon the Lord	175	With joyful praise and homage	130
We dedicate this house to Thee	394	With willing hearts we tread	397
Welcome, delightful morn	248	Worthy the Lamb of boundless sway	43
Welcome, O Saviour! to my heart	404	Worship, honor, glory, blessing	193
We praise Thee, Lord, with earliest morning ray	242	Would I might love Thee more!	46
We praise Thee, O God	146		
What a friend we have in Jesus	182	Ye choirs of new Jerusalem	308
What cheering words are these?	165	Ye Christian heralds, go, proclaim	423
What grace, O Lord, and beauty shone	97	Ye messengers of Christ!	388
When as returns this solemn day	255	Ye saints, your music bring	416
When human hopes all wither	356	Ye servants of God, your Master proclaim	93
When I survey the wondrous cross	295	Ye sons of Light and heirs of Truth	413
When shall the voice of singing?	208	Yes, for me, for me He careth	181
Why should the children of a King?	118		
Wilt Thou me guide?	216	Zion, awake! thy strength renew	113

CHANTS.

And now we rise	407	Thy will be done	457
Come unto Me	331	With silence only as their benediction	455
Our Father, who art in heaven	267		

DOXOLOGIES.

Let God the Father and the Son	212	Sing we to our God above	22
O God, forever blest,	247	To Father, Son, and Holy Ghost L. M. 84, C. M. 140 and	245
Praise God from whom all blessings flow	459	To Father, Son, and Spirit blest	435
Praise the Father, earth and heaven	194	To God the Father, God the Son	114
Praise the God of all creation	160	To God the Father, Son	234 and 442
Praise the name of God most High	72	To Thee be praise forever	129

GLORIAS.

Glory be to God on High	290	Glory be to the Father	259

NATIONAL AND PATRIOTIC.

Breathe, balmy airs	454	My country, 'tis of thee	440
From everlasting, God	439	O Columbia, the gem of the ocean	453
God bless our native land	441	O God, beneath Thy guiding hand	444
God of our fathers! Bless	443	O, say, can you see?	451
God of our fathers, known of old	449	Our Fathers' God, from ancient days	445
Hail! Columbia, happy land	452	Strew all their graves with flowers	456
Mine eyes have seen the glory	448	When wilt Thou save the people?	450

INDEX OF SUBJECTS.

The figures refer to Hymn numbers.

Adoration, 10, 64, 211.

Baptism, 397 to 404.

Chants (see Chants in First Lines).
Christ, Born, 282 to 292.
   Coming, 208.
   Crowned and Enthroned, 61, 96, 103, 104, 159, 171, 172, 305 to 309.
   King (The), 32.
   Only, 44, 124, 207, 208, 209.
   Risen, 299 to 304.
   Suffering, 293 to 298.
   Trust in, 316 to 326, 364 to 373.
Church (The), 6, 108, 113, 385 to 395.
Communion (see Lord's Supper).
Conflict, 132, 134, 190, 231, 235, 236.
Consecration, 5, 68, 138, 139, 156, 165, 176, 177, 186, 189, 203, 231, 351 to 363.

Consolation, 4, 326.
Constancy, 239, 241, 242.
Creator (The), 55, 70, 90, 91, 111, 128, 178.
Cross (The), 15, 109, 177, 186, 228, 229, 416.

Dedication, 391 to 396.
Deliverance, 118.
Devotion, 159, 163, 179, 228 (see also Consecration).
Dismission (see Parting Hymns).
Doxologies (see Doxologies in First Lines).

Encouragement, 232, 233, 235 to 237.
Eternity, 82 (see also Heaven).
Evening, 271 to 281 (see Morning and Evening).

Faith, 106, 120, 125, 126, 229, 232, 235, 241, 316 to 326, 364 to 373.
Fellowship, 50, 166, 179, 181, 182, 197, 200, 205, 206, 207, 221, 225, 238, 240.

General Praise (see Praise).
God, 2, 10, 11, 14, 17, 19, 20, 21, 23, 33, 39, 41, 48, 51, 53, 66, 67, 81, 85, 86, 89, 92, 98, 108, 109, 110, 112, 119, 161, 162, 163, 178, 185, 193, 210, 215, 233, 235, 237.
God's Blessing, 139, 188.
   Care, 192, 225, 226.
   Creations, 70.
   Deliverance, 118.
   Fellowship, 75, 132, 169, 225, 226.
   Friendship, 12.
   Goodness, 121.
   Glory, 4, 6, 7, 15, 31, 64, 79, 99, 112, 166, 174, 181.

ALPHABETICAL LIST OF TUNES.

God's Grace, 51, 136, 196, 197, 199, 211, 226, 227.
Greatness, 10, 11, 41, 53, 175.
Help, 167.
Holiness, 110.
Kindness, 34, 201, 214.
Love, 14, 32, 89, 138, 145, 147, 196.
Majesty, 18, 26, 111.
Mercy, 24, 63, 183.
Peace, 144, 205.
Power, 48, 115, 140.
Wisdom, 107.
Grace (see God's Grace).
Guidance, 157, 177, 191, 194, 216, 217.

HEAVEN, 8, 27, 45, 50, 83, 94, 127, 157, 167, 168, 170, 219, 374 to 378.
Holy Spirit, 136, 142, 158, 231, 310 to 315.

INVITATION, 148, 327 to 336.
Invocation for
Blessing, 13, 38.
Grace, 246 (see God's Grace).
Guidance, 157, 177, 191, 194, 216, 217.
Help, 37, 231.
Inspiration, 71, 73, 161.
Knowledge, 137.
Love, 46.
Presence of God, 90, 221, 224.
Jesus, 63.
The Spirit (see Holy Spirit).
Success, 37.

JESUS, 12, 15, 26, 42, 46, 56, 58, 60, 65, 77, 87, 88, 97, 121, 123, 124, 143, 146, 150, 151, 152, 165.
Jesus' Beauty, 62, 97.
Care, 184.
Cross, 109, 180, 229 (see also Sufferings of Christ).
Friendship, 185.

Jesus' Guidance, 230.
Name, 153, 154, 190.
Power, 58, 146, 162.
Praise, 60, 123, 132.
Salvation, 227.
Support, 172, 173.
Triumph, 61, 88.
Universal Reign, 61.
Worship, 155, 244.
Joy, 108, 133, 156 (see also Birth of Christ).

LAMB (The), 32, 43, 94.
Lord (The), 1, 3, 4, 16, 29, 30, 36, 38, 40, 57, 74, 78, 80, 135, 137, 175, 209.
Lord's Day (The), 246 to 257.
Lord's Prayer (The), 267.
Lord's Supper (The), 405 to 412.
Love, 14, 25, 46, 115, 142, 144, 150, 162, 184, 209, 211, 213, 224, 227.

MEETING and Parting (see Parting Hymns).
Memorial Day, 454 to 457.
Missions, 87, 91, 93, 102, 108, 113, 215, 230, 421 to 430.
Foreign, 421, 423, 429, 430.
Home, 422, 424, 429.
Morning and Evening, 258 to 281.
Morning, 258 to 270.

NATIONAL and Patriotic, 439 to 457.
Flag (The), 451.
Memorial Day, 454 to 457.
Our Country, 439 to 441, 443 to 447.

OCCASIONAL, 413 to 420, 431.
Anniversary, 431, 432, 433.
Commencement, 413 to 415.
Corner Stone, 391, 392.
Dedication, 391 to 396.
Installation and Recognition, 417, 418.

Occasional.
Memorial Day, 454 to 457.
National and Patriotic, 439 to 457.
New Year, 433.
Ordination, 413, 417 to 420.
Thanksgiving, 431, 432.

PARTING Hymns, 69, 154, 155, 158, 194, 220, 221, 222, 223, 434 to 438.
(See also Doxologies in First Lines.)
Patriotic (see National and Patriotic).
Peace with God, 141, 198, 202, 204.
Praise.
General, 1 to 244, 458.
(See God, Christ, Jesus, and Subdivisions.)
Perpetual, 99, 100, 102, 201.
United, 200, 238.
Prayer, 9, 13, 37, 71, 73, 75, 91, 121, 130, 131, 134, 138, 174, 205.

REDEEMER (The), 116 to 119, 147 to 149, 153, 156, 173, 187.
(See also Christ, Jesus, Saviour.)
Refuge, 42, 47, 52, 62, 122, 124, 125, 126, 143, 148, 164, 169, 178, 180, 183, 186, 193, 217, 240.
Repentance, 338 to 350.

SAFETY (see Refuge and Security).
Saviour (The), 15, 18, 28, 31, 35, 47, 59, 76, 95, 149, 192, 199, 218, 227, 236.
Scriptures (The), 379 to 384.
Security, 2, 5, 122, 127, 128.

TRINITY (The) (see Doxologies in First Lines).
Trust (see Faith).

UNION with Christ (see Christ).

WARFARE, 190. (See also Conflict.)
Worship, 8, 21, 92, 93, 143, 216.

ALPHABETICAL LIST OF TUNES.

	PAGE		PAGE		PAGE
ABERHONDDU. 7s. 6s. D.	137	BALERMA. C. M.	51	Carol. C. M. D.	106
Adoration. 12s. 11s.	12	Bartimeus. 8s. 7s.	22	Casket. C. M.	150
Adrian. S. M.	156	Battle Hymn of the Republic	173	Caton. L. M.	118
Alford. P. M.	149	Beecher. 8s. 7s. D.	53	Cecilia. 8s. 7s.	120
All for Christ. 7s. 4l.	139	Bemerton. C. M.	172	Cephas. C. M.	90
Amazing Grace. C. M.	74	Benediction Chant	158	Christmas. C. M.	49
America. 6s. 4s.	170	Benedictus. S. M.	130	Christus. 8s. 7s. 6 l.	184
Amsterdam. 7s. 6s. D.	82	Bera. L. M.	124	Clyde. 8s. 4s.	150
Antioch. C. M.	107	Bethlehem. P. M.	104	Columbia, the Gem of	180
Anywhere with Jesus	140	Blessed Thought. L. M. D.	84	Comfort. 6s. 9s.	77
Ariel. C. P. M.	122	Blest Day. C. M.	95	Come let us adore Him. 11s.	28
Arlington. C. M.	61	Blumenthal. 7s. D.	11	Come unto Me. (Chant)	125
Armstrong. 8s. 7s. D.	68	Boardman. C. M.	43	Come unto Me. (Hymn) 7s. 6s. D.	126
Ashwell. L. M.	124	Bowring. 8s. 7s.	73	Come Ye Disconsolate. 11s. 10s.	54
At the Cross. C. M.	112	Boylston. S. M.	183	Conqueror. P. M.	115
Attitude. 7s. 6s. D.	135	Braden. S. M.	103	Consolation. 5s. 9s.	123
Aulé. 7s. 6s.	130	Bradford. C. M.	46	Coronation. C. M.	26
Aurelia. 7s. 6s. D.	133			Crucifix. 7s. 6l.	110
Austrian Hymn. 8s. 7s. D.	41	CAMBRIDGE. C. M.	157		
Autumn. 8s. 7s. D.	58	Canonbury. L. M.	120	DAY of Rest. 7s. 6s. D.	93
Azmon. C. M.	139	Capetown. 7s. 5s.	24	Dedham. C. M.	159

ALPHABETICAL LIST OF TUNES.

Tune	Page
De Fleury. 8s. D.	65
Dennis. S. M.	73
Desire. L. M.	95
Diademata. S. M. D.	116
Dix. 7s. 6 l.	107
Dolomite. 6s.	158
Doncaster. L. M.	111
Dover. S. M.	163
Downs. C. M.	37
Dudley. L. M.	98
Duke Street. L. M.	50
Dundee. C. M.	151
ECCLESIA. 8s. 7s. D.	10
Echo Hymn. 6s. 4s.	119
Ellacombe. C. M. D.	164
Elation. S. M.	20
Ellers. 10s.	168
Ellesdie. 8s. 7s. D.	67
Elvria. 7s. 4 l.	118
Emmanuel. C. M.	136
Ernan. 10s.	94
Essex. 7s. 5 l.	114
Evan. C. M.	73
Evarts. 7s. 6s. D.	78
Evening Hymn. L. M.	102
Eventide. 10s.	101
Ewing. 7s. 6s. D.	48
FABEN. 8s. 7s. D.	9
Federal Street. L. M.	18
Ferguson. S. M.	70
Ferrier. 7s. 4 l.	115
Flemming. 8s. 6s.	123
Forward, the Watchword. 6s. 5s. D.	86
Fountain.	113
Freeman. 8s. 6s.	129
GEER. C. M.	142
Germany. L. M.	100
Gloria Patri. (Chant).	96
Glory be to God. (Chant)	108
Glory to God. P. M.	109
God be with You	169
God of Our Fathers. P. M.	171
Golden Hill. S. M.	19
Gould. C. M.	119
Grace is Free. 7s. 4 l.	85
Gratitude. L. M.	38
Greenville. 8s. 7s. 4s.	83
HAIL, Columbia	178
Halladale. 8s. 7s. D.	60
Hanford. P. M.	158
Happy Day. L. M.	76
Harwell. 8s. 7s. D.	25
Haynes. 7s. 3 l.	129
Hebron. L. M.	97
Hendon. 7s. 4 l.	32
Herald Angels. 7s. D.	105
Holland. L. M. D.	27
Holley. 7s. 4 l.	123
Holy Cross. C. M.	91
Holy Voices. 8s. 7s. D.	108
Homeward. 7s. 6 l.	45
Horton. 7s.	66
Hosanna. C. M.	20
How I Love Jesus. C. M.	57
Hursley. L. M.	101
I'LL Live for Him	137
Invitation. P. M.	127
Invocation. 7s. 4 l.	168
Irene. P. M.	132
Italian Hymn. 6s. 4s.	34
JESUS, My Lord. 6s. 4s.	22
Jesus shall Reign. L. M. D.	17
Jewett. 6s. D.	59
KELSO. 7s. 6 l.	99
Kentucky. S. M.	62
Kimmel. 11s.	44
Kingsley. L. M.	161
LAND of Beulah. 8s. 7s. D.	64
Leave it with God	136
Lebanon. S. M. D.	142
Lenox. H. M.	92
Leominster. S. M. D.	146
Lichner. S. M.	23
Lischer. H. M.	40
Litlington Tower. L. M.	110
Louvan. L. M.	65
Loving Kindness. L. M.	56
Luther. P. M.	8
Lux Benigna. 10s. 4s. 10s.	66
Lyons. 10s. 11s.	36
MAITLAND. C. M.	70
Manoah. C. M.	79
Marching as to War. 6s. 5s. D.	72
Martyn. 7s. D.	69
Missionary Chant. L. M.	161
Missionary Hymn. 7s. 6s. D.	162
Monsell. S. M.	132
More Like Jesus. 7s. D.	134
Morgan. 10s.	81
Morgan Park. C. M. D.	155
Morning Praise. 11s. 10s.	96
Mornington. S. M.	94
NAOMI. C. M.	143
Nativity. C. M.	154
Navarre. 7s. 4 l.	98
Nettleton. 8s. 7s. D.	60
Nicæa. P. M.	97
Norwood. S. M.	87
Nottingham, C. M.	166
Nun Danket. P. M.	88
Nuremberg. 7s. 4 l.	15
OAK. 6s. 4s.	138
Offered Mercy. P. M.	125
Old Hundred. L. M.	184
Old, Old Story. 7s. 6s. D.	131
Olivet. 6s. 4s.	121
Olmutz. S. M.	159
Onset. C. M.	49
Opening Year. 6s. 5s. 12 l.	167
Ortonville. C. M.	14
PARADISE. P. M.	148
Park Street. L. M.	42
Pass Me Not	128
Peace. C. M.	52
Pelton. S. M.	40
Petrox. 6s.	151
Pilgrims. P. M.	147
Pilot. 7s. 6 l.	72
Pleyel's Hymn. 7s. 4 l.	82
Portugese Hymn. 11s.	44
Praise. P. M.	26
Praise the Lord. 7s. 4s.	7
Praise Ye the Lord	51
Praise Song. S. M. D.	80
Praises to Our King. 6s. 5s. D.	73
Precious Lives	182
RATHBUN. 8s. 7s.	85
Red, White and Blue	180
Refuge. 7s. D.	69
Retrospect. 7s. 6s. D.	166
Rockingham. L. M.	160
Rothwell. L. M.	163
Russia. 10s.	91
Rutherford. P. M.	145
SABBATH. 7s. 6 l.	30
Safe in the Arms of Jesus	141
Seelye. 8s. 7s.	100
Seymour. 7s. 4 l.	154
Sicilian Hymn. 8s. 7s. 4s.	13
Sing the Almighty Power. C. M.	23
Snelling. L M, D.	47
Star of Bethlehem. L. M. D.	21
Star-spangled Banner	176
State Street. S. M.	152
Stephanos. P. M.	127
Still Water. 11s. 10s.	71
Stockwell. 8s. 7s.	102
St. Agnes. C. M.	117
St. Albinus. 7s. 8s.	114
St. Alkmund. L. M.	33
St. Ann's. C. M.	152
St. Basil. 7s. 3 l.	152
St. Crispin. L. M.	132
St. Thomas. S. M.	153
Sweetly Sing	61
TAMWORTH. 8s. 7s. 4s.	117
Tappan. C. M. 5 l.	89
Thatcher. S. M.	62
The Grateful Song. L. M.	29
The Lord's Prayer (Chant)	99
The Lord is With Thee. 7s. 6s.	87
The Love of God to Me	54
The Peace of God. P. M.	76
Thy Will be Done. (Chant)	183
To-Day. 6s. 4s.	127
Toplady. 7s. 6 l.	45
Troyte. (Chant)	183
VALENTIA. C. M.	157
Valete. L. M. 6 l.	174
Varina. C. M. D.	63
Vaughn. C. M.	134
Vesper. 8s. 7s. 4s.	10
WALMER ROAD. C. M. D.	153
Ward. L. M.	24
Warwick. C. M.	39
Wavertree. L. M. 6 l.	113
Weariness. 7s. 4 l.	130
Webb. 7s. 6s. D.	165
We Praise Thee Again. 10s. 11s.	55
We're marching to Zion	16
Where He Leads, I'll Follow	144
Wilmot. 8s. 7s.	31
Wondrous Cross. L. M.	111
Woodland. C. M. 5 l.	81
Woodstock. C. M.	77
Woodworth. L. M.	90
ZION. 8s. 7s. 4s.	143

INDEX OF AUTHORS OF HYMNS.

Adams, Mrs. Sarah F., 359.
Alford, Henry, 230, 378.
Allen, George N., 186.
Allen, James, 86, 177.
Anderson, Mrs. Maria F., 422.
Anstice, Joseph, 309.
Archbald, E. P., 10.
Auber, Harriet, 16, 253, 314.

Bacon, Leonard, 444.
Baker, Sir Henry W., 3, 157, 316, 384.
Bakewell, John, 152.
Ballard, Addison, 330.
Barbauld, Mrs. Anna L., 105, 255.
Barber, Mary A. S., 176.
Baring-Gould, Sabine, 190.
Bartlett, Franklin W., 446.
Bathurst, William H., 178.
Beddome, Benjamin, 398.
Bernard of Clairvaux, tr., 123, 149, 243, 293, 317.
Bernard of Cluny, 127.
Bickersteth, Edward H., 247, 377.
Bickersteth, John, 154.
Blackburn, Alexander, 396.
Blacklock, Thomas, 111.
Bode, John E., 355.
Boden, James, 87.
Bonar, Horatius, 7, 147, 169, 181, 214, 229, 265, 283, 349, 366, 407, 437.
Bourne, Hugh, 404.
Bourne, Wm. Oland, 417.
Bowly, Mary, 399.
Bowring, Sir John, 228, 457.
Bridges, Mathew, 305.
Brooks, Charles T., 441.
Brooks, Phillips, 282.
Brotherton, Alice W., 418.
Brown, Jessie H., 364.
Brown, Mrs. Phoebe H., 205.
Browne, S., 134, 310, 435.
Bryant, William C., 392, 424.
Bullfinch, Stephen G., 252.
Burder, George, 213.
Butler, Nathaniel, 395.

Cary, Phoebe, 374.
Cawood, John, 289.
Cennick, John, 187, 218, 412.
Cobb, W. H., 391.
Conder, Josiah, 23, 29, 70, 128, 160.
Cook, William, 302.
Cotterill, Thomas, 30, 103, 246, 411.
Cousin, Mrs. Anne R., 44, 373.
Cowper, William, 298, 382.
Coxe, Arthur C., 386.
Crosby, Fanny J., 337, 351, 365.

Deck, James G., 321.
Denny, Sir Edward, 97, 409.
Dix, William C., 143, 288, 332.
Doane, George W., 278, 425.

Doddridge, Philip, 17, 28, 33, 100, 108, 117, 124, 131, 168, 203, 311.
Draper, Bourne Hall, 423.
Dudley, James H., 262.
Duffield, George, 429.
Dundee, Elsie, 202.
Dwight, John S., 441.
Dwight, Timothy, 390.

East, John, 367.
Eddy, Z., 85.
Edmeston, James, 208, 277.
Ellerton, John, 280, 434, 458.
Elliott, Charlotte, 324, 338, 356.
Elliott, Ebenezer, 450.

Faber, Frederick W., 139, 180, 210, 376, 377.
Fawcett, John, 55, 166, 222, 380.
Francis, Benjamin, 173, 240.
Franck, Johann, 242.
Fulbert, tr., 308.

Gellert, Christian F., 300.
Gerhardt, Paul, 233.
Gibbons, Thomas, 83, 136.
Gill, Thomas H., 37, 109, 432.
Gilmore, J. H., 225.
Goode, William, 159.
Gotter, L. A., tr. fr., 5.
Grant, Sir Robert, 92.
Grigg, Joseph, 2, 40, 328.
Guyon, Mme. Jeanne B. de la M., 370.

Hall, Newman, 76.
Hamilton, James, 233.
Hammond, William, 32.
Hankey, Catherine, 345.
Hastings, Thomas, 47, 145, 189, 236.
Hatch, Edwin, 342.
Hatfield, Edwin F., 442.
Havergal, Frances R., 206, 361, 433.
Havergal, Wm. H., 34, 36.
Haweis, Thomas, 129.
Hawker, Robert, 155.
Hawkesworth, John, 268.
Hayward, ———, 248.
Heber, Reginald, 71, 260, 421, 428.
Heginbotham, Ottiwell, 162, 201.
Herrick, George M., 445.
Hickok, Eliza M., 106.
Heginbothom, Ottiwell, 40, 162, 201.
Hinsdale, Mrs. Grace W., 42.
Hodder, F., 379.
Holmes, Oliver W., 171, 224.
Hope, Henry J. McK., 319.
Hopkins, John H., 443.
Hopkinson, Joseph, 452.
Hopper, Edward, 191.
How, William W., 204, 353.
Howard, Anna Holyoke, 46.

Howe, Julia Ward, 448.
Hudson, R. E., 357.
Hunter, William, 170.
Huntington, William R., 439.
Hutchinson, J. P., 414.

Irons, Miss G. M., 325.

Jenness, J. F., 415.
Johns, John, 426.

Keble, John, 272.
Keith, George, 120.
Kelley, Thomas, 13, 15, 56, 59, 60, 61, 220, 221, 257, 307.
Kempthorn, John, 74.
Ken, Thomas, 269, 274, 459.
Kent, John, 165.
Key, Francis S., 57, 451.
Killinghall, John, 239.
King Alfred, tr., 264.
Kingsbury, William, 88.
Kipling, Rudyard, 449.
Knox, William, 188.

Langford, John, 77.
Lavater, Johann C., 363.
Leeson, Jane F., 227.
Litzsinger, Louisa E., 130, 232.
Lloyd, William F., 175.
Lowry, J. L., 420.
Luther, Martin, 2.
Lyte, Henry F., 1, 8, 63, 153, 271, 315, 360.

Mackay, Wm. P., 146.
MacKellar, Thomas, 381.
Mant, Richard, 4.
Marriott, John, 91.
Mason, John, 254.
Mason, William, 251.
May, Wm. A., 216, 231, 202.
Medley, Samuel, 40, 148, 287, 323.
Millard, James E., 21.
Milton, John, 389.
Monsell, John S. B., 14, 348, 405.
Montgomery, James, 24, 50, 99, 393, 410.
Monro, Henry, 322.
Moore, Thomas, 115, 145, 368.
Moore, W. T., 35.
Morgan, Thomas J., 394.
Morris, George P., 11.
Mote, Edward, 123.
Moultrie, John, 39.

Neale, John M., 281, 318.
Needham, John, 51, 209, 401.
Nelson, David, 375.
Nevin, Edwin H., 179.
Newman, John H., 174.
Newton, John, 6, 12, 151, 193, 196, 436.

191

INDEX OF AUTHORS OF HYMNS.

Offord, Robert M., 346.
Ogden, W. A., 372.
Onderdonk, Henry U., 110.
Opie, Mrs. A., 82.
Osgood, George, 419.
Osler, Edward, 193.

Palmer, Ray, 65, 68, 250, 279, 320.
Patzke, Johann S., 270.
Perronet, Edward, 58.
Pierpont, John, 90, 223.
Pirie, Alexander, 96.
Pollock, William, 385.
Pott, Francis, tr., 301.
Prentiss, Mrs. Elizabeth P., 358.
Procter, Adelaide A., 352.

Raffles, Thomas, 256.
Rankin, J. E., 354, 438.
Rawson, George, 304, 405.
Read, Andrew, 416.
Reed, Mrs. Elizabeth, 329.
Rinkhart, Martin, 235.
Robert of France, 313.
Robinson, Charles S., 291.
Robinson, Robert, 158.
Rorison, Gilbert, 54.
Rothe, Johann A., 126.

Saffery, Maria G., 402.
Sampson, Miss J. W., 161.

Schmolke, Benjamin, 156.
Scott, Elizabeth, 246.
Scriven, Joseph, 182.
Seagraves, Robert, 219.
Sears, Edmund H., 285.
Shaw, David T., 453.
Shepherd, Thomas, 186.
Shirley, Walter, 43, 177.
Skene, Benjamin, 172.
Smith, Mrs. Caroline S., 276.
Smith, Samuel F., 335, 397, 430, 440, 454.
Steele, Anne, 95, 116, 275, 371, 383.
Stennett, Samuel, 18, 167.
Stephen the Sabaite, 334.
Stocker, John, 312.
Strong, Nathan, 20.
Stryker, P., 62.
Swain, Joseph, 200.
Swain, Leonard, 51.

Tappan, William B., 217.
Tate and Brady, 19, 84, 101, 140, 241, 245.
Tate, Nahum, 237.
Tersteegen, Gerard, 297, 327.
Thalheimer, Elsie, 27.
Thompson, Alexander R., 79.
Thompson, J. B., 387.
Thring, Godfrey, 192, 340.

Toke, Mrs. E. L., 306.
Toplady, Augustus M., 122.

Very, Jones, 456.
Vokes, Mrs., 388.

Wardlaw, Ralph, 119, 427.
Waring, Anna L., 207.
Watts, Isaac, 25, 26, 31, 38, 41, 48, 52, 81, 94, 98, 102, 104, 107, 112, 114, 118, 132, 133, 135, 168, 184, 199, 211, 215, 238, 244, 263, 273, 286, 295, 296, 347.
Wesley, Charles, 22, 71, 80, 89, 93, 138, 142, 164, 183, 197, 204, 266, 284, 303.
Wesley, John, 234.
Wesley, John, tr., 126.
White, Henry Kirke, 69.
Whitfield, Frederick, 150, 350.
Whittier, John G., 455.
Wigner, John M., 336.
Williams, Benjamin, 78.
Williams, Isaac, 341.
Williams, William, 369.
Wilson, Mrs. Caroline (Fry), 66.
Winkworth, C., tr., 242.
Wolfe, Aaron R., 408.
Woolfolk, Mrs. Ellen, 330.
Wordsworth, Christopher, 45, 75, 249.
Wreford, John R., 446.

www.ingramcontent.com/pod-product-compliance
Lightning Source LLC
Chambersburg PA
CBHW032138160426
43197CB00008B/692